Shen's Unlikely Journey

From Confucian China
to the Court of Louis XIV

ROBERT HENREY

Copyright 2024 Robert Henrey
All rights reserved.

Published by Robert Henrey

Library of Congress Cataloging-in-Publication Data
Robert Henrey

Shen's Unlikely Journey: From Confucian China to the Court of Louis XIV
Robert Henrey—1st ed.

ISBN 9798325940606

1. Jesuits in Imperial China. 2. Publishing Confucius in Europe.
3. Ancestral Rites Controversy. 4. Godfrey Kneller's Chinese Convert.

Front cover artwork:
Godfrey Kneller's portrait of the Chinese Convert (1687)—
Royal Collection Trust / © His Majesty King Charles III 2024.
Source: Wikimedia Commons—a faithful reproduction of a
two-dimensional work of art in the public domain in the
United States and in its country of origin.

Book Design: Caren Polner

Contents

Introduction 7
    I Shipwrecked 13
   II A Summer in Batavia 37
  III The Return of the Rains 95
  IV A Homecoming...131
   V Versailles...153
  VI The Eternal City..171
 VII Confucius in Paris 197
VIII An English Summer.......................................251
  IX Lisbon..287
   X Epilogue 297
Historical Notes 303
Author's Notes...321
Illustrations...327
Acknowledgements 333
About the Author..335

Shen's Unlikely Journey

Map of the World in 1684

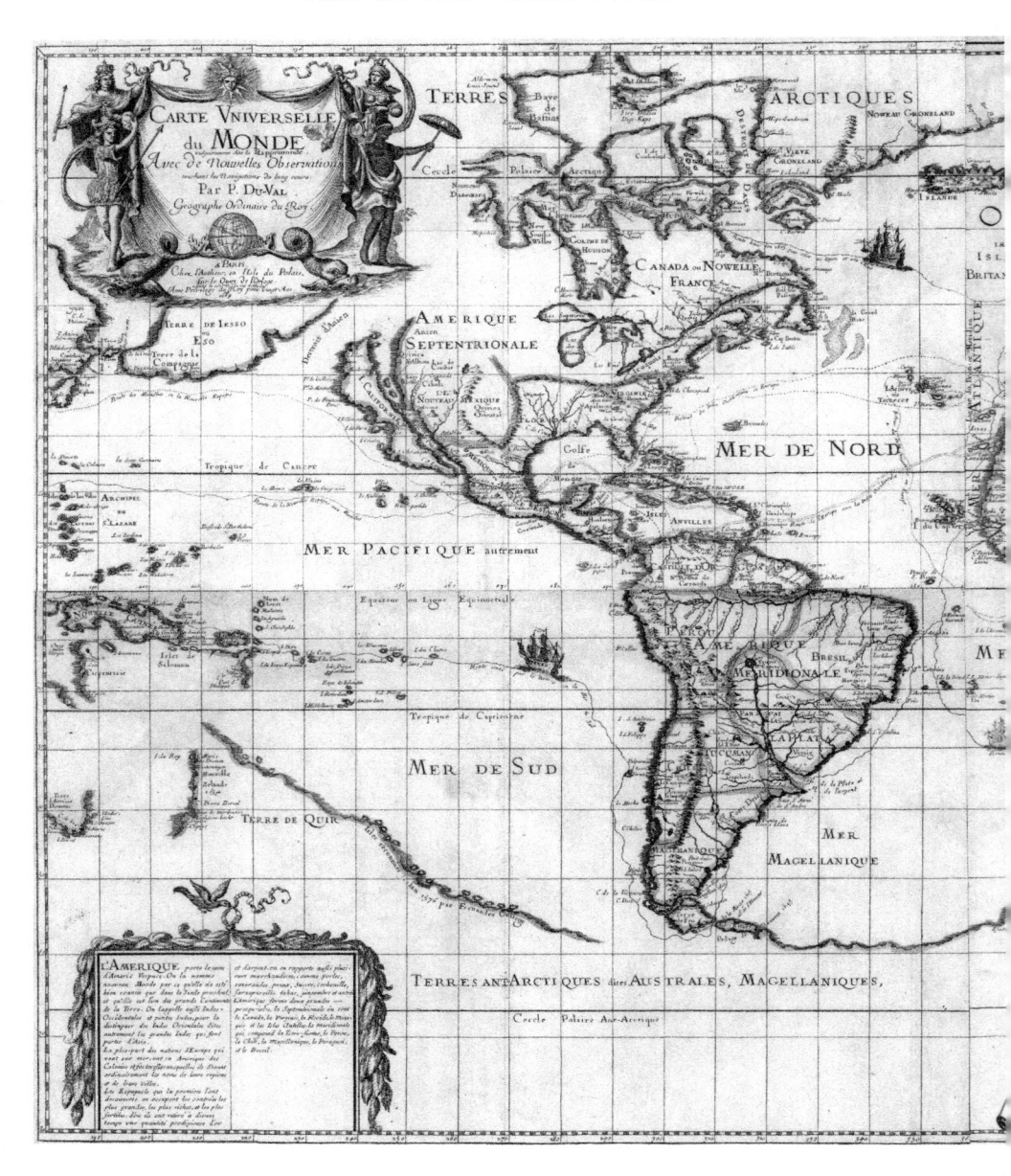

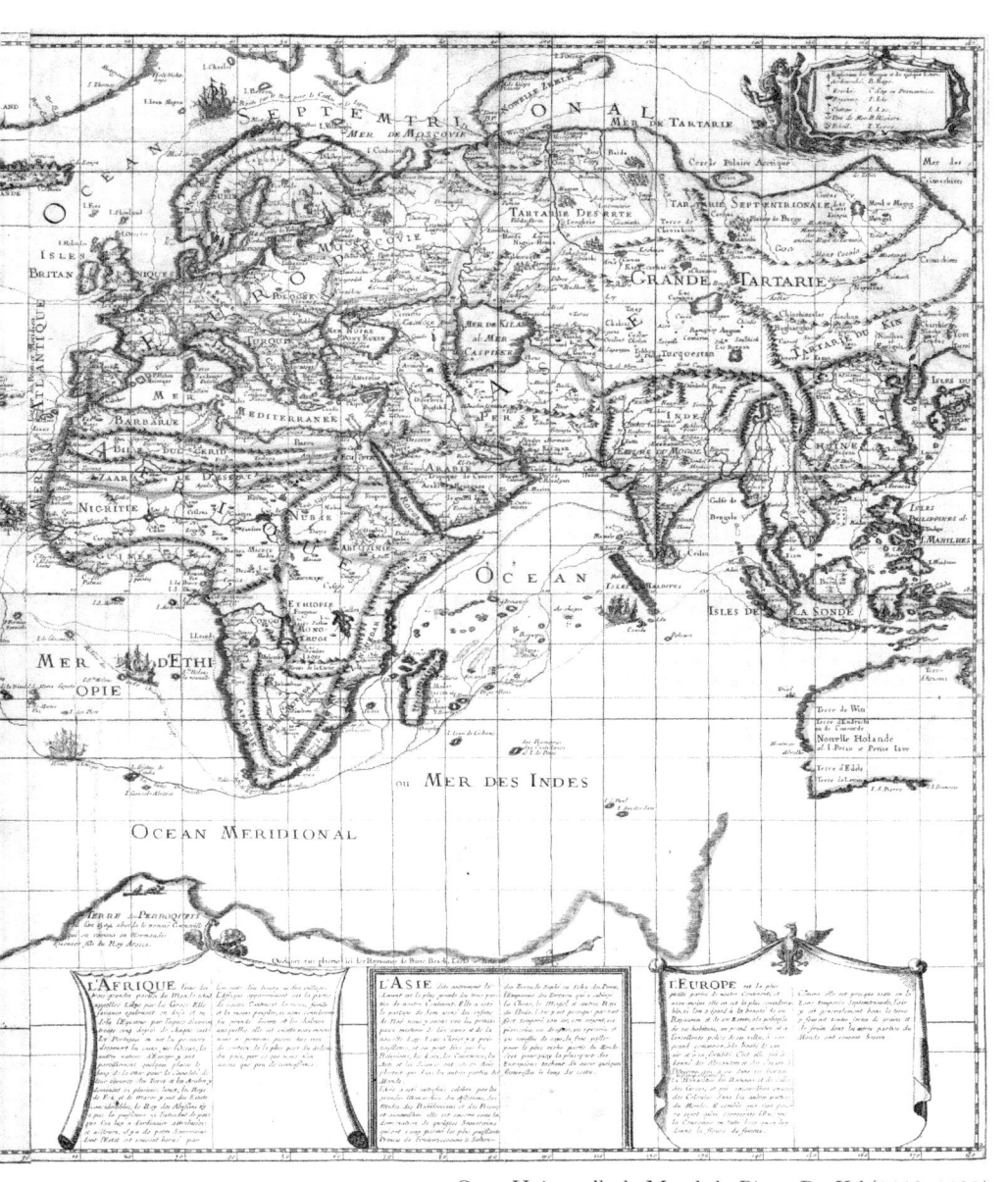

Carte Universelle du Monde by Pierre Du Val (1619-1683)

Introduction

$\mathcal{I}$t was thanks to an extended stay in Singapore in the 1970s that I first encountered Chinese culture. I'm grateful beyond words because it forever changed my worldview. Ever since, I've been curious about those who first set out to bridge the great cultural divide which had separated the West from the East for most of recorded history. Naturally enough, I came across Marco Polo and then the Jesuits. There were others, of course, but it seemed as though it was invariably those from the West who had undertaken the quest. Then, by chance, I came across young Shen. It was his portrait that made me want to imagine what it might have been like for him to embark on an adventure into Europe which led to his being so engagingly portrayed. I learned that, so far as anyone knew, he was the very first from his native China to have been taken on so extensive a journey. With Europe on the cusp of enthusiastically and uncritically embracing the promise of a scientifically-driven, enlightened wider world, it had to have been the most unusual of experiences.

The reason we have Shen's portrait is that James II, one of the several reigning monarchs into whose presence the young man had been ushered, commissioned it from one of the foremost painters of the time. The portrait shows Shen from head to toe, because the king had been moved by both the young man's disarmingly deferential manner and by the silken vesture he had brought from China. It was a dark, blueish-green gown richly embroidered with dragons, the most evocatively Chinese of images, subtly entwined into its very texture. It was otherwise quite plain, and the young man bore none of the insignia of rank or of princely status that would have been expected to grace one whose portrait had been commissioned by a reigning monarch. Rather than exhibiting it in one of the impressively gilded rooms gracing the great palaces within which King James habitually resided, he had it hung within the intimacy of his private apartments in Windsor Castle. It was commissioned in 1687, about three-and-a-half centuries ago.

We're lucky. Thanks to the portrait, we can look into the young man's eyes.

There is indeed something serene and wistful about Shen's pensive expression. The portraitist endowed his sitter with a touch of otherworldliness. Shen is shown pointing toward what might well be a distant, spiritually suffused horizon.

So, taken by the desire to tell the story behind the painting, I was moved to want to see it for myself. I therefore sent an email to the Royal Collection, curious to know whether the portrait was still on view in Windsor. To my surprise, a response landed in my inbox the very next morning. Regrettably, the curator informed me, Sir Godfrey Kneller's admirable painting of The Chinese Convert had been lent out by the trustees to the Louvre, not the Paris Louvre, but the one newly housed in an architecturally provocative structure built on a tiny island attached to Abu Dhabi, one of the Persian Gulf's hyper wealthy emirates. The helpful curator suggested I Google "Versailles and the World—Abu Dhabi."

An excellent suggestion! I visited Abu Dhabi virtually and there was Shen's portrait, hanging prominently in the fourth room of a special exhibition. It turned out to be a visually enriching experience featuring the glorious outpouring of art and science that had so characterized the long reign of Louis XIV. The Sun King had made a point of welcoming Ottoman, Persian and Siamese potentates in the most lavish of all palaces of the time, Versailles, and each visit had been memorialized by a great artist. The opulence of Versailles' Hall of Mirrors was unrivaled, as were the fountains embellishing the vast formal gardens surrounding the château. So, since Shen had visited Versailles and, as I later learned, famously initiated the Sun King in the use of chopsticks, and since his portrait was among the very best Godfrey Kneller had executed, it merited inclusion in the Abu Dhabi exhibition.

I was wowed by the sheer geographic span underlying Shen's story as well as that of those individuals he encountered: it ranges from his native Nanjing, an ancient capital city situated within China's traditional heartland, to Lisbon where his circuitous and long-drawn-out journey eventually took him.

I had other questions regarding Kneller's painting. Not long after Shen's visit to England, James II suffered the ignominious loss of his crown. His abandoned throne was handed over to his daughter Mary and to her Dutch husband William of Orange. They were both staunch Protestants and highly allergic to Jesuits. What had happened to Shen's portrait? I should have mentioned that Shen's linguistically gifted mentors and deft guides were Jesuits. They were the ones who had unreservedly adopted and exalted the wondrous culture that was China's. They would, it turned out, be very much part of the story I was inspired to write.

I need not have worried because Shen's portrait remained in Windsor Castle throughout the reign of three of the four Georges, and when it was eventually moved it was only as far as Buckingham Palace where Queen Victoria was happy enough to keep it for a good part of her famously long reign. It eventually made its way back to Windsor Castle.

Does the Royal Collection, vast as it is, include a full-length, formal portrait of a famous Chinese person? Of an emperor, for example, or of a distinguished general or of Sun Yat-sen, the founder of the Chinese Republic, or perhaps of one of China's wisemen of antiquity? What about Chairman Mao? Apparently not. It falls to youthful Shen to be the sole native of the Middle Kingdom to enjoy such an honor.

—Robert Henrey, 2024

To see what is right and not to do it is want of courage.
Analects II

Without knowing the force of words, it is impossible to know men.
Analects XX

—Confucius

Age of Sail Portuguese carrack: 1897 print

I
Shipwrecked
February 1682

They were shipwrecked. There was no other word for it. The Santo António, on approaching the shallow narrows leading into the straits, had been overtaken by a sudden and overwhelming squall. Gusts whipped up by monsoon winds had blown relentlessly the day before and the storm had intensified throughout the night. As the first light of dawn appeared above the nearby Javanese hills, the full extent of the damage became apparent. The mizzenmast had snapped near its base and the fractured spar, weighed down by the sodden sails lashed to its yards, had landed hard against the mainmast. The Santo António had taken on a perilous starboard list. It's doubtful anyone on board had slept that night. Couplet and Shen certainly hadn't. The haunting sound of the timbers of a drifting ship grating ominously against a rock-strewn sandbank is not easily forgotten. By daybreak, the crew of Portuguese and Goanese sailors had joined the handful of forlorn passengers huddled helplessly on the Santo António forecastle. There was nothing left to do but shiver, drenched and exhausted, and wait for the storm to run its course. And pray, of course, for a miraculous deliverance from the encircling waters. Many did so as they clutched hastily retrieved rosary beads.

Shen's Unlikely Journey

The straits of Sunda and of Malacca: 1683 French map

    Phillipe Couplet, a middle-aged Belgian Jesuit priest, and Shen Fuzong "Michael," the young Chinese scholar who was his unlikely companion, had sailed out of Macao barely a month earlier. The Santo António had weighed anchor in early December 1681, a mere three weeks before Christmas. She was a ruggedly built carrack, fully loaded with silks, porcelains, and other highly prized Chinese trade goods. It should have been a reasonably straightforward voyage and taken no more than a year. With luck and fair weather, perhaps even less. Their ultimate intended destination was Lisbon. The first leg of the journey should have taken them to Goa, the fabled Portuguese enclave and colony, on the Malabar coast of South India. Accordingly, from Macao the ship had set a southerly course. Portuguese mariners had been sailing their large capacity carracks in these waters since the early decades of the 16th century.

In the past, the master of a Portuguese ship such as the Santo António would have unhesitatingly headed for Malacca. Sailing through the long, narrow straits that bore the port city's name offered the best chance of successfully negotiating the many islands and peninsulas that had historically added difficulty to the challenge of reaching the Indian Ocean from the South China Sea. The Portuguese knew that all too well because shortly after their conquest of Goa at the beginning of the 16th century, they had sailed further East and crossed the Indian Ocean. In a strategic move, they had then committed all their available ships and firepower to ousting the Islamized sultanate which had hitherto controlled Malacca. The city, thanks to its deep harbor, had grown into a crucial commercial hub linking Chinese, Indian, Siamese, and Arab traders. The Portuguese had succeeded and Malacca had become a prosperous Portuguese and Catholic enclave within a largely Islamic world. Their hold, however, was precarious and had lasted no more than a century.

It was the Dutch who, some forty years before this most dispiriting of shipwrecks, had finally wrested Malacca from the Portuguese. Malacca's new masters were out to grab a lot more. They had set their sights on an even greater prize and had secured it by imposing themselves as a naval and commercial power to be reckoned with. They had extended their eastern reach immeasurably beyond Malacca. They had done so by cowering into submissive neutrality most of the Islamic sultanates established among the many islands of the impressively extensive archipelago that Europeans had taken to referring to as the East Indies. They were the Indies to the east because, from a European perspective, those islands lay beyond India. They were not to be confused with those to the west that Columbus had encountered in the Caribbean a century earlier and had fancifully assumed to be in India's immediate neighborhood.

The Dutch, lured by the profitability of the spice trade, had succeeded thanks to their formidably ambitious merchants and their lethally equipped and aggressively manned ships. It was an astonishing achievement for one of Europe's smallest nations. There was irony to the fact that much the same could also have been said of the Portuguese when, a century and a half earlier, they also had set out to master the shipping lanes connecting an unimaginably distant and hitherto virtually unknown East to a Europe that was awakening to the reality of a wider world.

There was another way of crossing from the South China Sea into the Indian Ocean. The largest of the islands comprising the mighty East Indian archipelago that the Dutch so coveted was Sumatra. To the east of it lay Java and, due to their closeness, the two islands form an impressive barrier to shipping. It was possible, though, to steer a ship along the body of water separating them which mariners commonly referred to as the Sunda Straits.

So, the master of the Santo António had chosen to avoid the long and narrow Dutch-controlled Straits of Malacca by trying his luck by way of Sunda. While the Sunda Straits are wider and shorter, a southbound ship can only enter them by negotiating a narrow passage rendered the more perilous by an abundance of submerged rocks and shoals. The Sunda Straits were also notorious for the unpredictability of volcanic eruptions that on occasions threateningly convulsed their waters. To the east lay a Javanese sultanate whose capital city, the ancient port of Banten, was advantageously sited in a sheltered bay lying a few nautical miles from the daunting narrows.

What the master of the Santo António knew was that over the years, Sunda had grown into a prosperous Islamized trading sultanate whose ships sailed as far west as India and as far north as Japan.

Thanks to the fertility of its well-watered lowlands and tropical climate, it was ideally suited to the large-scale cultivation of a type of elongated peppercorn that was particularly attractive to the Chinese. He'd headed for Sunda in the knowledge that the Dutch, although powerfully entrenched along the north coast of Java had, until now, refrained from overpowering the independently minded Sundanese. Portuguese ships could therefore still count on docking in Banten. What he hadn't reckoned on was the exceptional intensity of the monsoon winds the Santo António had had the misfortune of encountering. Couplet and Shen would come to regard João Atayde as their true savior. No, he wasn't the one to have physically rescued them from the waves breaking threateningly against the forsakenly beached hull of the Santo António. He was no seafarer and not even acting in an official capacity. He'd self-deprecatingly referred to himself as a mere merchant who, having become aware of the misfortune that had struck his fellow countrymen, had saddled his horse and hastened to the scene. All he had done, he had said repeatedly, was offer hospitality to those in need and reassurance to the forlorn. He was, however, the most resourceful of men and it was thanks to him that all was not lost.

Indeed not because all four—Dom João Atayde, his wife Dona Inês, Philippe Couplet and Michael Shen—found themselves only a few evenings later lingering over a fine dinner of curried shrimp reflecting on the chance events that had brought them together.

"Dom João," asked Shen, "tell us the truth. Were we lucky? The Dutch, knowing Father Philippe was a Jesuit, could have imprisoned us in their imposing fortress, demanded a ransom, simply done away with us…no one would have been any the wiser. Instead, they entrusted us to your care."

"You were very lucky that the listing Santo António, instead of drifting against jagged rocks and sinking like a cannonball, had settled itself, lame-duck-like, atop a sandy perch. You were lucky that it happened at daybreak, that Javanese fishermen caught sight of you and that they abandoned their nets in the expectation of a handsome reward. You were lucky that they knew these waters better than anyone else. You were also lucky that the winds had suddenly died down, and you were even lucky that your precious camphor chests had been so well made that they survived the drenching and dunking to which they were subjected. Yes, you were lucky but as to the Dutch, I don't think you need have feared for your lives. You weren't destitute. It has been your good luck to hold onto your impressive-looking possessions and, furthermore, Father Philippe speaks pretty good Dutch. Look, the reality is that the Dutch no longer feel threatened by their erstwhile European antagonists. A lot has changed since they first came here."

The two men in their misfortune had indeed been lucky. The Javanese fishermen had so skillfully maneuvered their flat-bottomed long boats into the shallow tidal waters surrounding the stranded Santo António that, within a matter of hours, the survivors had been ferried into the safety of Banten's sheltered harbor. In an act of laudable Quranic hospitality, they had then been taken to the great hall abutting the city's famed mosque. It was there that the women of Banten had cooked up a hefty pot of peppered rice into which they had thrown a generous portion of coconut milk.

Batavia was only fifty miles to the east of Banten so that by nightfall the following day word of the shipwreck had reached the Dutch stronghold. What João Atayde had then done, however, was no small thing. On hearing the news, he'd resolved to ride out the very next morning from Batavia to Banten. He knew that the Santo António would be carrying valuable cargo. Could it be salvaged? Was the ship still seaworthy? What Atayde hadn't bargained for was the presence, among those rescued, of a bedraggled Jesuit Father accompanied by a youthful and solicitous Chinese acolyte.

They struck Atayde as the oddest of couples. There was Couplet, tall, and slightly hunched over. What stood out was the priest's wizened and furrowed face crowned by a disheveled shock of reddish hair. He was clad in somber shapeless robes belted tightly against his protruding midriff. The ordeal of the last few days had taken its toll, and he was visibly anxious—shaken and distracted to the point of straightaway confiding in a startled João Atayde that what he feared above all else was the loss of the irreplaceable contents of the camphor wood chests that had been part of his voluminous baggage. Atayde's greeting had, however, elicited a broad sigh of relief. They were compatriots. Almost, that is! Atayde, despite his Portuguese name, had spent his childhood in Rotterdam and Couplet, despite his French name, was from the Flemish speaking Southern Provinces. And then Atayde had promised to go in search of the chests.

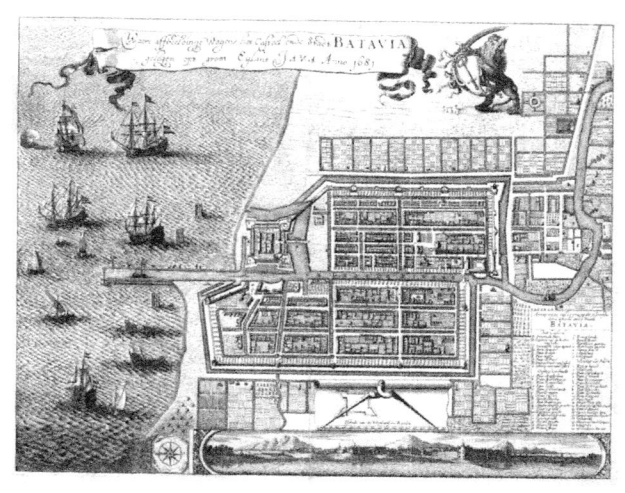

Plan of Batavia showing Dutch kasteel and docks: 1681 Dutch engraving

Shen, in striking contrast, radiated the muscular agility and optimism of youth. His hair was jet black and tightly cropped. He wore a snugly fitting, buttoned cotton tunic with broad sleeves. It was dyed a slightly fading indigo blue. His trousers were narrow legged and cut ankle high. His confident yet respectful manner immediately struck Atayde as a mark of high birth.

Atayde had lost no time in going about his business. Was the Santo António repairable and some of its cargo recoverable? Apparently yes. The Sundanese were capable shipwrights. No question, however, of sailing her on to Goa, let alone Lisbon. The Santo António's chastened and humbled master would be lucky to muster his rescued crew and, thanks to a hastily spliced mizzenmast and freshly caulked hull timbers, make it back to Macao. As to the salvageable cargo, Atayde was in the enviable position of offering a fair price. The Santo António's ill-fated voyage would not have been totally in vain. And, yes, the Javanese fishermen had recovered Couplet's chests, or at least most of them. They'd shrewdly held on to them. They could tell this was no ordinary baggage. In Atayde, though, they'd encountered an equally shrewd negotiator.

What about Couplet and Shen? No point in their returning to Macao with the patched up San António and still less remaining in Banten. Banten was no place at which to tarry, the well-informed Atayde had told them, for the notable reason that one of the aging sultan's brash and rebellious sons had challenged his father's benevolent rule and civil strife was in the offing. The Dutch had no intention of standing idly by. This was the chance they had been waiting for and they were ready to pounce. Best to keep out of harm's way, was how Atayde had put it.

Besides, if Couplet was hellbent on reaching Europe, and he clearly was, then moving on to Dutch Batavia was the only viable option. Even then, there was no obvious way of reaching Lisbon or even Portuguese Goa. This meant he and Shen would have to resort to negotiating passages on a Dutch ship bound for the Netherlands. In addition there was the severity and frequency of the monsoons to be reckoned with. So Couplet had reluctantly come around to the unwelcome realization that he and Shen would most likely have to wait things out in Dutch Batavia. For how long? Hard to tell. Atayde had enjoined patience. As much as a year? Couplet had asked anxiously. Atayde had just nodded.

Now there was the thorny issue of just how Couplet, given his weakened state, was going to make it all the way to Batavia. Atayde was prepared to accompany him on horseback. It was the least he could do. What about the chests, though? Their salvage and ransoming had gone a long way toward lifting Couplet's spirits, but he'd vowed that from this moment on he'd never again let them out of his sight. Well, as Atayde had explained, they'd have to be loaded onto a couple of carts each hauled by a pair of lumbering water-buffaloes. What about Shen? Might he not be trusted with accompanying the beasts of burden all the way to Batavia? A mere fifty miles! Being young, he surely wouldn't mind spending the next few nights under makeshift thatched roofs and subsisting on a diet of rice gruel and coconut milk. The men driving the buffaloes would take him along terraced rice fields and groves of climbing pepper bushes. Java during the rainy season is humid but resiliently green. He'd catch sight of an abundance of brightly plumed birds, hear their songs, cross paths with frogs and scampering lizards, observe butterflies and watch monkeys at play in distant treetops. Of course Shen wouldn't mind! The young thrive on adventure…the more unpredictable the better! It would be part of the journey.

❦

In Batavia, Atayde had taken it upon himself to pay his respects to the Dutch officials who occupied cavernous premises within the great walled Kasteel. He'd cheerfully agreed to sign a document drafted in Dutch legalese vouching for his guests' good behavior.

Atayde, with an unmistakably Portuguese name, was a most resourceful man of means who was well known to the pipe-smoking Dutch administrators with whom it was his business to entertain cordial relations. He'd been brought up in Antwerp and given his trading savvy, he'd at first tried his luck in Portuguese Goa. Events beyond his control, however, had led to his eventually seeking to establish himself beyond the reach of Goanese officials. The Dutch East Indies offered such an opportunity. He'd never imagined himself doing so, but he would have been the first to admit that he'd eventually run into some good luck. That, together with hard work, had earned him the respect of the tightly knit community of traders that operated out of Batavia. He owed his success in no small part to his uncanny ability to strike up engaging conversations with those he encountered in his business dealings. He also had the most charming of Portuguese wives. Dom João and Dona Inês were the most hospitable of couples and being engagingly curious enjoyed the company of their fellow human beings.

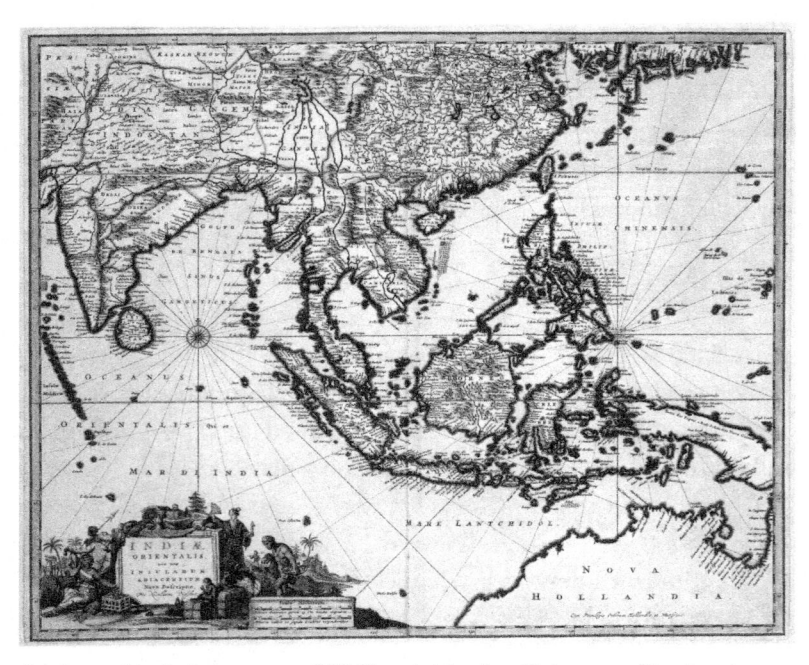

❖

Southeast Asia depicting range of VOC's activities: late 17th century Dutch map

It was Dona Inês' suggestion to bring out the maps. She'd sensed the extent of young Shen's utter wonderment at finding himself in such a strange place as Batavia. It couldn't have been otherwise. This was the most unexpected of beginnings to a journey that had held out the promise of taking him halfway round the world.

Turning to her husband, she said, "Why don't you spread one of your maps right here over our dining room table? Then I think you should help our guests find their bearings. Tell them about this strange place we find ourselves living in."

It was an excellent idea. Atayde loved maps. He collected them. Their accuracy had improved significantly of late and Dutch cartographers and printers had made a virtue out of publishing them in ever greater numbers. Atayde liked to think of them as contributing to bringing the world into ever sharper focus. That's something he took pleasure in talking about. He warmed to his wife's suggestion and called for one of the house servants to bring in the large teak chest he used as a map box.

Atayde began by pointing out Banten and the very spot at which the Santo António had run aground. It was obvious from the map that its commanding position at the narrowest point of the Sunda Channel, while contributing mightily to the prosperity of the local sultan, had also excited the envy of Europeans. The Portuguese during their heyday had coveted it and so had the English, who for a time had fondly dreamt of cornering the spice trade. That is, until the Dutch had made a surprise appearance. Thanks to their mighty gunships, they'd bullied their European rivals into submission and sent them packing. Yes, they'd held back from overrunning the Sundanese but, as Atayde had predicted, their patience had now run out and they were about to extend their domination over the whole of Java.

"Tell Michael about the VOC," suggested Dona Inês referring to Shen. "It runs this place, and he needs to understand why."

The Dutch had organized themselves under the aegis of their

Amsterdam-based East India Company. It was called the Verenigde Oost-Indische Compagnie, but given that name's grandiloquent un-pronounceability, everyone referred to it as the VOC.

"The Dutch," Atayde explained, "chose to build their mighty fort here rather than in Banten. It's a far larger emplacement and it overlooks a sheltered deep-water bay. There was a time, so I'm told, that the ancient ruins of a walled stronghold erected by a local sultan could still be seen."

"The other reason the Dutch chose Batavia," continued Atayde, "is that the area is well watered and habitable. Marshy, yes, but ideal for growing rice. To the south there are richly wooded hills abounding in iron-wood teak. These are things that enhanced its attractiveness to would-be settlers. The Javanese have a name for this place that sounds something like Ja and Karta. In Malay, those words are said to refer to the existence of a powerful fortress."

Why so strange a name as Batavia? The traditionalists in charge of the VOC, Atayde went on to say, had chosen a name inspired by the Batavi, a militaristically inclined Germanic tribe that in Roman times occupied the area later described as the Netherlands. The Dutch, Atayde remarked with a wry smile, were in the habit of choosing those kinds of nationalistic names for their colonial outposts.

Mention of the aggressive ancient tribesmen led Couplet to ask himself whether his maternal ancestors might have had more than few drops of Batavi blood running through their Flemish veins. The Dutch, after their conquest of Malacca, had further consolidated their hold over the many islands making up the three-thousand-mile-long archipelago. It was then that the VOC had made Batavia into the administrative hub of its expanding commercial empire. The Dutch built up the old fortress into a massive walled compound and, since it was adjacent to the harbor, mounted it with guns. It was there that their mighty vessels docked, were careened and repaired and restocked their galleys with locally produced food.

Batavia in short order became the transshipment point for the spices destined for the European market.

"Were it not for spices," observed Atayde, "there would be no reason for any of us to be here. There would be no Batavia. Did you notice the warehouses along the canals? That's where the spices are stored. And then, look around you: this place is teeming with people. There's no reason to be in Batavia other than to work. Men, women, and children do so day-in-day-out; right here in the docks, warehouses and surrounding fields and marshes. There's also timber to be harvested in the wooded hills to the south. There's cooking and cleaning to be done in the houses of the Dutch. There are streets and alleys to be swept and canals to be dredged. The Javanese, together with their kith and kin from Sumatra to the west and from the many islands to the east are, it stands to reason, most obviously present here. They are the ones that speak Malay. Their ancestors, I'm told, reached these shores by sailing, generation after generation, from island to island."

Then there were the Chinese who, according to Atayde, were valued for their resourcefulness and tenacity. They had been recruited by the Dutch as indentured laborers. Most came from southern provinces such as Guangdong and Fujian and had emigrated in the hope of a better life in the wake of the Manchu invasion. So naturally enough, Batavia had within it a thriving Chinatown with temples, teeming alleyways, shops, and market stalls. To Shen, it was boisterous and brash and certainly a far cry from the gentility of his native Nanjing but, nonetheless quintessentially and nostalgically Chinese.

Dutch Batavia, the way Atayde put it, seemed to have a near insatiable need for able bodied laborers. It was the Portuguese, he reminded his guests, who thanks to their commercial acumen and maritime knowhow, had been the first to transport captives over long distances. The trade had grown gradually and initially involved Portugal's coastal enclaves such as Goa, Malacca, Nagasaki, and Macao. Enslaved Asians had early on been exported not only to

Europe but also to eastern colonial outposts such as Batavia. That accounted for the presence of numerous Indians from the subcontinent's southern shores. Then, following the Spanish and Portuguese colonization of Brazil and of the Caribbean, the trade had expanded beyond recognition and abruptly changed direction. European colonizers had come to look on Africa as though it were a near inexhaustible source of much needed manpower. Yes, there were even Africans in Batavia.

Yes, Couplet freely admitted, there were Africans in Macao. Even the Jesuit fathers had one or two at their beck and call. They treated them well, of course and they had baptized and instructed them in the faith.

"Saved their souls!" exclaimed Atayde, a touch defiantly.

"So," Shen exclaimed, "all this is due to spices! Tell me something, Dom João, where do the spices grow? I don't, admittedly, know exactly what to look for but, so far as I can tell, I have yet to catch sight of anything remotely resembling a nut…other than a coconut that is…nothing, other than peppercorns, that might be ground down to produce a pleasing flavor. What am I missing?"

"Why, Michael, do you think that Dona Inês prevailed on me to bring out my precious maps? Here, take a look."

Had it not been for their name printed in large lettering at the easternmost section of Atayde's map, the Moluccas might have passed for near insignificant blotches within the most intricate and extensive of the world's archipelagos. They were, however, Atayde explained, home to tall evergreen trees whose flowers produced nail-shaped buds.

"Those, Michael, are cloves…that's right, much coveted cloves… and the Moluccas according to this map are more than a thousand miles from here. That's why you and Father Couplet could spend the next twelve months wandering around Batavia and the only cloves you would catch sight of would be either in sacks stacked in warehouses awaiting shipment to Holland or in Dona Inês' kitchen."

Spice Islands East of the Straits of Sunda: 1683 French map

The section of the map devoted to the Moluccas bore yet smaller specks. They were, Atayde explained, mere volcanic peaks jutting upward from the vastness of the ocean floor.

"They may appear to you as insignificant specks, Michael, but let me tell you that they are the only place in the whole wide world on which grow even taller trees that produce nuts that weigh their proverbial weight in gold. Until maps like this one came along, the whereabouts of those specks, veritable treasure islands, had been shrouded in secrecy."

These were nutmegs which, as Atayde explained, gave forth a double bounty. It was customary, before grinding them down to produce the most valuable of powdery spices, to strip them of their outer fibrous coating. This envelope, which had a strangely crimson-like color, was yet another condiment that had become highly prized for its subtle fragrance. That was mace. Spice traders were in the habit of offering it to their customers together with nutmegs and cloves. They complemented their shipments with ginger root acquired from Chinese coastal traders and with cinnamon and cardamom obtained during stopovers at southern Indian ports-of-call. Europeans eager to enliven their bland foods couldn't get enough of such riches.

Dona Inês had in the meantime asked her Hainanese cook to bring into the dining room a sampling of cloves, nutmeg, and mace. He'd displayed them on a small finely engraved silver salver. Shen was invited to do some sniffing which he did with youthful enthusiasm.

"Didn't the Dutch get greedy?" Asked Couplet.

"Father Philippe, are you prepared to listen to a story that puts us Europeans to shame? Do we risk scandalizing Michael whom you have presumably taught to expect Christians to treat their fellow human beings with a minimum of compassion and forbearance?"

"Let me put it this way, Dom João. Thanks to your hospitality and kindness you're going to do your utmost to help us continue our journey. If, thanks to you and Dona Inês, we do reach Europe, Michael will see for himself the way in which we Christians are all too often driven to treat each other in ways that blatantly disregard the principles we hold as sacred. I'd just as soon you be the one who prepares him for that dispiriting display of callousness."

"Very well then. I'll be brief. There's no need to dwell needlessly on shamelessness. These islands have been known to traders since antiquity. More recently, they were part of an Arab dominated trading network, thanks to which the spices they produced were funneled into the Middle East. You might not be aware of this, Michael, but the spice trade accounts for the Islamization of this vast archipelago. It was Arab traders who brought their religion to these parts."

"Their missionaries were profit-seeking traders?"

"I hadn't thought about it that way, Michael, but yes. Islam proved hugely successful in this part of the world. That's something Dona Inês and I have often reflected on. Has God abandoned us Christians? The fact is that Islam's message was appealingly straightforward. The other thing that might interest Father Philippe is that the Venetians were also part of this highly profitable arrangement. They were the ones who, at the westernmost point of the network, distributed the spices throughout the Mediterranean. Remember Marco Polo? He was Venetian. All that to say that when the Portuguese, and after them the Dutch, sailed into these waters they were not exactly welcome. They were interlopers. The Dutch, though, were more determined and consequently more strenuously opposed. It wasn't a fair contest. The Dutch had large ships mounted with state-of-the-art cannons. They invaded the islands I showed you on the map, methodically, one after another. Inhabitants who opposed them were either massacred or deported. The Dutch instituted a plantation system as a way of controlling production and monopolizing the business. They brought in indentured workers and even enslaved laborers. Commercially, they were extraordinarily successful. The British, though, had their own East India Company. We call it the EIC for short. It had, ironically, served as the model for the VOC. There was no love lost between the two countries.

The British deeply resented the Dutch for having beaten them to the punch. The EIC also had big black ships mounted with equally powerful cannons. There was a clash. It didn't go well for the British. The Dutch lost their cool and beheaded a group of EIC officials. When news of the beheadings reached England, it caused an outburst of self-righteous outrage and left a long-lasting impression on the public imagination. It was this embitterment that caused the Dutch and their British Protestant cousins to embark on a series of mutually punishing naval engagements—in Europe and as far as the Americas. That's it. I said I'd be brief."

Shen had listened intently. "It isn't," the young man commented reflectively, "as if we Chinese aren't inured to such atrocities. Our chronicles often read as though their sole purpose was to record the deeds of countless warriors hellbent on exacting ruthless revenge on each other. The Manchus more recently showed little mercy on the Ming loyalists who resisted their takeover of our homeland. No, that's not the issue. Father Couplet put it well. It's that none of this meshes with the ideals of forgiveness, forbearance, tolerance, and mercy that are supposed to distinguish Christians from the followers of other religions. I'm on a journey, Dom João. So, I'm learning. I'm grateful to you for being my teacher. One last question, though. You said that the spice islands were over a thousand miles east of here? I don't understand. Why did the VOC choose to entrench itself in Batavia?"

"You're not the first to ask such a question, Michael. Take a closer look at the map. Batavia is a good place from which to keep an eye on ships crossing from the Indian Ocean into the South China Sea. It's the gateway into the archipelago. The Dutch regard the entire East Indian archipelago as their private hunting grounds. They are not, as you now realize, about to allow other Europeans to muscle into a business they are determined to keep strictly to themselves. Have you noticed the cannons mounted on the walls of the fortress?"

Shen had.

❧

When Shen had asked whether he and Couplet had been lucky, given their Jesuit connection, not to have been jailed on arrival by Batavia's reputedly fiercely anti-Catholic authorities, Atayde had given as an answer that times had changed, and that the Dutch no longer felt threatened. Shen's question had given Couplet pause and caused him to remember a story that bore an uncanny resemblance to the predicament they presently found themselves in.

The story concerned a Frenchman who, having spent many years living with the Vietnamese, was on his way back to Europe. He was known for having perfected a highly innovative method for transcribing the Vietnamese language's highly complex writing system that was awkwardly based on Chinese characters. He'd proposed an alternative based on the western alphabet. Yes, he was another Jesuit, and his story likewise involved a shipwreck in the Sunda Channel following which he had been rescued and ended up in Batavia. The big difference was that his shipwreck had occurred thirty-five years earlier.

"Would you be interested in hearing the story?" Couplet asked the Ataydes.

They were, and most especially Dona Inês.

Couplet described the shipwreck as a traumatic and life-threatening event and credited the Frenchman's survival to his carrying a sacred relic. Couplet remembered a telling detail. Just like he and Shen, the Frenchman had been welcomed into a Portuguese family in Batavia. At their request he'd celebrated Mass and when word of it reached the Dutch authorities, he was arrested and jailed. After several months, he was sentenced to a flogging, but what troubled him most of all was the Dutch governor's decision to put on the equivalent of an auto-da-fe. It turned out to be a public ceremony during which the holy images, crucifixes and prayer books taken from him at the time of his arrest were solemnly burned. He mentioned in his memoir that for good measure a couple of thieves had been simultaneously burned at the stake.

"Only thirty-five years ago!" exclaimed Dona Inês, deeply moved by Couplet's telling of the story.

In the end, the Dutch governor relented, spared him the flogging, and allowed him to slip out of Batavia on a Dutch ship which, after more hair-raising adventures, landed him in India. That was just the beginning of his ordeals. He walked most of the way across Persia and Turkey and did in time reach Rome. His book had been published in Paris. It was written in French and Couplet now remembered reading it twenty-five years ago before leaving for China. He joked that it had indelibly impressed on his mind the importance of doing everything in his power to steer clear of Batavia.

"Your story, Father Philippe, has jogged my memory," commented Atayde. "I now remember being told about this Frenchman's misfortunes soon after my arrival in Batavia. Do you remember his name?"

"I do, Dom João and for the good reason that I was made aware of the unusual story behind it. It was Alexandre de Rhodes. Before joining the Jesuits he'd been brought up in Avignon. His family had emigrated from Spain. They counted among their ancestors Sephardic Jews who had been forced to wear a circular yellow insignia called a rueda—the Spanish word for a wheel—and refer to themselves by that name. The Ruedas, on arriving in Avignon, had adopted the aristocratic sounding de Rhodes. They'd escaped the Inquisition and the Avignonese were welcoming."

"Interesting indeed! Thank you, Father Philippe. Such details add poignancy to your story. Well, the thing about the Dutch," remarked Atayde after a pause, 'is that they've accumulated so much wealth that they can now afford to be much more open minded. They've begun to make a virtue out of political and even religious tolerance. The Dutch Republic has begun to advertise itself as a European haven within which no one will be persecuted for holding deviant religious or political views. I'm hearing my Dutch colleagues refer to a Dutch Golden Age."

"I'm sure," Atayde continued, "that you've heard of how the Japanese, after booting us Portuguese out of their country as well as you Jesuits and all other quarrelsome foreigners, made an exception for the Dutch. They have permission to occupy a tiny island inside Nagasaki Bay that is just about large enough to allow for the docking of a couple of VOC ships. In exchange, the Dutch have agreed to supply the Japanese with medical and scientific books published in Europe and never ever refer to the Christian religion. I happen to know that some of my Dutch associates make an unconscionable amount of money out of this arrangement. It's also given the Dutch publishing industry a boost. They increasingly boast of being the best educated and most scientifically inclined of all Europeans. So, yes, Father Couplet, times have changed. I can guarantee that you and Michael will be left in peace. No one will take the slightest interest in the fact that every morning you say Mass for us right here in our dining room. Our Dutch friends are too busy making money."

All that was true. Couplet and Shen did feel free to wander the streets, alleys, canals, entrepots, littered lots and backyards of Batavia. Out of a desire to not cause the Ataydes any kind of trouble, they did so with the utmost discretion and, in fact, spent a good deal of time reading, annotating and seemingly arguing over texts rescued from the camphor chests that had caused Couplet such anxiety. They did so, to the wonderment of their hosts, in pointedly tonal Chinese and in the spacious room they had so generously been given. They also conversed about the many questions that had arisen in Shen's mind since their arrival in Batavia which was, for the young man, despite its Chinatown and Dona Inês' Hainanese, Fujianese and Cantonese servants, the most foreign and disconcertingly thought provoking place he'd ever chanced upon.

Confucius says:

The doctrine of our master is to be true to
the principles of our nature and the benevolent
exercise of them to others, this, and nothing more.
Analects III

What I do not wish men to do to me,
I also wish not to do to men.
Analects V

What you do not like when done to yourself,
do not do to others.
Doctrine of the Mean

II
A Summer in Batavia
1682

"I'm curious by nature, Father Philippe," began Dona Inês.

She spoke over a dinner of steamed rice and crab dressed in a pungent chili-suffused sauce. It was a culinary treat and a celebration of sorts. It was now early May and several months had gone by since the shipwreck. The heavy rains had receded and Couplet, thanks to rest and a restorative diet, had recovered much of his energy. For good measure, the Chinese physician attending the Atayde household and consulted at Dona Inês' insistence had prescribed and formulated a particularly effective ginseng-based infusion. Night had fallen. In the tropics the sun sets early and abruptly.

"Dom João and I have been talking mostly about our own lives here in Dutch Batavia, but how about you? You've told us you were brought up in a Flemish speaking part of the Spanish Netherlands and yet you spoke French at home. What was your childhood like? You've spent almost the last quarter century of your life in China…the Middle Kingdom as you call it. You were, I think you said, in your mid-thirties when your ship docked in Macao. You mentioned, didn't you, that you never thought you'd ever turn back? But now you have…your shipwreck has brought you here. Would you mind telling us how you ended up spending so much of your life in China? If you care to bare your soul, we'll be eager listeners."

Couplet's memory of his birthplace was that of a well-watered, orderly city that had flourished since Medieval times thanks to the cloth trade. Its people were proud of their magnificent Gothic churches and civic buildings and the ladies of Mechlin produced the finest lace in all of Flanders. It was, therefore, only to be expected that such a beautiful city, set in such a prosperous land, should find itself perennially in the eye of storms whipped up by warring factions and rival empires.

Mechlin Cathedral: 18th century English print

Couplet explained that his paternal ancestors were Burgundian, hence his French name and French-speaking family. His father was a town official. Mechlin had at some point in its politically convoluted past been annexed by the dukes of Burgundy. They, in turn, had come under the sway of the Holy Roman Empire, only to end up as part of Charles V's inheritance. Charles, in addition to being elected Holy Roman Emperor, had, thanks to his mother, inherited the Spanish crown. He'd therefore set his heart on turning the northern Dutch provinces and the southern Flemish Netherlands into a single fiefdom. He insisted on unquestioned subservience not only to Spanish rule, but also to the Catholic religion. He was said to believe with dogmatically induced fervor that only then could his subjects hope to save their eternal souls. He'd thereby triggered a ruinous Dutch-Spanish conflict that had dragged on for the best part of eighty years. Mechlin had indeed been in the eye of the storm. When it was all over, Flemish-speaking Mechlin had ended up in the so-called Spanish Netherlands. It was south of the border which now cut it off from the Protestant and fiercely independently minded Dutch Republic.

Couplet's birth had coincided with a relatively peaceful spell in the city's history. He was the fifth of his mother's nine children. The Couplets, despite living in Flemish-speaking Mechlin, prided themselves on educating their children in French, which they regarded as the most genteel of all languages. That hadn't prevented him from learning on the fly the colorful but fluent version of Dutch spoken in Mechlin's scrappy back alleys. Couplet's mother had died tragically young, in childbirth. His father had remarried but only later in life. As a nine-year-old, Couplet, still mourning his mother's untimely death, had been sent to Mechlin's Jesuit college. From there, at age 17, without so much of a transition, he joined the Order as a novice.

"You were only 17. What made you want to join the Jesuits at so young an age?"

"A searching question, Dona Inês! Studying is what I did best. I didn't have a mother whose advice to seek and my teachers encouraged me in that direction. They didn't think I was cut out to be either a soldier or a sailor and yet I looked forward to the day when I'd find a way of escaping Mechlin. Adventure beckoned. I couldn't help looking up to the men I'd read so much about and who had founded the Order. To me they were conquering heroes. They were much more than saints."

"You were thinking of Francis Xavier? Tell us why he so inspired you."

"You're right about Xavier. I learned everything I could about him. He'd spent his childhood in a castle built atop the foothills of the mighty Pyrenees. That image stimulated my imagination. I was a lowlander and had never seen a proper mountain! He was highly intelligent, perceptive, charismatically persuasive, by nature restless and boundlessly energetic. At 19, he left the Pyrenees for Paris so he could study and he never made the journey back home. That made me realize that we don't always know where adventure will lead. In Paris he met with Ignatius—naturally, they were both Basque. Ignatius was fifteen years his senior and Xavier became one of the six students who, at his bidding, vowed to band together. They undertook to devote their lives to reenergizing the Church. It was in sore need of rejuvenation and risked being overwhelmed by the enthusiasm and intellectual standing of the reformers. These seven men adopted a simple but powerfully effective double-edged agenda. They appealed to Europe's leading families by promising to educate their sons with the utmost academic rigor—mathematics, astronomy, logic—as part of an effort to reassert the Church's intellectual credibility. Then they spared no effort in their attempt to encounter the wider world. It was turning out to be vast beyond what we Europeans had previously imagined. That's what I wanted to be part of."

"Didn't Xavier end up in China?"

"Almost…he was arguably the most intrepid of the seven. Within years of the Order's formation, he'd boarded a ship in Lisbon that took him across the Arabian Sea to Goa."

Couplet went on to evoke how men like Vasco da Gama and Afonso de Albuquerque had, with determination and at the risk of their lives but with luck on their side, contributed to establishing strongholds along maritime routes encompassing both African coasts and the Indian subcontinent. The Portuguese had done so by dismantling the network of Muslim traders that Atayde had talked about just a few days earlier. Their daring had indeed had momentous consequences. By sailing ships capable of rounding the Cape of Good Hope, the Portuguese had bypassed the Ottoman controlled Middle Eastern bottleneck and broken the Arab monopoly. They had pushed even further toward the South China Sea, secured Malacca, and embraced Japan. Distant China, however, was still beyond their ken. Its imperial policies had resolutely fenced it off from outside influences.

"So, Dona Inês, this is the world Xavier was eager to step into. He envisioned it as fertile soil ready for sowing. Gathering in the harvest would surely follow. He preached in India, but he was restless. Suffice to say that he moved on to Japan. Japan was a miracle of sorts. The Portuguese had come across its southernmost islands by pure chance. I'm telling you what you already know, but what the Japanese really liked about your countrymen was the trade potential of their big black ships. Given that the Japanese were in the middle of a miserably ruthless civil war, they were likewise bewitched by the effectiveness of European guns. Xavier seized the opportunity and his openness to conforming his preaching to Japanese cultural traditions contributed to the missions' spectacular early successes."

"But it didn't end well, did it? Not only that but am I right in saying that Xavier really had his heart set on China? Wasn't it where he really wanted to get to?"

"You're right on all counts, Dona Inês. Let's leave Japan for later. What Xavier knew about China was that there was no larger country to be encountered anywhere else in the world. It was a world the vastness of which was only just beginning to be better understood."

"That's a thought-provoking remark, Father Philippe," reflected Atayde. 'We humans hadn't until then had the means to be aware of such a mind-expanding reality."

"Well, yes, and so it occurred to Xavier that for the Church to be truly universal, it would have to be present in China. The Japanese had taught him that when it came to culture and religion, they inevitably looked to China for guidance. So, in blatant disregard of the difficulties he would surely face, Xavier attempted a stealth landing on a beach near Canton. He never made it. He was struck down by a fatal fever while still on an offshore island. He was only forty-six."

"How tragic! What happened after that?"

"At first nothing, but then, as you and Dom João know only too well, the Chinese eventually came to an agreement with your countrymen regarding the leasing of Macao. Am I correct, Dom João, in saying that once again it had to do with money? Isn't it a fact that the Chinese eventually came to realize that they could enrich themselves by exporting their high value silks, ceramics, and other luxuries? Europeans were flush with the silver they had extracted from the Americas. The Chinese wanted a piece of it."

"Yes, and that's still very much the case. You and Michael have spent enough time in Macao to know what it offers. It's a deep harbor easily accessible from the South China Sea. It's therefore an ideal place for us to dock our ships and repair them. And then, because it's close to Canton and at the mouth of the Pearl River, it suits the Chinese middlemen we deal with. Our Macao warehouses are a convenient drop-off point for their goods. At the beginning, Europeans weren't allowed to cross into China proper."

"That's right, but even though it was strictly a trade deal there was nothing in the lease preventing us Jesuits from using Macao as a base for our missions. It was a good place at which to learn Chinese and begin assimilating the Middle Kingdom's ancient culture. The Portuguese encouraged us and even built our schools, churches and residences. It was, they thought, in their self-interest to support our missions financially. I don't have to tell you, Dom João, that it is

Port of Macao: 18th century French drawing

an arrangement that has at times caused us untold misery. We're beholden to the hand that feeds us. The Portuguese Crown is our patronizing godfather, the famous Padroado. Enough said. I don't want to come across as bitter and disillusioned."

It was at this point in Couplet's story that another larger-than-life-character made an appearance. It would not be possible, Couplet said, to be a missionary in China and not look back to Matteo Ricci for both inspiration and guidance. The man was an intellectual giant. While still an aspiring Jesuit in Rome, he'd been taught by one of Europe's outstanding mathematicians at the Collegio Romano, the school founded by none other than Ignatius.

"On arriving in Macao, Ricci set out to master Chinese."

"How long ago was that?" asked Dona Inês.

"Almost exactly a century has gone by. That might seem like ancient history to you but not to us. We still face much the same difficulties, and the ways he set out to cope with them are as relevant as ever. Let me begin by telling you about the Chinese language. While fundamentally monosyllabic, it evolved early on into a highly flexible form of expression encompassing the full range of human emotions, no less than Classical Greek. It both delighted and challenged poets and still does. It relies on a writing system that expanded and flourished thanks to an equally ancient scribal tradition. So, imagine this, if you can. Chinese communicates its richness both through sounds and through visual subtleties inherent in its written form. Each written character has a colorful history underlying the strokes that make it up. While originally evocatively ideographic, it gradually evolved by incorporating phonetic elements. As a result, it grew ever more sophisticated. Scholars thrive in such an intellectually stimulating environment and Ricci was a scholar."

"Can you, Father Philippe, give us an example of the richness you speak of so enthusiastically?"

"Of course, Dona Inês, but it occurs to me that we would do well to ask Michael to tell us about the Chinese name he was given at birth. He's an accomplished calligrapher and since his writing brush and inkstone are at hand I'll wager that if you ask him he'll be only too happy to present you with an elegant rendering of his given name. Am I right Michael?"

"Nothing would give me more pleasure. As you all know, I was baptized Michael or rather Michael Alphonsus, but that's not my official name. I should mention that we Chinese like using nicknames. Back in Nanjing, my relatives and even many of my friends often referred to me affectionately as Little Brother, or Master Michael. At birth, though, my parents gave me a two-character Chinese name. It happens to be Fuzong or rather 'fu' together with 'zong'. That means that my full name is Shen Fuzong; Shen being my father's family name. I'll start with Fu. It's a thirteen-stroke character written thus (福). It connotes blessings, happiness, and good fortune. The component to the left which happens to be the character's radical, symbolizes a god-like spirit. The elements on the right below the horizontal stroke have traditionally been associated with a mouth and a field. It's very Chinese. We need a mouth to eat the rice grown in our fields. It's a matter of survival! Zong (宗) is an easier character to trace. It has only eight-strokes and it evokes propitious places such as ancestral temples and schools as well as notions connected with families and clans. As you can see it's made up of two components. The upper or radical element is the roof of a dwelling and the lower is most often used to designate an ancestral tablet. I like my name. Father Philippe has observed that it encompasses symbols that are connected with sacredness and ancestor worship. He's right. My parents chose wisely."

"Michael, you haven't said anything about your family's ancestral name."

"Forgive me. I should have. Most Chinese families refer to themselves by one of the names listed in a traditional text that we refer to as *The Hundred Names*. Most of them consist of a single character… and yes, Shen (沈) is one of those prominently mentioned. It's written using seven strokes. The radical on the left denotes water. You can easily imagine that those two dots together with that short downward stroke symbolize drops. That's right, water is very present in our culture. It thanks to our mighty rivers that we grow the rice that sustains us. The four strokes on the left are evocative of a figure on the move… swinging arms… a slender body arched forward and a foot leading the way. Calligraphers delight in the challenge of bringing such characters to life."

Calligraphic rendering of Shen's family and personal names

"So, Michael, you are well named…here you are on the move journeying to the other end of the earth and over water! Now, I'd be honored if you'd allow me to keep what you have traced as a reminder of your stay with us."

"I did so, Dona Inês, for that very purpose."

"How many written characters," asked Atayde turning to Couplet, "would Ricci have felt it necessary to memorize or, at the very least, recognize, and thereby stand a chance of teasing out their meaning?"

"There's no way of knowing, but at a minimum several thousand and by the end of his studious life probably close to ten thousand. Maybe considerably more! Ricci had, naturally, given priority to voicing the written characters in the so-called Mandarin manner. Imperial China insisted on its officials using that uniform way of pronouncing Chinese throughout the Middle Kingdom. It was the way people spoke in Beijing, home to the Forbidden City. That was Ricci's goal. He wanted to make it all the way to the Forbidden City."

The challenge, Couplet stressed, was not for the fainthearted, especially for Europeans whose classical education had exposed them to fundamentally differently structured languages such as Latin and Greek.

"Father Philippe," interrupted Atayde, "allow me a question. You and Michael speak to each other in Chinese. You said only the other day that you speak it as fluently as your native French. That's impressive. Now, living in Batavia, Dona Inês and I can tell that it isn't the way we hear Chinese spoken by my Cantonese and Fujianese business associates and certainly not by our household servants. Tell us, then, when you and Michael are together, how do you voice those characters you revere?"

"Much in the way Ricci would have learned them," replied Couplet. "He was hoping to converse with imperial administrators and scholars. Michael was brought up in a highly educated family in Nanjing, a city at the very center of the traditional Han heartland, so that's the way he spoke it at home. He'll tell you that he can also get by in Nanjing's markets and back alleys as well as in those of other cities around the lower reaches of the mighty Yangtze—cities like Shanghai, Suzhou and Hangzhou. I could, too, as well as in Canton, although at first that was a challenge. It helps that Macao is in a Cantonese-speaking region. Have I answered your question? Good! Let me get back to Ricci because he went beyond the language. He immersed himself in the Confucian texts that, according to the Chinese scholarly tradition, were the very embodiment of its ancient culture."

Couplet went on to say that before long, Ricci and a fellow Italian slipped unobtrusively out of Macao into China proper. They set out to befriend and gain the respect of scholarly Chinese officials whose language they were learning and whose culture they were making a point of scrupulously assimilating. Ricci was also a skilled mapmaker. His newfound Chinese friends soon recognized the immense importance of relating the Middle Kingdom's geographic position to the wider world of which he had knowledge. Thus armed, Ricci undertook the painstakingly slow process of establishing his scholarly reputation. He did so by moving from city to city as though they were stepping-stones leading him northward toward Beijing.

Shen recalled a family story he was only too happy to share with the Ataydes.

While in Nanjing, one of the key stopovers during the closing years of his progression toward Beijing, Ricci had, in fact, met Shen's great grandfather. Nanjing was a historic city which had intermittently served as China's imperial capital. It was strategically sited on the Yangtze, somewhat west of other cities which would in time likewise be welcoming of fledgling Christian communities. These included Shanghai, which was a growing but still small walled-in provincial town and Hangzhou, which, much like Nanjing, boasted a large population and a rich cultural and religious past.

Shen's telling evoked images of canals crossed over by elegantly arched bridges, elaborate temples with soaring, ridged, dragon-decorated hipped roofs, a gloriously tall eight-sided pagoda adorned with wondrously glazed glistening tiles, bustling markets, and the constant river traffic of junks, dhows, and sampans plying upstream and downstream of the mighty Yangtze, all set within a beguiling setting of lakes and distant hills.

Nanjing's porcelain pagoda: 1664 Dutch engraving

The meeting which had taken place over eighty years ago had, the way Shen described it, become part of his family lore. As a child, he'd heard it repeatedly told by his grandfather, who had in turn heard of it from his father. The venerable old gentleman, who was one of Nanjing's most prestigious physicians, recounted a discussion around Confucian ethics.

Ricci had politely and tentatively suggested that since there was such a thing as a Confucian Heaven, then surely it would have to have had a Lord ruling over it. In that case might not that Lord be none other than the God also worshiped by Christians? Wasn't that a logical hypothesis, given that strict Confucians were imbued with ethical principles that closely resembled those of Christians?

The story included details such as Shen's great grandmother

being present and having been given the honor of serving tea and sweet Nanjing-style dumplings. It was easy to imagine the young woman with her bound lotus feet shuffling respectfully in her ceremonial silken dress and the small talk revolving around the dumplings—they were a Nanjing specialty—with the host deprecating them and Ricci praising them effusively. Such were the ageless and essential rituals of Chinese life.

View of outskirts of Nanjing: 1683 French engraving

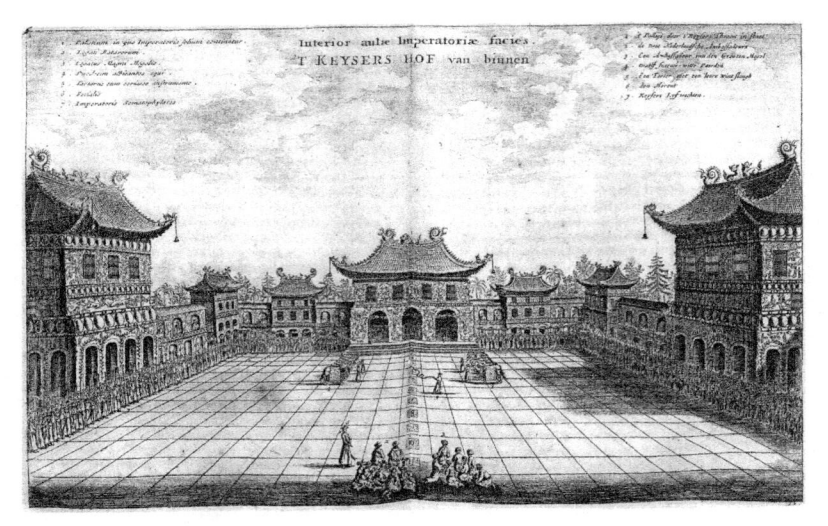

Inner Court of Beijing's Forbidden City: 1664 Dutch engraving

Couplet went on to say that thanks to Ricci's knowledge of mathematics and astronomy he had not only made his way to Nanjing but had in fact gone beyond and in time reached his end goal which was the Forbidden City. It had taken him nineteen years, but he is said to have been the first European to have been admitted within its walls.

"Why astronomy?" asked Atayde.

The observation of the heavens had, since time immemorial, played a leading role in Chinese imperial affairs. Officials overseeing the emperor's official observatory were responsible for publishing a calendar or almanac predicting the timing of observable celestial events. These included the phases of the moon, the movement of the planets, the change of the seasons, the appearance of comets, and the occurrence of eclipses. The calendar was used to determine the dates of festivals and celebrations and which days were or were not auspicious to the outcome of key human endeavors. Ricci was therefore the possessor of skills and knowledge within a discipline deemed essential to the proper administration of the empire. Since the ruling dynasty depended for its Confucian legitimacy on the quasi-religious concept of the Mandate of Heaven there was, Couplet explained, a ritualistic, almost priestly, aspect to the function.

❖

    Several weeks went by before an occasion presented itself for the Ataydes and their guests to continue their conversation. Couplet had celebrated Mass at dawn for the assembled household and the brightness of the early morning July sky held the promise of one of those luminous dry days that reminded those born in Europe of the magic of summer. They had broken their fast with a generous bowl of cooked spiced vegetables mixed into rice porridge. Atayde had decided to linger rather than set out hurriedly, as was his custom, for his quayside office. Couplet's recounting of Ricci's journey had sparked Dona Inês' curiosity regarding the different religious traditions he would surely have encountered as he immersed himself ever deeper in Chinese culture. And then, she freely admitted, despite being the most pious of Catholics, she couldn't help taking an interest in the spiritual well-being of her impressively large company of Chinese servants. They were the ones that swept, scrubbed, and polished every surface and cranny of her lovely teak-built breezy house. She was proud of it. It was a house, Shen had remarked admiringly, that rested harmoniously on mighty beams and rose well clear of the green and luxuriant vegetation that grew out of the humid soil beneath. So, yes, her gardeners climbed up and down the coconut trees that gracefully overhung the house's elegantly pitched palm-thatched roof, her amahs cared for her four young children, and her kitchen staff prepared and cooked the spicy delicacies that so appealed to her husband.

    All this to say that Dona Inês had also taken an interest in the many Chinese temples which added to the charm and mystery of

Shen's Unlikely Journey

Batavia's extensive Chinatown. Those temples might not have been as numerous as the neighborhood mosques, whose white-robed and white-capped Javanese muezzins chanted daily at the top of their solemnly monotone voices the five ritual calls to prayer, but they were the ones that commanded her attention. In fact, guided by her amahs, she took pleasure in visiting them, and most particularly the colorfully welcoming ones. She was only too happy to gaze at their great red paper lanterns and watch devotees thrust smoldering incense sticks into large sand-filled lavish bronze bowls decorated with slinking, sinuous dragons. She wanted to know more. Might Shen oblige?

There followed a hasty exchange between Couplet and Shen. It was, not unexpectedly, in hushed tonal Chinese. The upshot was that Shen excused himself and a few minutes later returned with a Chinese book. It was a traditional, butterfly-bound volume comprising alternating pages of woodblock-printed columnar text and attractive black-inked line illustrations. Shen obligingly pulled apart the slim volume's accordion-like folds and in so doing turned up an image of three old men standing behind what appeared to be a barrel.

At Couplet's bidding, Shen passed it around for all to see.

"Ah!" exclaimed Dona Inês, "the three religions. Isn't this the famous vinegar barrel visual parable?"

There was a whimsical quality about the woodcut. It did indeed depict three wise-looking dignified older men standing around a barrel. It was large and, yes, Dona Inês was not mistaken, it was filled with vinegar.

"There's much subtlety and subjectivity to the taste of vinegar," she remarked, "and it's an essential ingredient to any painstakingly cooked Chinese meal."

There was also something about the picture that jogged Atayde's memory.

"Isn't the point of the picture to get across that this vinegary life of ours can be perceived differently depending on how we approach it. It can be sweet, or sour or just bland. I'm going to guess that the gentleman on the right is Laozi, the founding father of Daoism. He's smiling and so to him the vinegar is sweet. Am I right?"

The three vinegar tasters

Atayde had indeed remembered correctly. Couplet commented that there were ancient texts attributable to Laozi that Ricci had no doubt studied. They reflected a lofty philosophical awareness that shouldn't be confused, he suggested, with the magical and colorfully extravagant beliefs of the temple devotees Dona Inês took pleasure in observing while in the company of her amahs in Batavia's Chinatown.

"True enough," observed Shen, "but the Daoist tradition nonetheless reflects the subtleties and delights of popular imagery. There are cranes soaring against backdrops of craggy limestone cliffs onto which cling ancient pines. Streams flow and sparkle below. The cranes symbolize long life and carry souls toward eternal bliss. The symbols that dominate are those of the Yin entwined and vying with the Yang. They complement each other in a mystical union. Dao in Chinese simply means The Way and the idea is to get through life by being realistic about the fact that we are all mixtures of Yin and Yang…tendencies mingle…some turn out better than others and in the end, coping with the conflicting motivations we're dealt with generally turns out to be the best strategy. We Chinese revere those images regardless of our beliefs. I remember as a child listening to the servants in our ancestral home speak of the gods, devils, and spirits that are very much part of our natural world. They'd tell me stories about how those spirits darted in and out of their everyday lives. They were harbingers of either good or bad luck and invited reflection. I know that as far as Father Couplet is concerned, all this is mere superstition and he's right, of course. I simply don't think that any great harm can come from indulging in such fanciful tales. Not if they can contribute in some small way to helping us navigate life's ever-changing challenges. What I always liked about Laozi was his benign way of counseling us to allow our better natural instincts to guide us. Lao, incidentally, is a pleasing homey ideographic character (老). It means 'old' and therefore benevolent. That just about sums up the venerable Old Man. He gives his advice with a smile and maybe a bit of a shrug. So, all in all, you're right, Dom João: to him the vinegar tastes sweet enough."

To Dona Inês, young Shen sounded homesick. There was, she reflected, a subtle sprinkling of sweet-tasting Daoist vinegar within the depth of his youthful Chinese soul.

As for Couplet, he wasn't nearly as enthusiastic about all those fleeting spirits and crafty little devils. He cautioned that Ricci would have been a lot more restrained in his appreciation.

Dona Inês took note. Next time she went to a temple in Chinatown she'd ask Shen to act as her guide.

Now for Siddhartha Gautama. He was the gaunt looking sage standing to the left of the barrel. His right hand was raised in blessing as a sign that he'd experienced nirvana.

Everyone in the Atayde household knew his story. He'd been brought up in a luxurious palace overlooking the loveliest of deer parks. Despite it being protectively fenced off from the outside world, he'd encountered disease, old age, and death. Those are the realities that inevitably accompany the human journey and resist being fenced-off. So, he studied philosophy, but it failed to bring him peace of mind. He practiced asceticism in the Hindu tradition, but that turned out to be impractical and excessive. What brought him serenity and understanding was meditation—seeking freedom from the mind's obsessiveness with impossible-to-satisfy desires. Thus did Siddhartha become a Buddha, or an enlightened one.

Dona Inês mentioned that she had grown accustomed to encountering statues of the Lord Buddha during her random walks through Chinatown and not just in temples but also in street shrines and homely nooks.

Couplet mentioned that the Lord Buddha had lived at roughly the same time as Laozi and Confucius. It had taken a good five centuries for his teachings to make their way from his native India into the Chinese heartland.

"It was a wonder they had," observed Atayde, "given Chinese wariness regarding all things foreign. There must have been something deeply appealing about Buddhism's spirituality."

"What do you think?" Dona Inês asked, turning to Shen.

"I think most of us would say that Buddhist imagery and even many of its rituals blended comfortably with our homegrown Daoist practices. The three men around the barrel aren't trying to push each other out of the way. They're accepting of each other. Buddhism's copious literate tradition appealed to my ancestors. Images of the Lord Buddha and of bodhisattvas spread soon enough across China. They were often accompanied by texts of sutras. We Chinese tend to revere what is written and have always taken great pride in the fact that we were the early inventors of both paper and mass printing."

"Can I assume," Dona Inês interjected, "that to the Lord Buddha the vinegar didn't taste of anything very specific? He'd just experienced enlightenment and he wasn't about to allow taste to distract him."

"That's exactly the way my grandmother would have put it. I probably shouldn't say this," exclaimed Shen, "but I know she kept an image of Guanyin, the Buddhist bodhisattva of mercy, in her Catholic prayer book. She once whispered in my young ears that Guanyin reminded her of Mary, the mother of Jesus. There was a Buddhist shrine in our kitchen. You know, the other thing about the Buddhist monks that came to us from India many, many centuries ago is that they had no reason to quarrel with traditional Confucian ethics. They weren't trying to talk us out of our existing beliefs."

"Perhaps not," objected Couplet, "but what our young friend Michael fails to point out is that there was nothing to commend Buddhism's logic-defying beliefs to those schooled in the rationally based discipline of Confucianism. Believe me, there wasn't!"

"No, of course not," observed Atayde, "but don't all religions, including our own, Father Couplet, invite their followers to accept as facts logic-defying events?"

The time for lunch was fast approaching and Dona Inês chose the moment to suggest that her husband serve their guests with a few drops of his precious genever liquor, the one drawn from the barrel that had been shipped all the way from Amsterdam. She noted in jest that its taste might turn out to be rather subjective. The genever, or gin, was indeed a welcome diversion.

By mutual consent, the Ataydes and their guests had left Confucius for a later occasion. August on Java's northern coast is, some would argue, the most pleasant month of the year. The sun is warm, but the air has a welcome lightness to it. Would Couplet be up to a ride along water buffalo cart tracks and forest trails? The Ataydes were in the habit of spending several weeks each summer by taking refuge from the bustle of Batavia in a secluded retreat in the southern hills.

How far away was this haven?

A sprightly horse, according to Atayde, such as one issued from the crossing of a Javanese pony with an Arabian might take no more than a day. Yes, it was true that the ponies had long ago come from Mongolia, hence their sturdiness. No more than a day? Perhaps, but that wasn't the pace at which Dona Inês, when accompanied by her young children and her retinue of servants, was accustomed to make this annual pilgrimage.

"Two days, Father Philippe, perhaps three. There's no need to rush."

※

There was indeed a calming and near-magical feel to the tall and gracefully elongated Javanese hill country pavilion that was the Atayde family's summer retreat. It was built of great teak rafters and bamboo struts and its thickly thatched saddle-shaped roof sloped steeply and majestically. It was set within a wooded wilderness of lakes and waterfalls, of monkeys, of deer, and of a great wealth of brightly plumed birds including flightless cassowaries. Yes, it was true that there were rhinoceroses and even tigers in the remoter areas but, Atayde had reassured Couplet, they were not to be feared. The villagers would be on the lookout.

So, it was on an evening in the southern Javanese foothills and in the sight of majestic Mount Salak's several volcanic cones that the conversation returned to Confucius. It was Shen who reminded everyone that the figure standing in the center of the vinegar-barrel woodcut was none other than that of the great Chinese sage. His towering scholar's headdress and his ample robes made him look rather large and imposing.

Couplet began by observing that even though Ricci and his Jesuit brothers had initially adopted Buddhist robes as a way of melding unobtrusively into the background of the provincial Cantonese cities into which they had insinuated themselves, they soon enough discarded them. The study and interpretation of Confucianism would, before long, become their major preoccupation. Scholarly gowns would not be confused with those of monks.

"Tell us again, Father Couplet," Atayde asked, "just what was it about Confucius that made his teachings so attractive to men like Ricci? Why, a century later, are you still placing such emphasis on Confucius?"

It was a searching and devilishly challenging question.

"Ricci," Couplet observed, "hadn't set out to preach on China's street corners. To do so would have invited trouble. Imperial China has always been intensely suspicious of preachers and of the sects that spawn them. They are regarded as rabble rousers. Provincial magistrates are inclined to have them flogged and paraded in bamboo cages. So, what Ricci did was to dialogue and engage intellectually with the learned rather than preach to those who huddled on street corners. He based his arguments on hallowed Confucian texts rather than relying on Christian narratives that would, inevitably, have been thought of as foreign-inspired and therefore highly suspect."

"You mean that he didn't use the gospels...that he hadn't translated them into Chinese...."

"Now, don't misunderstand me, Dona Inês. Ricci's idea was to initially engage with Chinese scholarly culture and establish credibility. It was never Ricci's intention to neglect the Christian message.

He did make converts—ask Michael about that. Not as many as our detractors would have had us make, but if Ricci had mindlessly rushed into China, preached on street-corners and ended up in a bamboo cage, where would we be?"

"You're both perplexed," Couplet continued following a long pause. "Understandably so! Would it help if I tried to summarize Confucius' philosophy? He based his teaching on relationships. He enjoined children to respect their parents. Wives should be faithful to their husbands no matter what, and citizens should be subservient and reverential in their dealings with the emperor and his ministers."

"It's a highly hierarchical view of society," remarked Dona Inês, a touch diffidently.

"It is, but it's rooted in being profoundly respectful of those we are beholden to. That's why Confucius was so insistent regarding ancestor worship. Such respect, in his view, was the bedrock on which rested piety and social harmony. He famously taught that if we wanted our children to respect us we had to begin by respecting the emperor and his ministers. Conversely, a man who failed to respect his father could never be a loyal subject nor a productive member of society. Don't neglect rituals and ceremonies, Confucius taught, because their purpose is to correctly channel your thinking and prevent you from straying. Now, let me ask you, Don João, what's not to like about such a teaching?"

Maybe it was the lateness of the hour or perhaps that Dona Inês had let out a deep sigh, but the fact was that Atayde just sat there meditatively puffing away at his long Dutch clay pipe. The Javanese pavilion's commodious upper porch faced south and that evening distant bursts of lightning flashed intermittently revealing the outline of the distant mountains.

"Let me put it another way," continued Couplet, "Ricci concluded that ancient Chinese sages had not only conceived of the God who was the one worshiped by Christians but that they had also developed an ethical framework reflective of humanity's most basic and profound spiritual yearnings. Thus, Confucius' teaching foreshadowed the eternal values on which Christianity had taken root. It was a dialogue Ricci had succeeded in engaging in with his learned Chinese friends. He had invited them to view their hallowed Confucian tradition from a Christian-inspired perspective. That was a major achievement. So, why not engage in such a dialogue with the emperor?"

"Is that why," asked Dona Inês, "Ricci was so focused on reaching the Forbidden City?"

"Undoubtedly. Confucius, he believed, had prepared the way…"

"…the way for the message of Christianity to be seen as the fulfillment of Ancient Chinese wisdom…that the time had come for the Son of Heaven to accept that message and do so on behalf of his people.…"

"I think you put it well, Dom João."

"Do you still believe that, Father Couplet? Or, given all that has happened since Ricci's day, do you think that we westerners harbor delusions in our assumption that the Chinese can be persuaded to see things our way?"

"You both ask searching questions to which I don't have ready answers. Let me just say that things didn't work the way Ricci hoped they would. The then emperor was one of the last to reign as a member of the then waning Ming Dynasty. He had succeeded his father as Son of Heaven as an eight-year-old and his coming of age had coincided with Ricci and his companions venturing out of the relative safety of Macao into China proper. As a young man, he was reputedly open to new ideas, and possibly instructed his provincial officials to turn a blind eye to the presence of the handful of unusual scholarly foreigners that had defied his orders. Sadly, in later life he tired of his sprawling and unresponsive bureaucracy. Dealing with stubborn issues such as floods, famines, and peasant unrest depressed him. He became a recluse within the vastness of the Forbidden City. It is said that Ricci had once been granted the honor of being led into the imperial throne room and thus into the emperor's symbolic presence, but that he never actually met him."

Couplet went on to say that life in the imperial capital can't have been easy for Ricci. It was hardly a haven of peace—not with its top-heavy bureaucracy and the intrigue-prone members of the imperial family that, in addition to the emperor's profuse offspring, included innumerable concubines. Then there were cohorts of power-hungry eunuchs and military commanders all vying for attention.

Ricci, however, had all along made it clear that Beijing was where he belonged. He had no desire to return to Europe and he never did. He'd sailed out of Lisbon as a 26-year-old and died at age 57. His hagiographers described death as having come to him quickly and caused by excessive fatigue. Contrary to strict precedent, according to which no foreigner could be buried within Imperial Beijing, an exception was made for Ricci. It was a great honor. To the Chinese he was Li Matou, an unassuming, but brilliant scholar of the first class.

What the Ataydes now knew for sure was just how much the Confucian texts meant to Couplet. Accordingly, Atayde, as he and Dona Inês made their way toward their sleeping quarters, thought fit to once again reassure Couplet that the camphor chests containing these texts had indeed been stored back in Batavia in the most secure of his warehouses.

❖

The next morning, Dona Inês greeted Couplet and Shen by expressing a troubling thought. It had occurred to her as she reflected on the preceding evening's extended dinner conversation. It had to do with the Confucian concept of a rigidly ordered society within which little mention was made of the role of women in shaping it.

"I'm trying to imagine, Father Philippe, what my life might have been like had it been my lot to be born into a well-to-do Chinese household. I gather that my feet would have been bound at a tender age and that around my sixteenth birthday I would have been informed by my parents that I was about to be given away in marriage to a man I was unlikely to have ever set eyes upon. I should, they would have reminded me, count myself as exceedingly fortunate given that my intended husband was from an upright family imbued with strict Confucian principles. Yes, I see you nodding in agreement. From then on I would have lived with my in-laws and been expected to lead a busy life seeing to the well-being of my husband and of my children. Were he to take on concubines, I would have been reassured, I would remain his first wife and continue to rule his household. That's right! So, I can also imagine myself to be so involved in the management of a domain teeming with servants and helpers that I would have few opportunities to venture into the world beyond the walls of my husband's ancestral mansion and certainly not find myself conversing with men I was not related to…unless perhaps in the company of my husband or of a brother?"

"Yes, Dona Inês, that's a fair summary and it does bring out one of the very real difficulties we Jesuits encountered when we first came to China. I think that we'd all agree that for faith to be solidly grounded it needs to take root within a nurturing family. That explains why women were nonetheless free to visit Buddhist temples, join religious sororities, and even speak with monks."

"But that wasn't an avenue open to you, was it? Didn't you tell me that Father Ricci had in time adopted a more scholarly approach that emphasized engaging with and gaining the trust of men who were schooled in Confucianism. Am I right? So, what happened?"

"Well, Dona Inês, our further hope was that having thus established our intellectual credibility, those men would then be impressed by the devotional practices underlying our spirituality…"

"I see. You are suggesting that since we women are more inclined toward such practices, the men would naturally want their wives, mothers, and sisters to be made aware of them."

"Precisely so that we would be given the opportunity to make that happen. Ask young Michael about how his mother, and his grandmother came to be the most devoted of Christians."

"What I remember," recounted Shen, "is that when one of the fathers visited us, my mother, my grandmother, my sisters, and our numerous women relatives were very present. It was an excuse for an extended family gathering and in our culture women enjoy each other's company. I remember them chatting, singing, and reciting poetry as they spun, weaved, embroidered, and sewed. The women in our family were well educated and so they also read. They did so together, and they often vied with each other as to who could compose the most evocative poems. They were never alone so the idea of studying devotional books together and even praying together came about quite naturally. We Chinese revere ideas that are worthy of being set out in writing. That had led Father Ricci and his fellow Jesuits to be the first from the West to write books in Chinese and have them printed. So, as you can imagine, these visits were an opportunity for the women in our family to add to their already extensive collections of edifying texts. Father Philippe will tell you that he never went around empty handed. That way our mothers and sisters became our teachers and we men listened."

"So that made a difference to your life Michael. Now tell me something else. I've also heard it said that Chinese women have a well-earned reputation for having a mind of their own and that their views are often respected and taken seriously; that when a woman is endowed by nature with a powerfully effective personality there is no Confucian principle preventing her from rising to prominence. Tell me more about that, Michael."

"You are right, Dona Inês. I was taught that one of the most accomplished and effective rulers of our gloriously cultured Tang dynasty was Empress Wu. She went from being a concubine of one of the earlier Tang emperors to marrying his successor and by dint of her personality eventually ruling over all of China. At her husband's death she extended her hold on power. She did so as empress dowager during the reigns of two of her own sons but then proclaimed herself empress in her own right. She even wore the yellow robes that are the exclusive prerogative of the one exercising the mandate of heaven. I'd also be remiss if I didn't tell you that China's present emperor Kangxi owes his own rise to power to his grandmother. It was she who as empress dowager convinced him to assert his right to rule by ordering the arrest of the most tyrannical of his regents. He was only fifteen at the time, but she turned out to be both wise and perceptive. Her grandson is on the path to greatness. He's restored harmony and prosperity to our Middle Kingdom and even expanded its borders. I don't say this lightly because I come from a family that was staunchly supportive of the Ming and regarded the Manchu invaders as destructive barbarians. We've been won over by our young emperor and the empress dowager commands our deepest respect. It's a story I can relate to. I'm barely three years younger than the emperor and if I'm here accompanying Father Philippe, it's thanks to the good advice my own grandmother gave me. She encouraged me to go in search of a wider world."

"Did I tell you, Dona Inês, that young Shen and I are the beneficiaries of the generosity of a remarkable woman who lived in Shanghai. It was my inestimable privilege to have been her confessor over the past ten years. She was indeed married off at a young age to a man she had never met and, yes, her feet had been bound. None of that got in the way of her engaging personality. She was energetic in the pursuit of causes that gave hope to those at the margins of society and her business acumen contributed to her eventually being recognized as one of Shanghai's leading personalities. I'd go even further and say that as far as we missionaries were concerned she went far beyond sustaining us with the financial support that we so desperately needed. She was an invaluable source of good advice, encouragement, and inspiration."

"You make her sound as though she was your patron saint."

"If I do that's because that's exactly what she was and still is. To my lasting sorrow she died two years ago. I'd already left Shanghai and was in Macao to prepare for this journey that Michael and I have embarked on and that, despite our inauspicious shipwreck, we hope to continue thanks to your help and generosity. It was a frustrating time for me. My superiors questioned my every move, but my greatest regret was that I was not at Lady Candida's side when she lay on her deathbed. She's inspired me and I'm determined to chronicle her life. We Jesuits are the only westerners living and working in all of China and there are probably no more than forty of us. We're a mere handful and vulnerable. We owe our continued presence to those among the Chinese who welcome the knowledge and the spiritual awareness that we bring with us. Traditional China is family-centered, and it's therefore thanks to women that its ancient culture has endured and thrived. Were it not for the example and dedication of women like Lady Candida all our efforts would have been in vain."

"You mentioned, Father Philippe, her business savvy. I'm curious," observed Atayde who had by now joined the conversation.

"Understandably so, Dom João. Let me put it this way. China is the most industrious of nations and I think it's fair to say that it is women who are responsible for producing its most coveted and revered handiwork. It is inestimably precious and thought of as a gift from the gods."

"Aha! You're talking, Father Philippe, about silk."

"Of course, I am. Let me tell you more about Lady Candida. She was raised within a Christian family. Her grandfather was a high official of the realm and he'd known Matteo Ricci. They were kindred spirits; both endowed with exceptional intellects. I've already mentioned that she was married at sixteen. It was a happy enough marriage to a man who chose to live a quiet life rather than pursue distinction and wealth by competing in the imperial examinations. She dutifully bore him eight children and was widowed while still in her mid-forties. She knew all there was to know about raising silkworms and, just like the women in Michael's family, was a talented spinner, weaver and embroiderer. She found herself at the head of a large household made up of daughters, sisters, nieces, cousins, and numerous attendants. This was an honorable pursuit. The Chinese take pride in the silks and cotton cloths produced by their womenfolk. Lady Candida was a widow. She was a dowager commanding the respect of every member of her extended family, and most particularly that of her sons, one of whom had been successful in the imperial examinations and whose high office added to her prestige. So yes, Dom João, she was free to go out into the world and achieve success as a businesswoman. To her eternal credit she used her wealth to succor the needy, feed the poor and help us found churches and orphanages."

"You said you were going to write a book about her?" Asked, Dona Inês.

"I've begun. You've no doubt noticed, Dona Inês, that I spend time every day studying and making notes. Confucius isn't my only preoccupation, although he does inspire me. I should have mentioned that Lady Candida was also artistically gifted. She designed sumptuous gowns and there's a quote from Confucius' Doctrine of the Mean that seems to capture the essence of who she was. It goes something like this:

> *Over her embroidered robe she puts on a plain single garment thereby forsaking the display of elegance for its own sake and imitating the way of the superior being who chooses to conceal his virtue.*

That she achieved what she did within a traditional Confucian-inspired society should also help us Europeans recognize that

Chinese culture is in no way inferior to our own. My notes are in French. It's my mother tongue and best suited to expressing my deepest thoughts."

❦

Atayde, accompanied by Shen, had taken long rides into the high hills beyond. Don João knew and spoke of distant volcanoes where a man could peer into smoldering craters and even tiptoe along shifting mud banks that led to sulfur-laden boiling lakes. The two men had likewise explored abandoned and long overgrown Hindu and Buddhist temples harking back to Java's pre-Islamic past. Shen had taken a lively interest in these remnants of erstwhile religious fervor, and this had prompted Atayde to tell him about the Javanese puppeteers who, as upholders of an ancient tradition, staged all-night reenactments of episodes from the great Hindu religious epics.

"I'll take you to one, Michael," Atayde had promised. "We'll sit in total darkness, and you'll be enthralled by the consummate skill of those who from behind a screen backlit by the flickering glow of a coconut oil lamp, project ghostly shadows. They bring mythical characters to life with extravagantly articulated shapes cut out of water buffalo hide. The puppet masters are accompanied by the pulsing of gongs, cymbals, and drums and the sounds of flutes and plucked strings. It all adds to the enchantment."

Yes, it would be something to look forward to on their return to Batavia. It would be a very late night. Some performances went on right up to the dawn hour. Even Couplet might feel well enough to join the party. What about Dona Inês? Why ever not? She had always, Atayde mentioned, taken pleasure in the rhythmic beating of Javanese drums, and of course she enjoyed a good yarn. Those Hindu storytellers of olden times were, she often said, every bit as imaginative as Homer.

Speaking of Dona Inês, she, while her husband and youthful Shen were out pursuing their adventures on horseback, took delight in whiling the hours away by exploring the magic that lay just beyond her doorstep. She did so accompanied by her children and amahs and guided by villagers. She listened to birds and watched monkeys at play in the treetops. She had taken to collecting strikingly colored plants which she discovered as she wandered lazily along the narrow trails that led through the dense forest to a nearby waterfall and beyond to stream fed lakes, gullies and canyons. Couplet all the while mused, meditated and dozed taking in the vastness of the cloud speckled sky above and the infinite green lying below. To him it was paradisiacal and seemingly boundless.

The days had drifted by with unaccustomed slowness. It was Dona Inês who, that evening and again over dinner, began the conversation. She was, as ever, both concerned about the wellbeing of her guests and curious regarding the tangled events that had led to their being stranded in Batavia.

"You were just the other day," she said turning to Couplet, "telling us about your upbringing in Mechlin and how, while still very young, you joined the Jesuits as a novice. I remember your saying that you had done so out of idealism. Naturally so, but you also said that perhaps an even stronger motivation was that, despite your studious nature, there was an adventurous side to your character."

"I did, Dona Inês. You were kind to take such an interest in me. As I recall, we went on to talk about Francis Xavier and Matteo Ricci. They were my heroes. I looked up to them and joining the Order seemed an obvious way of following their example and at the same time escaping from the narrow-minded provincialism of my native Mechlin."

"Do, please, continue from where you left off. How did you end up in China?"

"That's far from being a straightforward story. It took a long time. I was 17 when I joined the novitiate in Mechlin and by the time my ship docked in Macao, I was in my mid-thirties. Do you really want to hear it?"

"None of our stories are straightforward, Father Philippe," remarked Atayde. "We have plenty of time. Do please tell your story. Before you do, though, I'd like to ask our young friend Michael a question. Am I right in saying that you're twenty-four? Yes, so you're only a few years older than was Father Couplet when he became a novice in Mechlin. You've left your native country. We're going to do everything we can to help you get to Europe. So, you're about to attempt something which, if I understand correctly, few of your countrymen have ever done. Why did you undertake such a risky venture? You've already been shipwrecked once."

"Father Philippe and I have much in common. I was brought up in Nanjing. It's one of China's most beautiful and historic cities. I'm blessed with a loving family, respected and wealthy. My father wanted me to sit for the Imperial examinations. His dream was that one day I would be named a provincial governor or a senior imperial magistrate. Not unlike Father Philippe, I like to study. I'm Chinese, so I've been schooled in the Confucian classics since childhood. Why give it all up? I think you know the answer. Father Philippe has taught me that there's nothing straightforward about following through with the things we dream of…especially if they are worth doing. Have I answered your question, Dom João?"

Of course, Shen had. After a brief moment of reflection, Couplet went on to recount that during his novitiate in Mechlin he'd befriended a fellow Flemish student by the name of Ferdinand Verbiest, who happened to be an exceptionally gifted mathematician and astronomer. Years later, and after completing the extensive course of studies required of would-be members of the Order, they both asked to join the missions.

"There was an opportunity to do so in Mexico and that's where we were assigned by our superiors. I don't remember our being given much choice, but then we'd been taught as Jesuits that obedience was the greatest of all virtues. It was, however, not to be. The Spanish authorities, ever suspicious of allowing foreigners into their closely guarded New World possessions, turned us both down. So, Dona Inês, I was sent back home and told to teach. I was, quite frankly, dejected, and disillusioned. It was a low point in my life. Then, several years later, my luck turned. I attended a lecture at Louvain. Since my student days I'd always had good feelings about Louvain, where I'd studied philosophy and theology. The lecturer was a remarkable man who had just returned from the China missions and was on a recruiting tour in Europe. It was my good luck to be accompanied by my friend and contemporary, Ferdinand Verbiest, who was equally frustrated."

"It sounds as though what this man said changed your life."

"That's no exaggeration, Dona Inês. He was Martino Martini and I'd be remiss if I didn't mention the man's name. He was from Trent, a lovely Italian-speaking alpine city in Austria made famous by the great Council convened over a century ago to combat Protestantism. The man was amazing. He was barely forty at the time and yet he'd already spent ten years in China. His travels had taken him to so many places that, thanks to his mastery of mathematics, he'd become a consummate mapmaker. The famed Amsterdam cartographer Joan Blaeu had already undertaken to include his maps of China in his Atlas Mayor. Maps are your hobby, Dom João, I'm sure you've heard of the great Blaeu…of course you have. Anyway, Martini had also fallen in love with history and in talking to us made much of the books he was working on. One was destined to chronicle China's early history. It went back, he asserted, to an era predating the Biblical record and the other recounted the very contemporary drama of the fall of the Ming to the Manchus. Some Europeans still misguidedly believed that Marco Polo's Cathay and China we Jesuits had encountered were different countries, but Martini was emphatic in disabusing them. What perhaps fascinated us more than anything else was his use of a contraption he called a magic lantern. He used it to project images against a wall. It brought his words to life, and we were spellbound. Magic, indeed! Was it a Chinese invention, we asked? Apparently not. It was the Dutch who had figured the thing out with the help of lenses. They were much the same lenses, he told us, as those Galileo had used to look into the night sky and turn the world upside down. Yes, we were spellbound! I should also mention that one of the reasons Martini was in Europe was that he was on his way to Rome and that the question of the Chinese ancestral rites had already come up."

"So, Father Philippe," Atayde interjected, "a quarter of a century has gone by and here you are on your way to Europe so you can argue about the very same issue. Am I right?"

"Alas you are, Dom João. In any event, the prospect of being given the opportunity to learn Chinese and embrace so beguiling a culture proved irresistible. My friend Ferdinand Verbiest and I were both, I suppose, still struck by wanderlust. The prospect of going to China was a dream come true. It occurred to us that Divine Providence might have had a hand in inspiring the Spanish authorities to deny us the opportunity of spending the rest of our lives in Mexico."

A dream perhaps, Couplet went on to explain, but far from a simple one to bring about. By the time Couplet's ship had at long last sailed out of Lisbon for China, almost fifty years had elapsed since Ricci's death in Beijing. Those had been trying times for the fledgling Chinese missions. They were overshadowed by events in Japan. After a spectacularly auspicious beginning, the tide had turned against Japanese Christians. The wily and powerful daimyo who had found it expedient to support the Portuguese, was assassinated. It was no secret that he'd profited handsomely from his alliance with their traders and that they'd supplied him with state-of-the art musketry. The Jesuits and their converts suddenly found themselves on the losing side of the civil war. They were accused of being unpatriotic, committing treason and undermining the traditional values enshrined in Buddhism. They were caught up in the unforgiving crosswinds of human affairs.

The repression was both brutal and heart wrenching. It began with the crucifixion of twenty-six Christians in the city of Nagasaki, a strategically located natural harbor whose openness to foreign shipping and commerce had brought it great wealth. Thanks to its large community of Christian converts, Nagasaki had come to be known as the Rome of Japan. The Franciscans and Dominicans, who even at the best of times viewed the Jesuits with suspicion and envy, ascribed their rivals' undoing to their involvement in Japanese politics and to their pursuit of material gain. Shouldn't the Jesuits, they clamored, have devoted themselves single-mindedly to saving the maximum possible number of souls? They'd misguidedly relied on their intellect and pride was their undoing. Spain, now eager to expand its own sphere of Asian influence out of the beachhead it had established in the Philippines, was equally critical. It hoped to gain influence at the expense of the Portuguese.

The failure of the Japanese missions had put the China Jesuits on the defensive. In terms of numbers of converts, the progress made by Ricci and his superiors was deemed overly modest. As a result, the China Jesuits were accused of the sin of accommodation and nowhere more so than in Rome. Couplet placed much emphasis on that word. Accommodation had, he stressed, become a pejorative catch-all word for the much-criticized view forcefully advocated by Ricci that Christian converts should be allowed to continue to celebrate ancestral rituals and make offerings honoring their forebears. The Ricci view that the name of God should be rendered in Chinese by using characters that conformed with and respected China's highly developed culture was likewise excoriated.

"I haven't even mentioned the greatest of all threats that confronted me on my arrival in China twenty-five years ago." Couplet continued, "The country was in turmoil. The Ming dynasty had been deposed in the preceding decade. The new Manchu Qing rulers had their hands full. They were still repressing a loyalist resistance movement in the South. Initially, we Jesuits were caught in the middle. Most of the fathers had thrown in their lot with the victorious Qing, but not all."

"The perils of running afoul of politics as in Japan!" exclaimed Atayde.

"Exactly, Dom João, and there's an ironic twist to what I'm about to tell you. When I boarded the ship on the Lisbon-Goa leg of the long journey that would eventually bring me to Macao, I was entrusted to the care of a man by the name of Michael Boym. I wasn't the only one. There were, beside me, other inexperienced recruits on board. Boym was the Jesuit that had done the most to rally support for the southern Ming loyalists. He was returning to China even though his efforts to enlist help from the papacy and from Europe's crowned heads had met with abject failure. I remember him as an inveterate optimist."

Manchu archer on horseback: 18th century painting

The Ataydes wanted to know what had brought about the demise of the Ming. Couplet turned to Shen. The young man wasn't yet born when Beijing was overrun by the Manchus. He'd however been brought up in a loyalist family and had heard more than his fair share of stories told around those still recent events. That part of the narrative was his to tell.

"The Ming had thought of their rule as eternal," Shen began. "Their heavenly mandate felt secure. They were, after all, the ones that three centuries earlier had succeeded in overthrowing the upstart Mongol dynasty and restoring legitimate rule. They thought of themselves as the undisputed guardians of all that was authentically Chinese."

Shen went on to tell how the Ming hadn't counted on being challenged by the fearsome, horse-riding, Manchurian tribesmen that roamed the Eastern Siberian steppes. Nor had they given much heed to the half-starving peasants who, out of desperation, had rebelled and rallied around a strongman sympathetic to the Manchus. The rebels had convinced themselves that the Ming emperors were no longer worthy of ruling as Sons of Heaven. They had therefore earned the right to occupy and loot the Forbidden City. In battle, however, the well-trained Manchus were a lot more effective than the rebellious peasants. They were armed with powerfully strung extended bows, were skilled at shooting them from horseback and were highly disciplined.

"One didn't stand in the way of those kinds of people," exclaimed Shen.

Most threateningly of all, the Manchus had done their homework and were determined to step into the imperial shoes of the ousted Ming. They fully intended to rule as those to whom Heaven had now transferred its mandate. They were, for the most part, Buddhists, but hadn't completely cast off their earlier Shamanist inclinations. They also knew about the political expediency of paying their respects to Confucius. He was the mythically wise guardian of legitimacy, and the Manchus, like all invaders, were into acquiring self-serving legitimacy.

Shen quoted an old saying to the effect that while it was possible to conquer the Chinese by storming in on horseback, ruling them required dismounting. Kublai Khan, the fearsome Mongol, had conquered them several centuries before his latter-day Manchus cousins but even he had had to get off his horse. That's where Confucius came in handy.

"You couldn't," Shen joked, "study Confucius while on horseback and you couldn't lord it over us Chinese without invoking the principles enunciated by Confucius."

Couplet nodded approvingly.

That was when the Manchus adopted the dynastic name Qing. It was a Chinese character with reassuring meanings along the lines of clear, pure, and honest. Manchu men wore their hair according to a highly distinctive style that Europeans had come to refer to as queues. The name, Shen had been told by Couplet, derived from the French word for a tail. The front of the scalp was shaved off but the hair at the back was left to grow to great lengths. It was most often braided into a single swinging strand; hence it being tail-like. The style was unmistakably intimidating, and it was profoundly humiliating for those upon whom it was imposed. Shen spoke from personal experience.

How to make sense out of the chaos and bloodshed that ensued? Some, Shen stressed, had described the transition from the Ming to the Qing as cataclysmic. The harshness of the winters and the ensuing crop failures that had induced the peasants to rebel against the decadent Ming had hardly receded. The Manchus had made everything worse by taking for themselves the little sustenance that was available.

One of the first things that had happened as the peasants and the Manchus were closing in on Beijing was that the last Ming emperor turned his back on his frenzied household by walking unnoticed out of the Forbidden City into the nearby hills. There he strung a silk scarf tightly around his neck and jumped to his death.

It wasn't quite the end of the Ming, though. Surviving members of the deposed imperial family fled to Nanjing and then further south. Emperors in exile were named in quick succession only to be hunted down by ruthless and well-equipped Manchu horsemen. The loyalists did, however, eventually succeed in consolidating their tenuous position and exert an ephemeral hold over several southern provinces. These remnants of Ming legitimacy were vested in an emperor-in-exile who held court wherever it was expedient to do so.

Many of the stories Shen had listened to at family gatherings in his native Nanjing concerned an extravagant character who liked to be known not just as the Ming Empress Dowager but also as the emperor-in-exile's 'adoptive mother'. Under Jesuit influence, she had converted and taken on the highly symbolic Christian name of Helena. She set great store on her association with the Jesuits whom she viewed as emissaries of distant yet mighty western powers.

"Helena," Couplet interjected, "was the name of the Roman Emperor Constantine's notably meddlesome ultra-pious Christian mother."

This most Chinese of dragon ladies had also contrived to have the infant successor to the imperial-throne-in-exile baptized Constantine. Yet another symbolic name for the one who it was hoped against hope would one day be welcomed into the Forbidden City as the first Christian Chinese emperor. For that to have happened it would, of course, have been necessary for the Ming loyalists to have soundly defeated the now solidly entrenched Manchus.

"I'm beginning to understand," interjected Atayde, "why this small group of Ming loyalists would, in desperation, have resorted to seeking help from outside China. So, when all else had failed, why not play the Jesuit card? Why not let the good fathers use their political savvy to rally support from their powerful European friends. The Jesuits could, surely, be relied upon to spread the word that there was a Queen Helena involved and even a would-be Emperor Constantine in the wings?"

"I wouldn't have put it quite so bluntly, Dom João, but yes. That's where the man who I first met on the quayside in Lisbon came into the picture. He was another larger-than-life character but cast in a very different mold from Matteo Ricci. Are you and Dona Inês prepared to hear his story? Be warned, it will strain your credulity."

They were, and Couplet was only too happy to oblige.

Michael Boym was Polish, exceedingly enterprising, and it was he who had become the formidable Empress Dowager's most trusted advisor-cum-confessor. It was he who had prompted her to pursue the idea of sending him off as an ambassador to Europe. Boym was given duly signed and sealed letters of credence. They were redacted in Latin, and he was sent off on his mission single handed. He was to hold out the tantalizing prospect of a China over which the Ming would once again reign supreme and thus be on the cusp of becoming the world's most numerous and prosperous Catholic nation.

"Doesn't desperation have a way of breeding the wildest fantasies?" mused Dona Inês.

"Yes, and this particular mirage didn't end well," Couplet noted. The story had once again put him in a reflective mood tinged with sadness. "It couldn't have. Europe's Catholic monarchs, the pope included, had other more urgent matters on their minds. They always did when it came to China."

"Nor," observed Atayde, "can I imagine the Manchus standing idly by waiting for Boym's embassy to bear fruit."

"Of course not. It was the most implausible of adventures. Human affairs," reflected Couplet, "do seem to go in cycles, and the Ming era had irreversibly run its course. The thing about Boym is that he happened to be not only a linguist, but also a first-class naturalist and illustrator, and his father, being an illustrious physician, also had a keen interest in medicine. He was my senior by many years, but during that long journey from Lisbon to Goa he treated me generously and was only too happy to talk to me about the many years he'd spent in China. Not just in China; he'd hiked from India to Persia. He'd been to places like Mozambique, taken notes and illustrated everything. I felt I was in the presence of the most unusual of intellects. Against all odds, he'd found time to put together what I've been told is the most authoritative and original work on Asian flora and medicinal herbs. It was published in Vienna about thirty years ago and there's a copy of it in our Jesuit library in Beijing. I can confirm that the illustrations are lavish and that the book is a marvel to behold. Dom João, why don't you ask your Amsterdam agent to procure Dona Inês a copy. She'll enjoy it and use it to instruct your children. It shouldn't take much more than a couple of years to get to you."

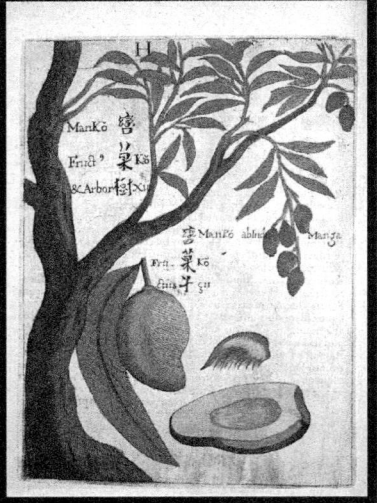

From Michael Boym's Flora Sinensis (1656): (left) Squirrel chasing a green haired turtle; (right) Mango

When the ship bearing Boym and Couplet eventually docked in Goa, the two parted company. Boym, strong headed and idiosyncratic as ever, had had a falling out with the Goanese Jesuits. They had looked askance on the misguided embassy the Empress-Dowager-in-exile had put him up to. Boym, unaware that the military situation of the southern Ming loyalists had, in his absence, further deteriorated, decided, in defiance of his Jesuit superiors, to return to China by the most unorthodox of routes that included hitching a ride on a ship operated by Viet pirates. He did, from Hanoi and on foot, cross into China but then fell sick on a mountainous trail.

Shen and Couplet concluded their storytelling by noting that Couplet's arrival in China had coincided with Shen's birth in Nanjing. It was also the time at which the last Ming emperor-in-exile had been hunted down and done away with by a Qing general sent for that very purpose to Yunnan from Beijing. And then, sadly, Michael Boym had not survived the trek along China's southernmost hill country.

"Could it be, Father Couplet," reflected Dona Inês, "that succeeding generations will look back on men like Boym and admire them for having left a mark on our world in the most unexpected of ways? Perhaps not so much for having saved souls but, well, for having had the genius to put together that remarkable book alerting us to the wonders around us. It may be no accident that it is while we are here in this most magical of gardens of Eden that we are evoking Michael Boym's true accomplishments. His surely was a life well lived."

❧

"Our evenings spent on this porch overlooking the mountains beyond are turning out, thanks to both of you, to be a heaven-sent opportunity for Dona Inês and for me to learn things about China that we should have been aware of long ago. If it's really true that the Middle Kingdom is the world's largest, most populated, and by the looks of things the most industrious of all kingdoms, then it strikes me that we would all be well advised to take to heart what you have to tell us. Isn't there a saying to the effect that to ignore reality is to live dangerously?"

"Yes, I think I've heard it said that while ignorance might be blissful it can also be highly dangerous," quipped Couplet.

"Of course, you have," continued Atayde with a cheerful chuckle, "but then when it comes to learning, you Jesuits are biased. It's your religion. All right then you've told us about the demise of the Ming. Now tell us about the Manchus, or rather about the Qing as you now call them by their adopted, dynastic, Chinese-sounding name. Tell us how the Jesuits huddled around Beijing survived the onslaught. I presume they did. I mean here you are, accompanied by young Michael, making your way to Europe as ambassadors of what you've described as Manchu-endorsed Confucian wisdom. We're curious as to how all this came about."

"I'll begin," Couplet responded, "by stating the obvious. It wasn't plain sailing, and the Manchus were not without challenges of their own."

Indeed, not and the big issue had to do with succession. The Manchu strongman who, having striven mightily and successfully to oust the Ming and take over the Forbidden City, died unexpectedly. He'd already declared himself emperor the year before the fall of Beijing when he was only fifty. The Manchus needed an emperor in a hurry because Confucian legitimacy was at stake. So the Manchu generals got together and designated one of the would-be-emperor's infant sons as his imperial successor. He was a five-year-old. It was the least the generals could have done to honor the tradition that Sons of Heaven were invariably chosen from among the deceased emperor's direct descendants.

They then squabbled among themselves until one emerged as regent. He was a brutally repressive character who went by the very

Manchu name of Dorgon. Buddhist-cum-animist that he was, he had little reason to pay much attention to the tiny number of Beijing Jesuits that, unlike their colleagues in the southern provinces still under Ming control, were lying low. Their hope was simply to remain out of harm's way. One of them did, however, come to Dorgon's attention. He was a German, and his name was Adam Schall.

"You're going to tell me, Father Couplet," joked Dom João, "that he was yet another towering intellect. That leaves me with the nagging question of why so many of these brilliant people became Jesuits and then gravitated toward China. Do you have an answer?"

"You've guessed correctly. He was an outstanding astronomer and mathematician. Why did he join the Jesuits when he could have made a name for himself back in his native Germany as a soldier or a statesman? He could also have opted for a more conventional church career and become a bishop, or why not a cardinal. The excitement, I think. I can relate to that. A feeling that the world was breaking out of its traditional confines. We Jesuits were willing to take on the risk of placing ourselves at the cutting edge of that irresistible force. It was and still is a dangerous place to be. But it is anything but boring. I've thought about that a lot. I'd still choose the risk of shipwreck over teaching Greek at the Mechlin gymnasium. That's what my superiors wanted me to do: teach Ancient Greek! Right now, I could be reading Aristotle's Metaphysics in the original."

"You could, Father Philippe, but what about Michael? Why don't we ask him why he let himself in for this journey?"

So, at Dom João's suggestion, Couplet turned to Shen.

"Michael, why did you agree to come to Europe when you could be sitting for the Imperial Examinations? You're from a good family. You might have become a provincial governor. You're not sure? Well, there you are, you chose the risk of shipwreck over the prospect of being a scholar of the First Class."

"The other thing, Dom João, is that once in China, we Jesuits were left largely on our own. No one knew enough to be in a position to tell us what to do. There was Adam Schall in Beijing asking himself how he was going to make the best of a seemingly hopeless situation. He wasn't just an astronomer and a mathematician with linguistic abilities, he was also a tinkerer extraordinaire with an uncanny ability to make things. He'd come to the attention of this Dorgon character because of the work he'd previously done on the official calendar. That was under the Ming, admittedly, but the upstart Qing needed to pay as much attention to the accuracy of the calendar as their predecessors, more perhaps. Remember, they were in search of legitimacy. They'd just gotten off their horses and were attending to the challenging business of ruling the Chinese. Then Dorgon heard something else about Schall that really grabbed his attention."

"I'll wager it was something practical and useful."

"It was, Dom João," continued Couplet. "Father Schall knew a whole lot about the mathematics of ballistics and the design and casting of cannons. Now, I'll grant you, Dona Inês, that we priests aren't supposed to involve ourselves in the design of lethal state-of-the-art military hardware, but these were no ordinary times. So, Father Schall went to work designing cannons for the Manchus. Dorgon returned the favor. Not only were the Jesuits allowed to remain in Beijing but they were even told they could build a church. It so happened that Father Schall knew a thing or two about designing handsome looking public buildings."

"A church for a cannon," quipped Atayde.

"Perhaps but better to be on the side of the victorious Manchus designing cannons than on that of rebellious southern pretenders embarking on hopeless embassies. We Jesuits had learned our lesson the hard way. You said it yourself. We'd been on the wrong side of the bitter struggle that had torn Japan apart. It spelled disaster for us. In any event, it was Schall's reputation as an astronomer and designer of useful devices that made him a respected presence within the Forbidden City's corridors of power."

There was a lot more to Couplet's storytelling. As the years went by, the child-emperor grew older and Dorgon, his regent, who fancied himself as the de facto emperor, continued to reign supreme. Now Dorgon was also a hunter, and it happened that one fateful day, he was mortally wounded while in pursuit of prey. By this time, the emperor was now a thirteen-year-old. He had given indications of being wise beyond his years, so he took Dorgon's death as a sign the time had come for him to rule in his own right. He prudently took Schall as his tutor and listened to what this father-figure of a Germanic teacher had to say. Thus did a German Jesuit, skilled in the sciences of mathematics and astronomy become the most listened-to man in all of China.

"Did Schall harbor hopes of converting the young emperor?" Asked Atayde.

"It couldn't have been otherwise, but the fact was that the young man was attracted to Chan Buddhism. Disappointing no doubt, but then, Schall found himself sadly confronting the most insidious of obstacles."

The conversation turned toward the ever-present threat of disease. If there was one thing that instilled sheer terror in the hearts of the European inhabitants of Batavia, it was the scourge of a sudden onset of fever. A random walk through the Dutch cemetery was the most sobering of experiences. It was impossible, when passing by each tomb, not to compulsively make a mental note of the difference between the date of the unlucky occupant's birth and that of his decease. This was no country for old men. Smallpox was just one among the many diseases responsible for so many premature deaths. It was known to have caused widespread misery at the height of the Roman Empire's territorial expansion. Couplet related that in Roman times, smallpox had almost certainly been present as far east as China.

What those around the dinner table were also aware of was that over the centuries, it had occurred to shrewd physicians that deliberately infecting a healthy person with a mild form of the dread disease conferred a degree of immunity. It was an insight that had gradually gained acceptance and the practice began spreading throughout Asia. Couplet referred to it as variolation and that was, as he explained, because variola was the name those Ancient Romans had given to the dread affliction. Variolation was risky, of course, but most Chinese seemed willing to take their chances. Not so, the Manchus. They feared the remedy more than the disease and instead hoped to survive by avoiding contact with those afflicted by the malignancy. Their invasion of China had, however, exposed them to a whole new level of infectious risk.

The tragedy was that, despite living within the relatively isolating walls of the Forbidden City, the promisingly alert and engaging young emperor succumbed to the dread disease and died. He was only twenty-two. His wives and many concubines had, notwithstanding his youth, assured him of a numerous progeny. The one chosen to succeed him as Son of Heaven was, of course, a mere child who had yet to reach his seventh birthday. Regents were once again named. Adam Schall, who by now was in his seventieth year, had lost a friend who revered his wisdom. He had also lost a much-needed protector. Regencies, by their very nature, breed political turbulence. Ambition, stoked by untrammeled greed, ran loose in and around the Forbidden City. A strong man did emerge, and many of those whom the deceased young emperor had favored were the ones the newly-empowered went about dismissing and persecuting.

Adam Schall had made enemies. It couldn't be otherwise. Astronomical predictions, calendrical calculations, the timing of rituals and the interpretation of what message a particular observed phenomenon might or might not convey were subjects of intense interest and potential controversy. Egos were all too easily bruised. Schall had promoted within the Astronomy Board those he deemed competent. So, inevitably, there were discontents and some of them had ties to the political factions spawned by the autocratic regent. And then there were those who for the longest time had been associated with the Islamic school of astronomy. China's ancient stargazing tradition had never completely closed itself off from schools originating within other civilizations. Thus had wise men over the centuries come from far-off India, Persia, Baghdad, and no doubt, even from Ancient Mesopotamia, the reputed cradle of observational astronomy.

"Allow me to express a sobering thought before I continue with the story," said Couplet. "I've come to realize in my old age—yes, I'm feeling older—that all too often those things that account for our early successes bear within them the seeds of our undoing."

"You have just voiced, Father Philippe, a truth we should all take to heart. But isn't it also understandable that Father Schall was resented?" exclaimed Atayde. "He was neither Chinese nor Manchu, and his competence inconveniently and dangerously brought out the shortcomings of others. That's something to be avoided at all costs. Sometimes it's safer to play the part of the dumb but useful underdog. I make a point of always deferring to my Dutch colleagues. We Portuguese are here in Batavia on sufferance. The VOC could send us packing at a moment's notice. Now, Father Philippe, tell me about Schall as a person. What was he like?"

"I met him when I first arrived in China. That was a few years before the young emperor's death. He was an intimidating figure, and I was a mere pup just off the ship. I was awed by the vastness of China and the wisdom of my superiors. He was very Germanic and I'm sure you know what I mean by that. So, yes, he wasn't the easiest of characters to relate to. Even some of the fathers experienced him as, shall we say, forthrightly opinionated. Jealousy, of course, came into play. He was brilliant and extraordinarily influential. Later, when he ran into trouble, there were those who stood ready to accuse him of indulging superstition. Stargazing, to some of our more conservative brothers, was by its very nature, suspect. Didn't aspects of it border on astrological idol worship? Some had even suggested that Schall deserved to be defrocked—booted out of the Jesuit Order, no less. He'd become vulnerable, and that brought out the blood-sniffing hounds. All we need for those corrosive thoughts to emerge from our collective bosoms is for some unanticipated trigger. His was a very human story."

Well, it did all fall apart. Schall was accused of many things. Some were mundane and petty while others were fanciful and conspiratorial. The least credible were among the hardest to dispel. They were certainly the hardest to make sense of. Schall's principal accuser and antagonist was a bitter and disgruntled rival on the Astronomy Board. He first contrived, with the implicit support of the hostile regent, to destroy Schall's credibility by challenging him to a trumped-up astronomical contest. Then, Schall and his close colleagues were essentially put on trial for causing the death of a Manchu princess who had been the recently deceased young emperor's favorite. There was even a suggestion that Schall might have caused the emperor's own death.

"Accused of murder!" exclaimed Dona Inês.

"It wasn't that simple. Here's what was said to have happened. The princess who was young, and reportedly, enticingly beautiful had borne the emperor a son. The infant survived barely a few months. The loss of one who might have been the next emperor caused the mother the deepest of unrelieved grief. Within a relatively short time, she also died, and this in turn drove the impressionable young emperor to the very edge of despair. Then, of course, he also died—of smallpox!"

"I still don't understand how Father Schall, who was the emperor's devoted tutor, could have contributed to this family tragedy?"

"There may have been other crimes imputed to Schall, but the one that stood out involved his presumed responsibility for having set the date at which the funeral rites for the deceased imperial infant had been carried out. Had the date been auspiciously chosen, in accord with tradition and with due regard to the alignment of the appropriate heavenly bodies? It had, Dona Inês, been Schall's responsibility, given his official position, to make such a determination. A grievous lapse had surely occurred. Clearly so, otherwise the princess would still be alive and not only the princess, but quite possibly the young emperor as well. Might Schall have added insult to injury by also casting powerfully malevolent spells in the strange languages he spoke when addressing his fellow Barbarians?"

"So, these spells might have brought about the smallpox? This is an unbelievable story!"

"I don't pretend to know, Dona Inês, exactly what evidence, nor what precise charges the judges considered, but the fact was that they found Schall guilty, together with six of his associates. He was thereupon confined to prison under absurdly harsh conditions. Do you remember me saying, Dona Inês, that when I joined the Jesuit novitiate in Mechlin, I made friends with a fellow student who was an exceptionally talented mathematician? We were close to the point that we had both volunteered for the Mexican missions and had both been rejected by the Spanish authorities for being suspiciously foreign. Then we'd sat together while listening to the lecture at Louvain given by Father Martini who'd clearly fallen in love with China. What I'd failed to mention is that he and I arrived in China the very same year. My friend's name, you might recall, was Ferdinand Verbiest. The years were beginning to weigh heavily on Adam Schall, and he needed an assistant. Verbiest's reputation for mathematical brilliance had preceded him, so not unnaturally, he was the one chosen to join Schall in Beijing. He was assigned to the imperial observatory as a full time astronomer and was therefore one of the seven accused of astrological malfeasance. It was a capital offense. He was confined to the same Beijing jail as Schall. I was devastated at the thought that he was going to die. Melancholy seized hold of me. I knew about melancholy, but I'd never experienced it as intensely as I did then. Verbiest and I were both 42 at the time. Father Schall was 74."

Schall had been too weak to speak at his trial, so it fell to Verbiest to defend him. It was to no avail since all were found guilty, and in Schall's case the judges recommended strangulation. The regent thereupon decreed that Schall's crime was such as to warrant the most outrageous of penalties, which was slow death by a combination of slicing and dismemberment.

At this point, Couplet's narrative took an unexpected turn. He hadn't witnessed any of these events directly. He had, at the time, been assigned to the Shanghai missions. Here are some of the things he had been told. There had been reports of a strikingly bright meteor streaking ominously across the sky and parts of Beijing, including the prison, had been rocked by an earthquake. Stranger still, a fire had broken out in a room adjacent to the one within the Forbidden City in which the trial had taken place. Had the Heavens spoken? Perhaps. It was also a fact, according to Couplet, that the Jesuits still had powerful friends at court. In any event, the regent, perhaps mindful of his own credibility, relented. Schall was freed, but all foreigners were either exiled to Macao or placed under house arrest in Canton. The five Chinese Christian astronomers trained by Schall, however, paid the full price. They were beheaded. This was rough justice indeed. Adam Schall died in Beijing shortly after his release from jail. He'd made it to his 75th birthday which, as Couplet remarked with a wry smile, was far more than any European toiling in China could reasonably expect. He'd most likely suffered a stroke brought on by the outrageous way in which he'd been treated. His had unquestionably been another life well lived.

"How, Father Couplet, could the China missions recover from this series of dire setbacks? Father Schall was dead. That was tragic because, as you describe the situation, he was the one man thanks to whose genius the Manchus had tolerated the Jesuit presence in China. Then didn't you mention that the reigning emperor was a helpless infant, and his regent a power-hungry tyrant hellbent on expelling foreigners and ridding the country of foreign ideas? What happened to you, Father Couplet? Were you expelled from Shanghai and exiled?"

"I certainly was, Dom João. I was one of the ones sent to Canton. It was, I suppose, a semi-exile. I was still in China. Canton is where the Order owned a spacious residence. We were told we could use it, but woe betide any of us caught outside the compound without permission. It could have been worse. We were allowed servants, ample provisions, and even visitors. You paint too bleak a picture. The emperor was no infant. He was a twelve-year-old and was rumored to be highly intelligent and to have a mind of his own. The regent was unpopular. There was a silver lining to our Cantonese semi-exile. For me, it was an opportunity to reunite with the three men with whom I had studied Chinese upon arriving in China. I'll talk about that later. We were all determined to survive the crisis."

"Was your old friend Ferdinand Verbiest with you in Canton?" asked Dona Inês.

"He wasn't. He'd managed to remain in Beijing, living in semi-hiding. It was an open secret that the Astronomy Board couldn't do without him. All was not lost."

Matteo Ricci, Adam Schall and Ferdinand Verbiest: Early 18th century French engraving

Shen's Unlikely Journey

Emperor Kangxi

The young emperor's name was Kangxi.
Couplet shied away from mentioning hard-to-remember Chinese

names to his hosts, though this one was different. *Kang* stood for health and *xi* for prosperity. A well-chosen name should also be a lucky one. The luck of a lucky emperor had a way of including within its beneficent aura those whom the Heavens had entrusted to his care. It was Kangxi's good luck to have a grandmother who was both sagacious and resourceful. She'd developed a hearty dislike of the autocratic regent, and on her grandson reaching his fifteenth birthday, counseled that the time had come for him to assert his imperial authority and do away with the man. This is exactly what Kangxi did.

The regent's demise was bad news for those who had brought about Schall's downfall. They were held to account for mismanaging the Beijing Astronomy Board and neglecting the imperial calendar. Verbiest emerged from hiding. With the help of influential Beijing friends, he'd stayed in contact with Macao. The exiled Jesuits needed no reminding of how vital it was for them to remain at the forefront of the rapidly developing field of astronomical observation. They'd prevailed on their colleagues at the Collegio Romano to do their utmost to obtain updated European star charts and optical instruments of the type pioneered by Galileo. The only way to get them to China was to ship them via Lisbon to Macao. The process was agonizingly slow, but successful. Schall's memory was rehabilitated and Verbiest was put in charge of the Bureau. It was a complete about-face.

Better still, Kangxi came to regard Verbiest as his tutor. The young emperor was intellectually alert and intensely curious; mathematical and scientific concepts intrigued him. Verbiest dreamed up ways of stimulating the emperor's practical turn of mind. He would have made an excellent engineer. He designed an autonomous steam-powered wheeled device. It was toy size, but it worked. Chinese craftsmen executed his design with laudable precision.

Couplet and his guests took pleasure that evening in speculating whether such mechanical contraptions might one day replace push carts and horse drawn carriages. Shen was inclined to think so.

The missions had been granted a reprieve, and there was Verbiest tutoring an emperor. Verbiest was a modest man, Couplet knew. He and Verbiest were like brothers. Their friendship stretched back to being classmates in the Mechlin novitiate. Verbiest claimed to have simply done what was expected of him. He'd been lucky. Was it luck or Divine Providence?

"You know, Dona Inês, young Michael and I have the same question regarding our shipwreck. Thanks to the shipwreck we have come to know you and thanks to your hospitality and good conversation we've had the opportunity to reflect on the momentous and chance events that have brought us to where we are. Thanks to you, Michael's journey has had an auspicious beginning. Luck or Divine Providence? You tell me!"

Confucius says:

I will not be afflicted at men's not knowing me;
I will be afflicted that I do not know men.
Analects I

The scholar who cherishes the love of comfort
is not fit to be deemed a scholar.
Analects XIV

They occupied the places of their forefathers,
practiced their ceremonies, and performed their
music. They reverenced those whom they honored
and loved those whom they regarded with
affection. Thus, they served the dead as they would
have served them alive; they served the departed
as they would have served them had they been
continued among them.
Doctrine of the Mean

III
The Return of the Rains
Autumn of 1682 to February 1683

The Ataydes and their guests looked back on the time spent among the magically wooded foothills of Mount Salak as one of those rare retreats from the numbing routine of everyday cares. They were grateful for having been afforded the opportunity to converse and reflect on how circuitous and seemingly chance events in each of their past lives had led to the present. Life in Batavia had for Shen and Couplet resumed its daily routine of meditation, study and waiting. There's much strangeness to waiting Shen had observed. We're never sure exactly what it is that we're waiting for and despite knowing we should be wanting it to happen we'd nonetheless just as soon remain enfolded within the reassuring sameness of the present. He'd voiced his thoughts to Couplet as might an overly scrupulous penitent, to a weary father confessor.

Then, one evening, something did happen. Atayde took Couplet aside, muttering that one of the more senior members of the VOC's governing board had approached him earlier that day. He wanted to see Couplet at the earliest opportunity. For what reason? Atayde hadn't thought it prudent to pursue the matter. He was a German by the name of Andreas Cleyer. Atayde knew him well. They'd arrived in Batavia at roughly the same time and Cleyer, who held himself out to be a physician skilled in the arcane study of medicinal plants, had by dint of ambition allied to political savvy, become the VOC's chief pharmacist and surgeon. All Atayde knew was that he'd just recently been promoted to an even more senior position at the Dutch enclave of Dejima in Nagasaki Bay, and that he'd soon be leaving for Japan. Couplet was flustered. He'd done his best to keep a low profile. Atayde went out of his way to be reassuring. Maybe Cleyer simply wanted to ask him something about China but then, he'd added as an afterthought, this was not a man to be trifled with. It would be best if the very next morning he and Couplet were to present themselves at the chief surgeon's office in the Kasteel Batavia and pay their respects.

Couplet that night had tossed and turned. Then it came to him. There was something familiar about the name. Yes, that was it! He'd even corresponded with Cleyer, years ago and then only briefly. He'd quite forgotten. Couplet's apprehension was well founded. There was an unresolved issue that, despite the passage of time, still haunted him. It went back to Michael Boym and to the interminable ocean voyage that a quarter of a century ago had first brought Couplet to China. He and Boym, despite the older man being his ecclesiastical superior, had become close friends. Boym on his many past journeys hadn't only studied plants and animals, he'd also put together a remarkably comprehensive and illustrated digest of Chinese medical practices. He'd brought it with him. The meticulous care he'd put into the illustrations had dazzled Couplet. Had Boym not joined the Jesuits he would surely, just like his Polish father, have become a famous physician.

Boym, once in Goa, had come up against the harsh reality that, given his unwavering loyalty to the Ming rebels, the Portuguese were not about to allow him to continue on to China. The Jesuits had made their peace with the Manchu invaders and Boym, given his uncompromising personality, would have caused trouble. Boym was undeterred. If need be, he'd walk to China. So, he'd entrusted his treasured papers to Couplet asking him to find a way of getting them back to Europe for publication. This Couplet had done only to learn later and to his eternal regret that the consignment, although placed in the care of a Portuguese master mariner, had been intercepted by the Dutch and had most likely ended up in Batavia. So, after all those years, might Boym's precious medical manuscripts have ended up in this fellow Cleyer's possession?

Indeed, they had and by the time Couplet had made it back only a few hours later to the relative safety of the Atayde residence he was not only accompanied by a boxful of papers but was also the bearer of unexpectedly good news.

```
                CLAVIS              56739
                  MEDICA
                     ad
              Chinarum Doctrinam
                       DE
              PULSIBUS,
                   AUTORE
         R. P. MICHAELE BOYMO, è Soc.
             JESU, & in China Missionario.
       Hujus operis ultra viginti annos jam sepulti fragmenta,
       hinc indè dispersa, collegit & in gratiam Medicæ Facultatis
                 in lucem Europæam produxit
         CL. DN. ANDREAS CLEYERUS,
           M. D. & Societatis Batavo - Orientalis
                  PROTO-MEDICUS.
          56739      A quo
                  Nunc demum mittitur
        Totius Operis Exemplar, è China recens allatum
              & à mendis purgatum ,        56739
                    Procuratore
         R. P. PHILIPPO COPLETIO,
           Belgâ, è Soc. JESU, Chinensis missionis
                    Romam misso.
              ANNO ɔɔ bc LXXXVI.
```

Michael Boym's Clavis Medica ad Chinam Doctrinam de Pulsibus as edited by Couplet: title page

Shen's Unlikely Journey

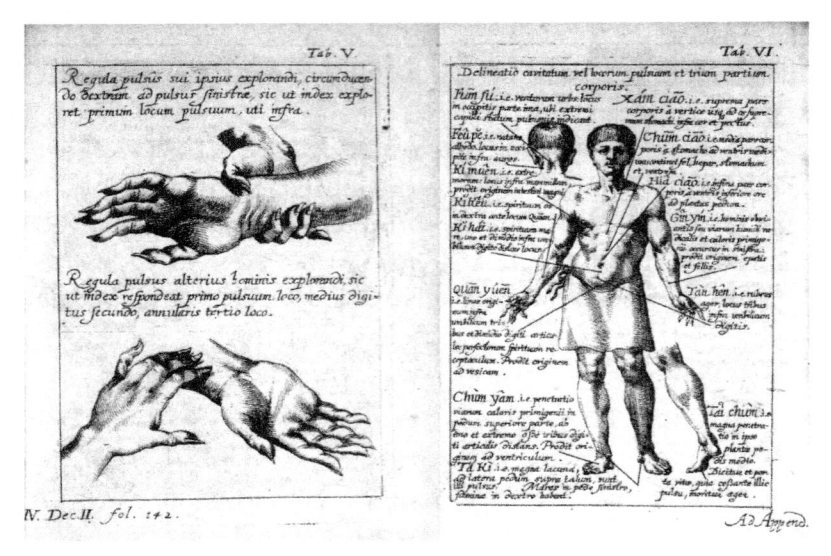

Clavis Medica: illustrative plate

    Cleyer, Couplet reported, had come right out with it. Thanks to his Germanic temperament and to the many years he'd spent working with the Dutch, he was a man of few words. He had absolutely no time for social niceties. Of course he'd come across Boym's papers. He'd found them quite recently when, on being promoted by the VOC, he'd taken over the office within the Kasteel that by rights belonged to the chief surgeon. They were gathering mold induced by tropical humidity in a forgotten drawer. He'd immediately realized their value, and yes he'd decided to publish them under the lofty title of Specimen Medicinae Sinicae with himself as the purported author! Whyever not? No one would ever be any the wiser. The first batch of edited papers were already in the hands of a printer in Frankfurt. The VOC had deep pockets and since they were propagators of Dutch science and ingenuity they'd enthusiastically bankrolled Cleyer's publication. The problem was with the remaining batch of Boym's yet-to-be-edited papers. Cleyer had run out of time. He was on his way to Japan. So, Cleyer had leaned over in Couplet's direction and outlined a proposal that he knew the good Jesuit was in no position to turn down.

"You take them. Your Latin is better than mine. You're also interested in Chinese medicine. My informants tell me you have a young man with you who is of a scholarly bent and whose father is a renowned physician in Nanjing. So, go to work and by the end of your stay here in Batavia, hand the edited manuscript to my colleagues at the VOC. They'll do what it takes to have the book published. It will be in Nuremberg. Don't worry, it's as prestigious a center of learning as Frankfurt, if not more so. Yes, of course, you can attribute the authorship to Boym and I know you'll want to make sure everyone knows he was a Jesuit—another of you crazy people! Then do yourself a favor by mentioning that you are the chief editor. Just don't forget to add my name on the title page—in appropriately large print, of course. So, there you are my dear father Couplet your superiors will thank you for having done your Order a favor. We heretics know when to be magnanimous and are not beyond doing you Papists a favor. We'll all be famous! That's it. Now please don't take up any more of my time than you have to."

Couplet had bit his tongue and swallowed hard remembering Atayde's good advice. He could see from the papers Cleyer had spread out on the spacious worktable set before him that this would be a book of intense interest to Europeans. They dealt with the most intriguing aspects of Chinese medicine, namely herbal traditions, diagnoses based on analyzing the subtle gradations of a patient's pulse and even acupuncture. This would be a key to understanding Chinese medicine—a clavis medica. Yes, that would be the book's title! Besides, wasn't this a way of honoring the memory of his old friend Boym who had died so soon after the two men had parted company in Goa twenty-five years ago?

So, there it was. A done deal and one on which Couplet reported that evening as he told Dona Inês of this strangest of developments.

This was another project for him and indeed for Shen to work on as they waited out their time in Batavia while enjoying the Ataydes' prodigious hospitality.

"Life," Dona Inês reminded everyone, "is nothing other than a journey into the unknown."

"It's just a roll of the dice," Shen had added for emphasis. "It nudges our inner yin and yang in the most unexpected of ways."

Atayde had, all the while, been puffing away contentedly on his long Dutch clay pipe enjoying the tropically induced lethargy of the late hour.

Tiger's Canal (Tijgersgracht) in Batavia : Late 17th Century Dutch Engraving

The Return of the Rains

By late October, the inevitable came to be. Atayde, after making extensive inquiries and considering other means by which his guests might reach Europe, had secured passages for both Couplet and Shen aboard a Dutch ship that had recently docked in Batavia and was still being unloaded. It would take several months for the East Indiaman to be placed back in service, provisioned, and its hold replenished with valuable cargo for the return voyage to Holland.

The skies had clouded over and the rains, as is their wont, were about to return to Batavia in full force. There was a predictable routine to the comings and goings of the Atayde household. Atayde was an early riser. He'd break his fast by gulping down several cups of strong, warm, sweet tea followed by a bowl of glutinous rice porridge cooked in coconut milk, a slice of papaya and perhaps a rambutan or a mangosteen. That done, he'd be ready to make his way to work. On most mornings he did so walking alongside his principal clerk and trusted scrivener so they could talk over what business the day was likely to bring. A young boy bearing a sturdy Chinese umbrella secured atop a long pole trotted dutifully behind them. It was an ingenious device consisting of oiled paper stretched over collapsible bamboo struts. He was ready to jump into action should they run into a squall. It was a short walk as the Atayde residence was within sight of Batavia' principal canal along which ran the city's busiest thoroughfare. The docks, warehouses and trading posts were no more than a block further to the north at which point the walls of the imposing Dutch Kasteel were very much in evidence.

Couplet and Shen likewise made an early start to their day. They devoted time to prayerful meditation and then, of course, study, that now included working on Boym's precious manuscript. As for Dona Inês, she also was up shortly following the dawn hour. She presided each morning over her assembled household, reviewing the day's events, resolving conflicts, and allocating tasks.

With the change of season conversations over dinner now tended to gravitate toward weightier matters of immediate concern.

There was an occasion on which Dona Inês had asked Couplet why it was that he'd been named procurator. Having pursued the matter further by asking him to explain just what a procurator was expected to do, the mood had turned decidedly somber; despite, that is, the excellence of the Hainanese coconut chicken and its accompanying spiced rice noodles. It also happened that the air following on that evening's dusk had felt even more oppressively humid than usual.

It was, Couplet set out to explain, the strangest of titles and one typically given to those charged with difficult missions. In Roman times procurators were senior provincial officials empowered, while far away from Rome, to act on behalf of the emperor. The Church, having modeled its bureaucracy on the centralized and authoritarian structure of the Roman Empire, had adopted many such legalistically sounding names. So, having been chosen by his brother Jesuits in China to represent them in Rome, where they had been maligned and misunderstood, he'd been named procurator. He'd at the same time been entrusted with bringing to a successful conclusion the publication of what Couplet referred to as the Confucian Treatise.

"Are you the first, Father Philippe, to have been given such a title, and given so weighty a responsibility?" asked Dona Inês.

"By no means. Might you have any interest in listening to yet another of my stories? If so, I could tell you about one of my distinguished predecessors, the good Nicolas Trigault. It's an old story. Although men like Adam Schall and Michael Boym were older than me, I did get to meet them. Trigault, I never met. He'd set foot in China a good fifty years before my own arrival. The point of my telling you Trigault's story is that he was charged with much the same thorny issues and tasks as those Michael and I will be facing. That is, if we ever reach Europe. Some things, it seems, never change."

The similarities were indeed striking. Nicolas Trigault, like Couplet, was from the Flemish Netherlands, had been entrusted with the publication of a book, and while he hadn't faced shipwreck, his journey had entailed a harrowing overland trek through stretches of India and Persia. He'd eventually reached the Mediterranean by way of Egypt.

"Was his book also about Confucius?"

"It wasn't, Dom João, it was Matteo Ricci's journal. Ricci had written it over the nineteen years it had taken him to reach the Forbidden City. It was exceedingly long and written in Italian. Trigault, who was a lot younger than I am today, was told to edit it down and produce a Latin version for publication in Europe. It had the makings of a best-seller. It was a first-hand account of what it was like to live in China, and was written by one who was intimately familiar with the culture. Until then, Europeans curious about China would have had to make do with Marco Polo's extravagant yarn that was over two centuries old. What Trigault achieved single-handedly was truly remarkable. The reason for the Latin was that it would ensure the book a much broader, European-wide readership. I don't know how he managed to work on the manuscript and hold on to his voluminous papers during his harrowing overland journey, but he did. Within months of his arriving in Europe, he'd found a publisher. It was in Augsburg, a Bavarian city known for its thriving book trade. He'd done so despite the impending outbreak of the Thirty Years War which, as I'm sure you are painfully aware of, turned out to be a disastrous religiously inspired European-wide conflict. The printing and distribution of Ricci's journal under those circumstances was an awesome achievement. I'm humbled."

Despite its length—it was over six hundred pages long—the book was a resounding success, and before long was translated into several European languages. It served, Couplet continued, a major purpose, which was to publicize to a broad and European-wide readership the challenging, and yet exciting and potentially rewarding, nature of the Jesuit enterprise in China. It became part of a public awareness campaign directed toward recruiting fresh blood

Ricci's De Christiana Expeditione Apud Sinas (Augsburg 1615), edited by Nicolas Trigault: title page

and raising funds for the missions. Trigault traveled to Europe's major capitals promoting it. Its title—A Christian Expedition among the Chinese—had an adventurous ring to it and no doubt contributed to its popularity.

"So, in a sense, you and Michael have a similar goal."

"We do, Dom João, because we need to emulate what Trigault did sixty years ago. It's high time for a follow-up. In those six decades, the China missions have made significant strides, but in some ways we face even greater obstacles. To publish a book showcasing Confucius' wisdom is an opportunity for us to demonstrate that the Chinese have developed a culture perhaps even more ancient than our Greco-Roman tradition. Confucius is an important symbol of that culture. He probably lived at the same time as Socrates. We're out to convince our fellow Europeans that dialoguing with the Chinese requires that we learn to speak their language. By language, I don't mean just memorizing the stroke order of those thousands of characters and the impossibly difficult challenge of knowing how to voice them. That's something our friend Michael does almost effortlessly. No! It's far more complicated than that. We're asking Rome to listen to what Confucius has to say. If his wisdom is taken seriously by the Chinese, then it behooves us to also heed his words."

"Was Confucius, whose sayings you are so committed to publishing, a saint?" hazarded Dona Inês.

"Perhaps, but that's not a conversation I would want to be drawn into. With you, Dom João and Dona Inês, in Batavia and at a safe distance from those who might seek to hold my words against me, I'll dare say something I would otherwise keep to myself. Confucius did say things that would not be out of place in our Christian scriptures. He spoke, for example, repeatedly about the wisdom inherent in not doing anything to others which one would not want to have done to oneself. That didn't make him popular with his contemporaries."

"I suppose," reflected Atayde, "that such truths are more easily accepted when voiced by those who are long dead and have acquired an aura of sanctity."

"You're onto something there, Dom João, but the fact is that we Jesuits need to renew our efforts. It's more than ever incumbent on us to make our European compatriots aware of the vital role China will eventually have in their world. We're all, I'd argue, going to have to pay much more attention to each other's cultures."

"You're suggesting, Father Philippe, that everyone is in for a surprise."

"I hadn't thought of it in those terms, Dom João, but yes, and the Chinese are also in for surprises. There is a world beyond their self-contained Middle Kingdom, and like it or not it's stirring, and doing so aggressively."

"So, Michael," said Dona Inês, turning to Shen, "I suppose that this journey you have embarked on is going to be full of surprises."

"It already is, and I'm increasingly conscious of the strangeness of journeying alone—in the sense of being cut off from my fellow Chinese—and away from my family. It's the strangest of feelings."

Silence fell on the assembled company.

Atayde eventually asked, "Won't the readers of your Confucian Treatise be rather different from those who were interested in Ricci's journal?"

"This treatise we have in mind will, I'll grant you, have a more limited readership. Ricci's famous journal had a wide appeal. We're addressing the philosophically curious. We'll be seeking out more intellectually committed readers. We see that as appropriate to our changing world. Europe isn't what it was sixty years ago. New ideas are threatening the old ways of doing things. We're caught in the middle! To the traditionalists, we're corrupting the true faith by seeking to engage with new ways of looking at the world and to those who are hellbent on challenging those same traditionalists we come across as diehard autocrats."

"Speaking of your detractors, Father Philippe, how did this predecessor of yours make out in Rome sixty years ago?"

"Well, Trigault was dealing with similar issues. The question of the appropriateness of Chinese Christian converts being allowed to continue honoring their ancestors in accordance with their traditional rites was already in the wings. Trigault's more immediate aim was to have the Church relax its universal rule regarding the exclusive use of Latin in liturgical celebrations. His Holiness was, we are told, sympathetic. Trigault thought he'd won out, except that sixty years later we still face much the same problem."

"So," Atayde observed with a smirk, "papal sympathy isn't enough."

"Apparently not. This was, you might be interested to know, the same pope who had chided Galileo and suggested it wasn't a good idea to upset people by telling them so unequivocally that the sun and the planets weren't gyrating around Mother Earth. You don't make friends by telling people what they don't want to hear. Humans, by and large, make a virtue of clinging to denial. It's comfortingly reassuring to think of the sun revolving around us humans. It's cozier."

"Did Trigault return to China?" asked Dona Inês.

"He did and let me tell you what happened to him. On his return he came up against unanticipated difficulties. I'm telling you this because those difficulties were uncannily like those that would years later lead to Adam Schall's distressing undoing. You remember Schall's tragic story?"

"The German astronomer who was condemned to be flayed alive," exclaimed Dona Inês.

"That's right. An unforgettable story! Well, I would go so far as to argue that even though we presently enjoy Emperor Kangxi's favor, those kinds of risks are still very much with us. The wind doesn't blow forever in the same direction. So, bear with me. I'll be brief. I promise!"

Shen's Unlikely Journey

Nicolas Trigault, by Peter-Paul Rubens, likely sketched in Antwerp in 1617

Trigault, according to Couplet's narration, had hoped to return to Hangzhou. It was a city that even Shen would have to agree rivaled his native Nanjing in natural beauty and antiquity. Its West Lake had been the backdrop of many a spiritually inspiring legend. He had spent time there before being sent to Europe with Ricci's journal. It was not to be. Trigault, on arriving in Macao was greeted with the most distressing news imaginable. An investigation initiated by a senior minister with the Department of Rites had led to an imperial decree the effect of which was to exile all missionaries from China. The Jesuits had been accused, both in Nanjing and in Beijing, of spreading false and potentially seditious practices and doctrines. The Christians had been singled out as a dangerous fringe sect promoted by hostile foreign powers. The missions were, to a degree, victims of their own success. They had made increasing inroads among a small but influential circle of imperial officials, thereby attracting unwanted attention. They had inevitably made enemies of opposing, and even more powerfully connected, political factions. They were viewed as rivals to be ruthlessly crushed.

"It pains me to say so," Couplet had gone on to say, "but the most disturbing aspect of this persecution was that it could be traced back to the good work begun by Ricci with the Astronomy Board. Ricci's successors had redoubled those efforts so that their astronomical competence was unrivaled, particularly when it came to revising the highly visible imperial calendar. So, yes, they were viciously attacked by politically connected officials whose technical incompetence in the realm of celestial observations was at risk of being exposed. It was a prefiguration of the Adam Schall tragedy. I've said it before. There's a moral here worthy of both Aesop and Confucius. That which brings about success often carries within it the seeds of its undoing. All the wisdom in the world wasn't going to do away with that stark reality. It's still haunting us."

The Jesuits were rounded up and put on trial. One of the fathers, a particularly zealous and vocal Italian who had compiled respected educational and catechetical texts in Chinese, was singled out. He was flogged and then confined to an exiguous bamboo cage for public display. That was a standard Chinese punishment meted out to petty criminals by provincial magistrates. Worse yet, he was carried off to Canton in the cage, at which point he was released and expelled to nearby Macao. Of the dozen or so Jesuits present at the time in China, those not shipped back to Macao were allowed to remain in China, but under strict orders to cease all activity. It could have been far worse, and the crisis did subside. The dreaded inquisitor from the Bureau of Rites who had started it all eventually fell out of favor and was banished to a provincial dead-end. His punishment took the form of a face-saving appointment to a minor bureaucratic posting.

"I hate to say it," muttered Shen, "but that is the most Chinese of outcomes. I should know. That's the culture I was brought up in."

"What happened to Trigault?" asked Dona Inês.

"He had the good sense to lie low and use the time to concentrate his linguistic talents and intellectual energy on a project that would make him famous. He compiled a remarkable reference book entitled, Aid to the Eyes and Ears of Western Scholars. The purpose was to provide foreigners learning Chinese with a handy pronunciation guide. It resembles a dictionary, except that instead of providing meanings for the Chinese characters listed, an approximation is given, using western alphabetic letters, of how they should be pronounced. The characters are not listed by reference to how they are written, but alphabetically by how they are pronounced. They are, in other words, set out in a Romanized sequence and not according to the traditional method that relies on identifying the pattern of the strokes used to write them."

Couplet spoke with feeling. He'd packed a copy of Trigault's masterpiece in one of his famous camphor chests. He was confident it would come in handy in Europe. Shen nodded in enthusiastic approval.

Trigault had continued to write and reflect on the Chinese classics. He was an intense thinker and, like Ricci, became convinced that the early settlers of China's fertile river valleys had correctly intuited the existence of the one and only, all-powerful personal creator God. Not everyone, of course, agreed, and disagreements went beyond the Roman curia and the influential cardinals that had been egged on by the critically inclined Franciscans and Dominicans. Even some of Trigault's Jesuits colleagues had voiced misgivings, his superior included.

All this proved overly depressing to Trigault. The last straw had to be that the Manchus were increasingly threatening the stability of the Ming dynasty and that China was suffering from the prolonged effects of a deadly combination of floods and periods of extreme cold. It was all made worse by the callous neglect of regional Ming imperial administrators. China was drifting into chaos. The Jesuit presence in China hung upon a thread.

His confessor had tried to talk him out of it but to no avail: Trigault was only fifty-one when he committed suicide. For those who knew of his brilliance and dedication, it was the cause of great sadness.

"Wasn't it, just like Michael Boym? Wasn't his yet another life most intensely and purposefully lived?"

"Of course, Dona Inês. It was well lived indeed, despite the mental anguish and the moments of inevitable loneliness. Hope for us all!"

❖

"I'm curious. Tell me something else, Father Couplet. You've mentioned that this Confucian Treatise publication project you and Shen have undertaken has a long history. You keep saying to us that all you are doing is trying to bring to a fitting conclusion something that many great minds have worked on before you. You're unduly modest, but yes, I'm curious. It can't have been easy. Tell us more, beginning perhaps with Father Ricci."

Atayde had posed a searching question and one that caused Couplet to consider just how he felt about the precarious position he now found himself in. Advancing age was taking its toll. Since arriving in Batavia, he'd reflected more deeply on what it had been like for him to come to terms with the strongly expressed views of the many larger-than-life personalities that over time had claimed ownership of the Confucian Treatise. It had turned out to be a dauntingly controversial project and it was now his by default. Events had conspired to shift its full burden onto his increasingly frail shoulders.

Couplet couldn't help beginning with Matteo Ricci. He was, after all, the very first westerner to have encountered the Confucian texts. He'd done so while studying Chinese in Macao almost exactly a hundred years ago. Ricci had immediately sensed that there was a prophetic quality to Confucius' writing. Confucius had been rejected by his contemporaries for daring to confront them with unpalatable home truths. His message was essentially that it behooved good and wise rulers to act primarily in the interest of those entrusted to their care. They could only do so if they disciplined themselves to resist the twin corrupting influences of power and greed. It was, and always would be, an unpopular message, but it was incumbent on everyone, not just the Chinese, to heed Confucius' advice. Could it be that such a prophetic message was of an inherently religious nature? It was a seductive message and while Ricci wouldn't have put it that way, he had become a disciple.

Ricci's companion in those early days in China was a fellow Italian by the name of Ruggieri. They worked together selecting texts from the Confucian Four Books and figuring out how to express them in Latin. Interestingly, the China Jesuits came up with the idea that having the Pope send a high-level mission to Imperial Beijing would work wonders for the fledgling missionary effort.

Ruggieri was the one entrusted with the unenviable task of presenting the idea to the Roman curia. Before leaving China, he'd packed in his bags a copy of the Latin rendering of some of the Confucian texts he and Ricci had worked on so assiduously. He most sensibly hoped to have it published. It didn't work out that way, because in Rome his enthusiasm was gradually ground down by the spirit of inertia that so characterized the workings of the Papal bureaucracy. He failed miserably on both counts. The idea of sending a Papal mission to Beijing was dismissed out of hand and the Confucian project failed for want of a patron. Dispirited and by then too old to make the return trip to China, he wisely retired to his native Puglia where he dedicated his waning years to composing Chinese poetry. Some have since thought of Ruggieri as the first true sinologist. His, Couplet remarked, had been yet another life well lived.

"That may come across to you as old history, Dom João, but to me it wasn't because when I first arrived in China a full half century after Ricci's death, I was lucky enough to get a hold of a copy of that first translation. It came in extraordinarily handy because, joined by three other recruits, I was assigned to a highly effective teacher who, in the Ricci tradition, used the Confucian Four Books as texts to drum into his students the subtleties of Classical Chinese. All four of us were in our mid-thirties. One was a native of Maastricht and by sheer coincidence had been another of my classmates in the novitiate. Another was Sicilian and the fourth a native of Austria."

"Was the teacher Chinese?"

"He wasn't, Dona Inês; he happened to be Portuguese. In the Ricci mold, he'd made China his cultural home and was renowned for his ability to inculcate his students with lasting feelings of reverence and love for his adoptive language. His approach to learning was to tutor, coax and pressure all four of us students into painstakingly parsing each of the characters making up a given text. He would insist on our weighing and considering the full range of potential meanings. Then he would engage us in a spirited and prolonged debate to determine which Latin phrase best conveyed the agreed-upon meaning. I remember the process as interminable and exhausting. Our Sicilian fellow student, on the other hand, had seemingly boundless energy. His name was Próspero Intorcetta. At the end of each session, he'd be the one to produce a rigorously drafted bilingual Latin and Chinese annotated version of the debated text. Its purpose, he would assert, was to mirror the group's collective efforts. Perhaps, but it was also reflective of his resourcefulness. Intorcetta was masterful in his ability to cheerfully adapt himself to whatever situation he found himself in. We admired him, grudgingly so, I'll admit. We who live by our intellect are the ones most likely to be enmeshed in petty rivalries."

Latin and Chinese bi-lingual edition of Confucian-inspired Sapientia Sinica: 1662 printed in Jiangxi with woodblocks on double leaves and published at Próspero Intorcetta's initiative

Before long, Couplet recounted, Intorcetta had compiled a book-length Latin commentary on Confucius. He titled it Sapientia Sinica, the most apt translation of which might be The Meaning of Chinese Wisdom, and caused it to be printed in the southern province of Jiangxi that had long been a center of Confucian scholarship. It was produced using high quality traditional woodblock printing. Couplet described it as an ancestor of the precious translations carried in the one camphor chest he and Shen always kept close at hand.

At the end of those many months the four had spent together analyzing, reflecting, and debating, they parted company. The time had come for each of them to join one of the still struggling missions that the Order, typically under the most challenging of circumstances, had established in and around the capital and along the lower reaches of the Yangtze.

There was, though, several years later a reunion. An involuntary one, certainly, but a reunion, nonetheless. It was in Canton during the great exile that had followed Schall's tragic trial in Beijing. It was, as Couplet had pointed out, a repeat, but on a far more extensive scale of the persecution that had confronted Trigault on his return from Europe half a century earlier.

It gave the Four Translators an opportunity to resume the challenge they had been confronted with on their arrival in China. It was the impetus of what would become the Confucian Treatise project. Intorcetta had suggested they focus their efforts on honing and perfecting the Latin rendering of what was arguably the most quoted of Confucius' Four Books. It was The Doctrine of the Mean. Intorcetta had once again risen to the occasion. He added a Latin introduction together with a brief life of Confucius to the bilingual text. Then, despite the interdiction and the rigors of house arrest, he persuaded a Cantonese printer to publish the first half of the book.

"What about the second half?"

Intorcetta was unstoppable. Following the fifteen-year-old

emperor's dismissal of the tyrannical regent, the strictures imposed on the exiles were gradually lifted. The time had come for the China Jesuits to not only resume their missionary work but also send one of their own to Rome to report on the situation they now found themselves in.

"Another procurator!" exclaimed Atayde.

"Yes, and because it had to be someone young and forceful they chose, not unsurprisingly, the resourceful Intorcetta to represent them. In Goa, on his way to Europe, he ferreted out a printer capable of taking on the second part. In time, a few copies of both the Cantonese and the Goanese volumes ended up in the hands of European collectors. Further proof, as if any were needed, that interest in China was on the rise and that the time was ripe for pursuing the publication of the Confucian Treatise in Europe."

By the time Intorcetta had returned from Europe, Verbiest was tutoring the young emperor and the exiles had been allowed back into China proper. Intorcetta was sent to Hangzhou. Despite the interdiction, the Christian community of this thriving historic city had grown appreciably. For Intorcetta, it was a promotion. He was placed in charge of the entire area that in addition to Hangzhou encompassed Suchow, Shanghai, and Nanjing. Shen remembered Intorcetta visiting his family. Yes, Shen's father had presented him to the engagingly charismatic Sicilian and even mentioned that his son Michael had begun to study Latin.

"It's fair to say," continued Couplet, "that while the Cantonese confinement had contributed to infusing the Confucian Treatise project with renewed vigor, it was no longer looked upon with a sense of urgency. Over the next few years it became depressingly evident that our detractors were still out to gain the upper hand, and this realization revived the project. We needed to face up to the challenge."

"So that what you refer to as the ruinous affair of The Chinese Rites had resurfaced?" interjected Atayde.

"It certainly had. Once again, we needed to send one of our own to Rome as procurator, so why not also entrust him with the Confucian Treatise?"

"Why, oh why," Dona Inês asked of both Couplet and Shen, "has such a seemingly virtuous custom as honoring one's forebears become such a stumbling block? Would you reprehend me if I were to light an incense stick instead of a candle and place it on an altar in front of my sorely missed mother's portrait?"

"On the contrary, Dona Inês, I would encourage you to do so! Why don't we ask young Michael here what he thinks of this affair that I'll continue to refer to as ruinous?"

Shen did indeed have his own story regarding ancestral rites. The young man recounted that Ricci's memory was still very much alive within his family. In Nanjing and on the altar auspiciously situated in the grand south-facing reception hall of the four-sided walled-in family compound, Shen's grandmother had made room, among the many ancestral tablets placed on it, for an image of Matteo Ricci printed from a finely engraved block of pear wood. She'd slipped the thin translucent sheet into an ornate silver frame and propped it to one side against an incense bowl. She'd done so on the tearful occasion on which Shen had taken leave of his assembled family. The young man had honored the image together with those of his ancestors. He'd done so with the most heartfelt of incense offerings. Ricci's blessing, together with that of the assembled company of the Shen family's ancestral ghosts, had been invoked by all present. Shen had set out the very next morning for the long southbound journey that would take him to Canton and thence to nearby Macao, where he was to join Couplet and prepare for boarding the Santo António. It was the most intense of memories and among those the young man imagined he would recall at that solemn moment when a living being faces the inevitability of impending death.

"This ruinous affair," continued Couplet, "is really about the competitiveness that blights our nature. We're political animals. We take sides and accuse each other of absurdly petty things that have little to do with the deep resentments that really set us apart. I don't want to preach a sermon. Sermons are boring, but allow me to go over some history."

The controversy's origins went back to the years following Ricci's death when Spanish friars established in the Philippines began insinuating themselves at several points along China's southern coast. They were, for the most part, Dominicans and Franciscans. Making their way to China from Manila wasn't difficult as there was plenty of local shipping. The Spanish were buyers of Chinese luxuries. They paid for them with Mexican and Peruvian-mined silver and, at great profit to themselves, shipped the silks and other fineries on to Europe via Mexico. The Spanish friars' backdoor approach to China, however, proved to be exceedingly troublesome. The Portuguese treated them as poachers contravening the Padroado.

"We Jesuits," explained Couplet, "regarded their preach-to-the-masses approach as horrendously inappropriate. We were proud of our Confucian acculturation. Until then, the Chinese hadn't realized that there were competing brands of Christianity. Competing preaching sects had always been regarded by Confucian Chinese officialdom with suspicion. You remember my story about the persecution initiated by the official with the Bureau of Rites? Yes, well, sects invariably appealed to the oppressed, and Chinese centralized authority abhors dissent. The friars were sent packing and they subsequently blamed us Jesuits for their undoing."

"Did they have a legitimate grudge?" asked Atayde.

"We weren't, I suppose, blameless. Of course, we resented their meddling. That said, we felt we'd been unfairly ensnared in a situation that was entirely of their making. Our problem was that the friars were well connected in Rome. They went on the attack. We Jesuits had it all dangerously wrong, they argued. There was no similarity between ancient Chinese awareness of the deity and the God of the Hebrew Bible. Nor was there common ground between

Confucian ethics and the natural law of the Abrahamic tradition. Confucius was at best a deferential agnostic. We were indulging in wishful thinking and were subverting the true faith by being overly accommodating. Our willingness to allow the Chinese to continue making sacrificial ritual offerings to their ancestors and to the emperor was tantamount to tolerating idol worship."

Couplet at this point became apologetic. He was asking the Ataydes to take an interest in the subtleties of Church politics. This was not something devout laypersons should be exposed to. It might endanger their faith. And what about Shen, young, impressionable, and hitherto sheltered from much of this ecclesiastical politicking? He was hopefully a candidate for the priesthood. Why risk putting him off? But then, Couplet reasoned once again, in time he'd be exposed to all of this. He might as well hear about it now.

"Here's what had happened in Rome. The papacy had recently set up a special office, the purpose of which was to centralize the oversight of the worldwide missions. It was referred to in Latin as the Propaganda, which was natural enough, since its purpose was to 'propagate the faith'. As far as the Portuguese were concerned, this Propaganda was a brazen political maneuver on the part of Rome. They saw it as an attempt to circumvent the authority they had previously been granted to fully control the missions in areas over which they had jurisdiction. Since Macao was Portuguese, China, despite the momentous changes that had occurred over the past two centuries, was by their reckoning still within their Padroado. The Jesuits, whose Order was the most international of organizations and who had a well-earned reputation for doing things their own way, felt caught in the middle. At first, Rome sided with the friars, but then the Jesuits convincingly made the case that the Confucian rites were of a civil and familial nature, rather than ritualistic in a religious sense."

"I'll wager that you're going to tell us that wasn't the end of the story."

"You're perceptive, Dom João. Did it bring an end to Portuguese-Spanish rivalry and reconcile the Jesuits and the friars? Did it resolve the conflicts between the Portuguese Padroado and the recently established Propaganda? Absolutely not. The pot simmered along with each side adding further flavor-enhancing spices into the giddy mix. The latest broadside was delivered by a highly articulate Spanish Dominican, who had ironically been forced to hole up with us Jesuits in Canton in the aftermath of Adam Schall's trial. I met the man. All of us did. We got on well enough. The exile had brought us together. He was even interested in Chinese history, so we had a lot in common. The persecution over, he went on to Rome, and to our intense disappointment turned against us. He added fuel to the anti-Jesuit fire. I'm told he's been rewarded with a bishopric and, despite his being well-versed in Chinese history, has been sent to the Caribbean Island of Hispaniola."

"The Lord's ways are indeed inscrutable," mused Dona Inês.

"Depressingly so," quipped Atayde.

So yes, this was the thorny political thicket into which Couplet and Shen had been charged with jumping into. Lest anyone forget, there was the unresolved imbroglio regarding the language in which it was appropriate to celebrate the Christian liturgy in China. Couplet had included in his famous camphor chests drafts of missals translated into Chinese. Might the Pope, at the very least, allow Chinese priests, of which there were so far precious few, to use their own language? Might Shen get to meet the Pope? Dona Inês could hardly repress the excitement she felt at the thought that she was talking to two people who might possibly have reason to be summoned into the Holy Father's presence. She would have given anything to kiss his feet.

Couplet was more tired than usual that night, but anticipation was in the air. Christmas was but a few weeks away. It was a reminder that the Santo António had sailed out of Macao also a few days ahead of Christmas. A full year had gone by. The other looming reality was that the Dutch ship Couplet and Shen hoped to board had by now been unloaded. It was being careened, repaired, and provisioned. According to Atayde, it would be ready for the return journey to Europe within a month or two at the most.

The Ataydes had turned in for the night and Couplet, despite his tiredness, was in an unusually mellow mood. Shen took his chances and asked the question he'd recently been mulling over.

"Isn't it strange, Father Philippe, that you and I should be the ones chosen for this mission?"

"It was, in a way."

That evening, Couplet freely admitted that he wasn't an obvious choice. He was in his late fifties and arguably too old to undertake such a journey. Previous procurators such as Trigault and Intorcetta had been far younger. It was true that his heart had a way of periodically reminding him that he'd irreversibly crossed over from a vigorous midlife into old age.

"My heart speaks to me in throbs," was the way he put it. "Then I was criticized for wanting to make this into too grand a mission. As you well know Michael, you were originally chosen to be one of a delegation of seven. You're a survivor. The others were deemed either not youthful enough to make up for my infirmities, or not sufficiently scholarly in demeanor to project the image of the ideal Christian Confucian gentleman. Then there were those who simply gave up. I understand that. It's the hardest thing in the world to take leave of the nurturing cultural wellspring within which we've been raised, especially if you're Chinese. You're surrounded by such beauty! I don't blame you for wanting to avoid dealing with Barbarians. We're an unnecessary complication."

"So, I was the one who persevered!"

"Yes, even after the shipwreck! I'll be eternally grateful to you, my dear Michael. Then I was taken to task for all the baggage…the chests! How could we afford such largesse when the missions were perennially short of money and depended on the generosity of our

European patrons? It didn't do me any good to point out that Lady Candida from Shanghai, whose confessor I was privileged to have been, had shown herself to be exceedingly generous to us. Thanks to her kindness, I hadn't been put in the position of having to ask the missions to make any great financial sacrifice. And then hadn't we been charged with asking favors of powerful people? Wasn't it common knowledge that those in high places expect that those they deign to receive will come bearing gifts? I'm told the Holy Father loves books, so wouldn't a gift of finely calligraphed manuscripts make sense, as well as silks and glorious Ming dynasty porcelains. Well, my dear Michael, I didn't make any friends among my brothers. They made a virtue out of holding themselves out to be Spartans of the first order."

"But Father Philippe, you make no mention of the Confucian Treatise."

"I'm coming to that. If I was too old, then so were the other translators. We were all born within a year of each other. Besides, Intorcetta had become too important, and Herdtrich, the Austrian, was too good a mathematician for Verbiest to spare him. François de Rougemont, my compatriot from Maastricht had, to my great sadness, recently died in Shanghai. I visited him on his deathbed. It was one of those fevers that come about with unexpected and brutal intensity. Such is life!"

"But you and Father Verbiest are the closest of friends, and he is one who has earned Emperor Kangxi's trust. Surely…"

"You're right Michael, I do have reason to believe that it was he who finally supported me. Not because we were the same age and not because we'd stood side-by-side on the dock in Cadiz only to be told by the Spanish that we were both unfit for the Mexican missions. No, no, I do know my Confucius and I'm the last man standing. Everyone knew I was open to risking my life to see this grand project through. It was conceived of by Ricci, and I owe it to his memory to at long last make it happen. I may not have been the best choice, but my old friend Verbiest knew I was committed. As for you, Michael, you're a wonderful choice. You're a living embodiment of Confucian values. Father Intorcetta did well to put you up as a candidate. You know that Verbiest has brought this mission to the emperor's attention. You're correct in saying that he still has Kangxi's ear. It's a mission to bring Confucius to Europe. It was fitting that the emperor be made aware of it. I was told before we left Macao that I was to mention to our colleagues in Europe that the emperor wants more mathematicians. He's worried about Verbiest's eventual demise. He should be. Verbiest and I are the same age. So procuring mathematicians is going to be part of our mission."

Couplet thereupon fell asleep right there in his chair and Michael Shen gently propped a puffed-up pillow under his weary head.

※

The entire Atayde household had gathered on the quay to wish their honored guests well. There was much sadness at the parting. All Couplet and Shen could do was express their heartfelt gratitude again and again. It was the Ataydes, Dona Inês said repeatedly and tearfully, who had been blessed by the presence of their providential guests. Everyone expressed the fervent hope that at some propitious future time and place all would meet again. Yet deep down all knew, on that overcast early January morning, that this was likely wishful thinking.

It was a moment when the mere thought of just how long it took to cross over from one end of the world to the other induced feelings of awe, bordering on dread and helplessness. It most particularly affected those left behind to watch the men who had become dear and close to them disappear slowly and inexorably over the horizon. Such feelings were surely rooted in a deep awareness of the brevity of the human lifespan. The attendant perils were many. There were storms, pirates, injuries, drownings, starvation and perhaps most perfidious of all, debilitating and life-threatening diseases. These things were not spoken of on such occasions, but they were unsettlingly present. So, yes, there was much crying and hearts were indescribably heavy. All knelt by the quayside. Dona Inês sobbed and Father Philippe gave a final blessing. His and Shen's year in Batavia had ended. It felt, on that clouded-over morning of the rainy season, as though it had gone by far too quickly.

Their ship was named after the city of Apeldoorn. It was a three-masted East Indiaman and part of the regular fleet used by the VOC to annually transport cargo and passengers from the spice-rich archipelago to northern Dutch harbor-towns. If all went well, the voyage would take somewhat less than a year. That meant that after being careened, cleaned, and repaired in one of the VOC's many Dutch boatyards, it would once again be loaded with merchandise and provisions for the return journey. So, with a lot of effort and a great deal of good fortune it would, two years from now, once again be docked in Batavia, perhaps at this very spot within sight of the Atayde warehouses.

The Apeldoorn was a modestly proportioned, double-decked, ocean-going vessel. The crew occupied the lower or orlop deck, used to store the supplies that would be needed on the voyage. It also housed the galley and mess. It was the deck on which the Apeldoorn's twenty-four heavy guns had been mounted and therefore by far the busier of the two. Depending on the number of passengers taken on for a particular voyage, it was possible to squeeze the less fortunate into nooks and alcoves built into the spaces adjacent to the orlop deck's inner storage rooms. Thanks to Atayde having recourse to some of his better-connected VOC business associates, he'd managed to secure an upper deck cabin for Couplet and Shen. It was, for sure, one of the more exiguous of those reserved for higher ranking passengers and they would have to share it. They were lucky, though, because it did offer the relative luxury of a narrow porthole and a modicum of privacy. There was just about enough space to allow for one of the passengers' precious accompanying camphor chests.

In packing the chest, Couplet had considered at great length which of the manuscripts and lexical references he and Shen would most likely want to have handy during the interminably long voyage. The other chests had been consigned to the cavernous depths of the east Indiaman's below-the-water cargo space. They were tightly and irretrievably stowed beneath an impressive accumulation of bales, crates, and barrels, within which were packed the silks, spices, porcelains, and other fineries whose values, when transported halfway around the world, were destined to increase by perhaps as much as a hundredfold.

Couplet had made his selection in the hope that the voyage would afford him the opportunity to devote significant time to further reviewing the Latin translations of the Confucian texts he hoped to publish. Shen would, of course, be at his side and be only too willing to assist in the linguistic interpretation of some of the more esoteric Chinese characters. It would also be a time for Couplet to reflect on the content of the comprehensive introduction that would be very much part of the Confucian Treatise. It was a daunting task since its purpose was to acquaint European readers with the richness and depth of Chinese culture. Couplet also hoped to make time to expand the early draft he had put together extolling the exemplary life of Lady Candida. That explained why a not inconsiderable amount of the chest's space had been taken up by blank quires of fine grain paper, steel writing pens and blocks of high-quality Chinese ink. Shen had brought with him a set of goat-bristle bamboo writing brushes. Then, and that had in some ways been the hardest part, room had been made for a change or two of the clothes that would have to be worn on the journey until ragged and threadbare. Just the strictest minimum. The Ataydes had most generously given Couplet and Shen woolen coats tailored in the Dutch manner with which to soften the unforgiving hardness of their box-like bunks. The coats would come in handy at the journey's end.

Another privilege enjoyed by upper deck passengers was somewhat freer access to the ship's strictly rationed fresh water, not just for drinking, but also to allow for an occasional soapy scrub-down of accumulated viscous bodily grime. Then there was the head, so named because it consisted of a narrow, grating-like assembly of latticed planks suspended above the waves below the bowsprit. In calm weather, using the head presented no great challenge. Not so during storms, when threateningly powerful rollers could be expected to periodically wash imperiously over it. It was, at such times, incumbent on a squatting man to hold on to whatever rope-end or railing was at hand.

Had the Santo António not lost its mizzenmast and drifted against a sandbank, it would, after negotiating the Sunda Channel, have pursued a westerly course across the Bay of Bengal, navigated the straits separating Sri Lanka from the southern tip of the Indian subcontinent and thereafter steered north hugging the Malabar Coast as far as Goa. After an interlude in Portuguese Goa, the challenge would have been to traverse the Arabian Sea, at which point it could have called at friendly stopover harbors on the African Swahili Coast—among them Mombasa and Mozambique. Then it would have been a question of rounding the Cape of Good Hope, heading north once more and eventually reaching Lisbon.

Not so the Apeldoorn. Dutch mariners were inclined to head more directly for the tip of Africa: the Cape of Good Hope that had originally been rounded by Bartolomeu Dias and following him, even more famously by Vasco da Gama. Much later, and around the time that Batavia had come under Dutch rule, the VOC had settled the Cape with a small colony of farmers brought over from the Netherlands. It was a strategically located emplacement, and its land was exceptionally fertile. The idea was to produce enough food to provision the VOC's East Indiamen as they made their way to and from Batavia. So, instead of hugging the coasts, most VOC ships took the more aggressive course of sailing across extended stretches of the Indian Ocean and Arabian Sea. Far from land, they relied on their charts and on the accuracy of their instruments. It was no secret that by Couplet's and Shen's time, the world's leading cartographers and plotters of ocean currents were Dutch. Mercator was a name that stood out but others, spurred by the economic incentives held out by the VOC, had followed his lead. So the Dutch had an advantage, and they kept their detailed maps and navigational charts under wraps, treating them as though they were state secrets as indeed, they were.

This is precisely the course the Apeldoorn had embarked on with Couplet and Shen as passengers. After a stopover at the Cape Colony, it had called on one of the west African ports friendly to the Dutch and thereafter, on reaching Europe, had given a wide berth to the Iberic Peninsula. After running into storms in the Bay of Biscay and despite losing part of its rigging, the Apeldoorn had made its way without further incident through the English Channel and into the North Sea. By October of 1683, almost two years after leaving Macao aboard the Santo António, Couplet and Shen, to their immense relief, watched from the Apeldoorn's quarterdeck, as, on the last leg of her eight-month voyage, she entered the relatively calm waters of the well-protected Zuider Zee. Days later she docked in the ancient city-harbor of Enkhuizen.

Couplet had had plenty of time to get used to the fact that he and Shen would now be landing in the Dutch Republic rather than docking in Lisbon. The more he thought about it, the more he allowed himself to rejoice that a shipwreck had set in motion events that were leading to an unanticipated homecoming. He would, after all, be on his home turf. Almost, that is, given that his native Mechlin was only a hundred miles or so to the south of Enkhuizen. Besides, northern European roads and canals were in a lot better shape than those along which long-suffering travelers trekking through Spain and southern France on their way from Lisbon to Rome would have had to put up with. Yes, this was a godsend!

Confucius says:

Filial piety and fraternal submission are they not the root of all benevolent action.
Analects I

Learning without thought is labor lost; thought without learning is perilous.
Analects II

The superior man has dignified ease without pride. The mean man has pride without a dignified ease.
Analects XIII

IV
A Homecoming
October 1683 to the Summer of 1684

*I*t was perhaps a godsend but a complicated one. As Couplet stood on the Enkhuizen quay along which the Apeldoorn had berthed, watching the eleven camphor chests that had been rescued from the shipwreck at Banten being unloaded, he was in the most reflective of moods. He and Shen were certainly grateful that before leaving Batavia, their good friends and rescuers the Ataydes had procured them warm, woolen, Dutch overcoats. Not only had the coats protected them against both the rough weather encountered along the Bay of Biscay and the cool winds blowing into the Zuider Zee from the North Sea, but they were now affording them a measure of much-needed anonymity.

Couplet, while thankful to have arrived in Europe after a two-year journey, now faced the disquieting question of where to take Shen, the camphor chests, and himself. There had been no welcoming delegation. How could there have been? While the two men took comfort from knowing that the Santo António had indeed been patched up in Banten and, relieved of its cargo, had made its way back to Macao thus bringing news of their having survived the shipwreck and chosen to remain in Batavia, no one would have been any the wiser regarding their ultimate destination.

The reality was that with the passage of time no one in Lisbon or in Rome was expecting either Couplet or Shen. The more realistic expectation was that they had not survived the journey. So where to go?

Couplet knew by now that there were Jesuits in Enkhuizen. Over the eight months the voyage had taken, he'd spoken to every passenger and crew member on the Apeldoorn. He'd found out that Enkhuizen had a clandestine Catholic church and that, yes, it was a Jesuit mission. The Dutch, as Couplet had learned from his stay in Batavia, had grown somewhat more tolerant. The church, he'd been told, would be barn-like and quite ordinary, and Catholics, priests included, were expected to dress like everyone else. There was no ringing of bells or displays of piety such as statues of Our Lady or the clutching of rosaries in public, or anything like that. But, yes, Couplet's informants had assured him, once in Enkhuizen, he would surely find a carter willing to take him to the church and since it was Jesuit it was most likely dedicated to Saint Francis Xavier.

That's exactly what happened. The rector was quite taken aback by the unannounced arrival of a father who spoke both Dutch and Chinese, accompanied by a young man from China disguised as a Dutchman in borrowed britches. His reticence overcome however, he proved quite welcoming. There was also reason to be reassured by the discrete sound of the silver jingling in Couplet's finely woven Chinese silk purses. Room was found within one of the church's storehouses for the eleven camphor chests and since Couplet was unwell, tired by the voyage and, as he said repeatedly, feeling his age, he was given a good bed with a feathered mattress, and ministered to by a knowledgeable physician loyal to the Catholic cause.

It was by now late October and good food and good company was doing Couplet a world of good. Shen's engaging manners had made him into something of a local celebrity. He had picked up a few words of Dutch in Batavia and at Couplet's urging was now

A Homecoming

accompanied by a young man capable of tutoring him in Latin. He was shown around the polders and windmills surrounding Enkhuizen. He spoke of being quite taken by the sturdy charm of Dutch houses, and the polders reminded him of the beauty of the rice fields surrounding Lake Tai in the vast lowlands watered by the lower reaches of the Yangtse. The beauty of it all made him quite homesick. Shen also admired the canals, and he knew from his experiences of the Dutch efforts to build canals in Batavia just how much pride they took in them. He spoke of the grand canal his ancestors had built linking the Yangtse to the Yellow River. It was over a thousand miles long and the result of much human effort and ingenuity. Shen, though, being schooled in Confucian ethics and good manners, described the canals of his native land as far inferior to those he was being shown. He was, after all, a guest, and modesty is the mark of a good guest. It wouldn't have done, for instance, to remark on the fact that the entire population of the Netherlands would have been embarrassingly outnumbered by just one of the Middle Kingdom's smaller provinces.

As Couplet's health recovered, he set about writing letters. He needed to. It was a matter of where he and Shen should present themselves next in pursuance of the weighty embassy they had been charged with. The rector had given Couplet a piece of welcome news. Just a year earlier, a native of Brussels had become the Jesuit Order's Superior General. It was a responsibility so awesome that the holder was frequently referred to as the Black Pope. Charles de Noyelle had been elected unanimously following the death of his long-lived predecessor, who was Genoese. Couplet had known him before leaving for China twenty-five years earlier. They were compatriots and close in age. Couplet took this as a good omen and immediately wrote to de Noyelle explaining the strangeness of the circumstances that had led to his finding himself in Enkhuizen instead of Lisbon. Couplet made much of the importance given by the China Jesuits to the eventual publication in Europe of the

Confucian Treatise. Couplet mentioned Shen, describing him as a scholarly assistant whose presence would surely help convince those that needed convincing that the Chinese were eminently civilized and were the inheritors of a divinely inspired ethical tradition.

Charles De Noyelle: 17th Century Flemish Print

The Superior General resided in Rome, so it would take a while for Couplet to receive an answer to the pressing question of which European city he and Shen should journey to. Rome, presumably, but not before hearing from de Noyelle that doing so would not cause undue problems with the Portuguese authorities. Couplet had taken the liberty of mentioning in his letter that he hoped to leave Enkhuizen shortly and proceed south toward his native Mechlin. He craved de Noyelle's indulgence. He expected no objection to his visiting his family following a twenty-five-year absence. Might de Noyelle kindly address his answer to Couplet care of colleagues at the University of Louvain? Couplet had a nostalgic fondness for Louvain. It was there that he had studied theology and later it was at Louvain that he and his classmate Ferdinand Verbiest had heard Martini's lecture that had convinced them that they were destined for the China missions. The fact that the Spanish colonial authorities had opposed their going to Mexico had turned out to be providential. So it was a long letter, and Couplet didn't expect a quick answer. He didn't want a quick answer. His health was still frail, and he was tired of traveling. Why attempt to do so at the onset of winter? There was misery to being tossed around inside horse-drawn carriages and dragged over the Alpine passes of southeastern France and northern Italy, and then there were all those precious camphor boxes! Just then, Couplet believed himself to have been extraordinarily lucky to have been given the opportunity to revisit the country of his birth. What he hadn't mentioned in his letter to de Noyelle was that it would have been foolhardy to embark on as delicate a mission as the one with which he had been entrusted without pondering the events that over the past quarter-century had shaped the current European political environment. He needed time.

   So, it was at a leisurely pace that Couplet and Shen made their way southward along the great cities of Amsterdam, Utrecht and Rotterdam that had enabled the United Provinces of the Dutch Republic to withstand the eighty-year struggle against what they regarded as unwarranted Spanish religious and political oppression. The Republic had indeed emerged as Europe's preeminent commercial and artistic and scientific clearinghouse. As always, the travelers relied on the hospitality of the Jesuit houses that, despite taking pains to avoid all overt displays of religiosity, seemed to have found ways of thriving within the bustling diversity underpinning an era that was generally referred to as the Dutch Golden Age. It may have been Golden, but as Couplet and Shen learned soon enough it wasn't without its challenges and moments of seemingly unrelieved gloom.

Having come from Batavia, Couplet and Shen knew only too well about the bitterness that had dragged the British and the Dutch, Europe's two leading maritime and colonial commercial powers, into a succession of bitterly contested naval engagements with no clear winner. The Dutch had at one point pulled off the unimaginably humiliating feat of sailing up one of the river Thames' tributaries knowing that it was where the English had imprudently docked most of their mighty fleet, imagining it to be out of harm's way. The pounding sustained by the Royal Navy had been horrific. But then there was 1672, a year, so far as the Dutch were concerned, of disasters—the Rampjaar. The Royal Navy blockaded their coast and French armies had marched victoriously into the Netherlands.

"This had happened some ten years ago," Shen had exclaimed during a particularly festive dinner in Rotterdam, "and why such aggressiveness on the part of the French?"

Hadn't France become Europe's preeminent Catholic nation? Hadn't Father Couplet mentioned that to satisfy Emperor Kangxi's request for mathematically trained astronomers of the first order to be sent to Beijing it was increasingly likely that it would be necessary to have recourse to the French king? Was this what Christians did? Was it not surprising that the French had unleashed their armies on their seemingly peaceful neighbors?

Well, yes, Shen's spiritual mentors explained, but Louis XIV, like all powerful monarchs, had territorial ambitions and he'd set his sights on the nearby Netherlands. At the time it seemed to Louis XIV like an opportunity to expand France's northern borders and the prosperous Dutch were a tempting target. Hadn't Emperor Kangxi done much the same by subjugating most of southwestern China, and wasn't it rumored that he was intent on extending his rule to more distant lands such as Tibet and Mongolia and that he even coveted the fertile and strategic island of Taiwan?

It was all, admittedly, rather perplexing, but luckily things hadn't exactly gone the way Louis XIV had hoped. It was at this point that Shen was told that Louis XIV rather liked to be known as the Sun King. That was understandable; powerful monarchs were fond of such monikers. The two Chinese characters making up the name Kangxi, let it not be forgotten, stood for Peaceful Harmony. One of the Jesuit fathers remarked at that same dinner that some of the Chinese emperor's recently subjugated subjects might not exactly relate to that title. All sighed. Such was the imperfect world the Lord had called everyone to live in.

What had happened? Well, the Sun King had come up against geography and Dutch obstinacy. The Dutch Republic is a country predominantly at the water's edge. There was a way of releasing enough water into a succession of bogs and marshes to transform them into a virtually continuous line of treacherous slush that effectively shielded key cities such as Amsterdam, Utrecht, and Rotterdam from invading armies. Louis XIV had met his match when confronted with Dutch engineering savvy. Then the English decided to pull out of what had been at best an uneasy alliance with the French. The English made a separate peace with the Dutch.

Shen wanted to know more about the English. They didn't seem to figure very prominently from a geographic point of view, but in Batavia he'd of course heard all those stories about their harrying the Dutch in the spice islands and their taking altogether too much of an interest in India. Weren't they heretical Protestants? Indeed, they were, and no friends of the Jesuits. It was complicated though, and Shen couldn't be expected to understand all of this. He'd been in Europe barely six months. Let's just say that their king went by the name of Charles II and that he was thought to have Catholic sympathies. So, naturally enough, many staunch British Protestants feared he might be plotting with the Sun King to reinstate Catholicism in England.

It wasn't fair to complicate Shen's life with any of this since he was unlikely to ever go to England. He might, however, be interested to know that the English King had no male heir and that his brother James was a Catholic. That was a detail that clearly interested Couplet, but enough about the English. Back to the French. The upshot of it all was that the Sun King reluctantly pulled his horses and men back from the impassable Dutch bogs but, by way of a consolation prize, grabbed southern Flemish cities such as Dunkirk and Lille. He thereupon declared himself to be invincibly victorious, following which he and the Dutch negotiated another uneasy truce. That was five years ago. The truce had held.

From Rotterdam, Couplet and Shen made their way further south to Antwerp, crossing from the Dutch Republic into the so-called Spanish Netherlands. As far as Couplet was concerned, this was old history. The border had been established some eight years before his departure for China. It was part of the negotiated peace that had put an end to the gut-wrenching Thirty Years War that had contributed to the tearing apart of Christian Europe. Shen remembered João Atayde mentioning that his family was from Antwerp and that he'd been raised there. But wasn't he Portuguese?

Couplet explained that Antwerp had once been a prosperous trading city with access to the North Sea. It had dealt in spices and all things exotic so that enterprising merchants had flocked to it from all over Europe. Disaster had hit when the famously barbarous Duke of Alba had unleashed his Spanish troops on the citizenry massacring untold thousands in retaliation for Antwerp having aligned itself with the Protestant cause. Couplet did his best to be reassuring by pointing out to Shen that this also was ancient history. The massacre had occurred over a century ago and Antwerp had ended up south of the border in the Spanish Netherlands. What Couplet could have added to his historical recounting of events but chose not to, was that Mechlin, the beloved city of his birth, had also been pillaged by the Duke of Alba's mercenaries and that the man's ruthlessness had no doubt contributed to its remaining on the Catholic side of the border.

All this put Shen in a pensive mood.

"Weren't the Spanish Catholics?" he asked rhetorically. Wasn't this a bit extreme and then why would João Atayde have left Antwerp when he was from a Catholic family and the city had ended up in the Spanish Netherlands?

Couplet thought of himself as a patient man more than willing to address complex ethical issues, but this was trying. He hadn't up till now found himself in the unenviable position of justifying the actions of co-religionaries to those steeped in Confucian ethics. Back in Nanjing, Beijing, Suzhou, Shanghai, and Hangzhou, no one knew about any of this painful history. Couplet could have brushed Shen off with a vague comment and told him to go back to studying his Latin declensions, but to his credit, he didn't.

"There's something about João Atayde I haven't told you. Yes, he's a good Catholic and married to a pious woman, but there were Jews among his ancestors. You remember my telling the story about Rhodes, the Avignonese Jesuit who'd run afoul of the Dutch for saying Mass in Batavia? Do you remember Dom João asking me about his name? It's when I explained it had a Sephardic ancestry that he told me about his own forebears. Antwerp was known to be one of the cities to which Jews had moved from their Portuguese homeland."

Yes, Shen had heard about the Inquisition. Not much, admittedly, and not enough for him to ask a lot of questions but enough for him to now catch on to what Couplet was hinting at. He could sense the depth of Couplet's embarrassment.

"Let me put it this way. Dom João is a capable and ambitious man. He thought that in Goa the Portuguese authorities would have other things to worry about besides the purity of his ancestry. Yes, that's right. The issue was framed in terms of the Christian purity of the blood running through a man's veins. Jewish blood failed the purity test. His optimism was unjustified. So, you've guessed correctly, Michael. He moved further yet to Batavia where he had to worry about his adopted Catholicism rather than his Jewish roots. In this instance the Dutch turned out to be more forbearing. Don't, please, ask me to comment on any of this, Michael. You may know that my hero Matteo Ricci, while in Beijing, was visited by members of a Chinese Jewish community established by Jewish merchants perhaps as far back as the Tang dynasty. These Jews were from Kaifeng, a city in faraway Henan province. They and Ricci treated each other with great civility and mutual respect. Let me leave it at that."

❖

Mechlin is half-way between Antwerp and Louvain. The extended Couplet family had been given ample notice of the arrival of their distinguished relative and his Chinese companion. They were treated as conquering heroes. Couplet's parents were no longer alive. He was the fifth of his mother's nine children and she, sadly, had died while giving birth to that ninth child almost six decades ago. Couplet's father, Pierre, had remarried after a surprisingly long widowhood. He was in his seventies by then and Couplet was in China. Despite his advanced age, he'd sired five more children. Couplet learned, to his surprise, that he had an eight-year-old half-brother. His father, though, had died five years earlier. Not all of Couplet's siblings and half-siblings had survived, but there remained a mighty tribe consisting of dozens of nieces and nephews and to top it all there were cousins in the hundreds.

A civic celebration was organized, the high point of which was a Mass held at the church dedicated to Saint John the Baptist. It was the most solemn of occasions. The venerable Gothic church boasts a magnificent high altar enhanced by a triptych depicting the Adoration of the Magi. Couplet had childhood memories of his family praying before this great painting, awed by the knowledge that it was the work of the already famous Peter-Paul Rubens. Couplet had opened several of his precious camphor boxes and had chosen to wear the splendidly embroidered vestments he had brought with him all the way from Shanghai. These had been both designed and worked on by Candida Xu. She had lavished them with particular care and expressed the hope that they might one day be used to celebrate Mass in the Eternal City. The possibility that they might be used in the very church in which Couplet had been baptized had never crossed his mind. It was indeed the most emotional of moments. Couplet offered the Mass for the repose of the many deceased members of his family. He was particularly mindful of his beloved mother and of his father who had been regarded in Mechlin as something of a latter-day biblical patriarch. Couplet had added to his list of intentions the name of Candida Xu as well as that of her venerable Shanghainese grandfather Paul Xu, who had been known to Matteo Ricci. This homecoming was an occasion on which to be particularly grateful to Lady Candida for having devoted her later years, her exceptional intellectual acumen, and her considerable financial resources to supporting the Jesuit missionary effort in China. Couplet was more determined than ever to tell her story. He and Shen had tearfully reminisced that just before her death and as they prepared for the journey, they had made a point of visiting her in Shanghai to ask for her blessing.

It crossed Shen's mind that, had tradition allowed, it would have been comforting to the Couplet family to have dedicated within their Mechlin family home an altar to the memory of their ancestors.

All good things come to an end and now the time had come

for Couplet to turn his mind to the serious question of how to best approach his embassy. Louvain is but a short distance from Mechlin and it was there that he hoped to find both an answer to the letter he had addressed to the Order's superior general in Rome and guidance from politically astute fellow Jesuits. He was in sorely need of their good advice.

In Louvain, there was indeed a letter awaiting him. He was in luck because de Noyelle had responded promptly. Couplet was also in for a surprise. Yes, he and Shen were to make their way to Rome and were advised to do so with reasonable dispatch but, and surprisingly, they were to do so by way of Paris.

What Couplet didn't know was that shortly after he and Shen had sailed out of Macao on the ill-fated Santo António, the Emperor Kangxi had further and insistently impressed on Father Verbiest the necessity of dispatching competent mathematicians to the Forbidden City. In the more than two years that had gone by, it had been Verbiest's good fortune that the letter he had urgently addressed to Rome had taken a mere nine months to reach the superior general. Impressed by the urgency of the matter, he'd passed on the request to the French Jesuits, knowing that they were the ones in the best position to take care of such a delicate matter. Lady Luck had once again smiled on the initiative in that not only had Charles de Noyelle, Couplet's compatriot, just been elected superior general of the Order, but it also happened that the French King's confessor was a Jesuit by the name of Père la Chaise. The two men knew each other well and had every reason to work together. For reasons that were about to be revealed to Couplet, the idea of sending mathematicians to Beijing was greeted in Paris with unusual enthusiasm. Thanks to Père la Chaise's excellent connections, a group of promising candidates had been hastily assembled. So, there it was: Couplet and Shen were to hasten to Paris and were charged with delivering a crash course in Chinese civilization to the mathematicians.

François de La Chaise: 17th century French engraving

Why such enthusiasm? Here is what Couplet's learned advisors in Louvain brought to his attention. The French were particularly keen on establishing a political and trade beachhead in China. It must have been particularly galling to the Sun King that the grandeur of his reign was virtually unknown in a part of the world within which upstarts such as the Portuguese and then the Dutch had long been active. Spain had suffered from similar feelings of inferiority in the preceding century and had remedied them by grabbing hold of the Philippines. They had done so by spectacularly sailing galleons westward and across the Pacific from Mexico's Pacific east coast. Even the English, as of late, and thanks to their peskily aggressive EIC, had stolen a march on the French. They were insinuating themselves along the two Indian coasts. The Sun King was determined to catch up, come what may.

Now for the challenging part of the story. There was a tradition going back over a millennium that the French nation was the 'eldest daughter of the church'. Perhaps so, but that didn't mean that Louis XIV and the then pope saw eye-to-eye on the political issues that were currently challenging European unity, namely how to deal with the Turkish threat. Worse still, the king was at loggerheads with the pope when it came to who should have the last word over policies affecting the governance of the Church in France. Couplet was warned in no uncertain terms that whether he liked it or not, he would most likely be dragged into policy conflicts that, while having no direct bearing on events in China, nonetheless affected the issues he had come to Europe to address. Couplet, and by force of circumstances, young Shen, who was an increasingly eager and inquisitive listener, were thereupon treated to a master class in the current subtleties underlying the age-old conflict bedeviling the relationship of religion to secular power. To whom did bishops owe their appointment and their ultimate loyalty? To king or to pope? The conflict pitted Gallicans against Ultramontanes.

The term Gallicans was a historical allusion to ancient Gaul. Gaul was indeed ancient and distant and therefore lent itself to being fantasized as the immutable bedrock upon which those who claimed to possess a truly French identity could stand secure. No matter that France had been unified and territorially enlarged by Charlemagne who, much like the Manchu Qing emperors of China, was a foreigner. He was a Germanic Frank, hence the change in the country's name from Gaul to France. That was fine with Louis XIV because he thought of himself as Charlemagne's divinely inspired successor and thus entitled to rule undisputedly and absolutely.

Why Ultramontanes? They were accused of looking for guidance in the management of ecclesiastical affairs to a pope who resided beyond (ultra) the great Alpine mountain range separating France geographically from the Italian States. The Sun King looked upon their supporters as belonging to a dangerous fringe of intellectually warped idealists.

According to Couplet's friendly advisors, a lot of this had to do with the Sun King's personality. He was undoubtedly a single-minded pursuer of policies that not only redounded to the glory and primacy of the French nation but were also in accord with the highly traditional concept that the notion of statehood reached its zenith when embodied within the person of a ruler endowed with absolute powers. *L'état c'est moi.* Louis XIV undoubtedly had a high opinion of himself. Athenian democracy had been an intellectually intriguing but impractical aberration.

Didn't such a definition, Shen observed, match almost word for word the way Confucians described the role of the Son of Heaven? Absolutely, neither Confucius nor Mencius nor any other Chinese political theorist had so much as imagined a governance system like that practiced by the ancient Athenians. It would, in the Chinese context, have been inviting anarchy. China had a long history of peasant revolts and drifting apart at the seams only to swing back seeking the sense of cultural security that could only come from feeling attached to the umbilical cord of centralized imperial power. So, religion, quite naturally, was integrated within such an absolutist and person-centered concept of sovereignty. The way it was put to Shen was that as far as the Sun King was concerned, the practice of religion was essential to fostering a spirit of reverential submissiveness essential to the proper functioning of a divinely ordered body politic. Shared religious beliefs were therefore regarded as the glue that bound an individual citizen to his ruler. How else could a sovereign rely on the unquestioned loyalty of his subjects? Shen went so far as to remark that he was familiar with such a view, since it was again essentially Confucian. The emperor presiding within the splendor of the Forbidden City didn't think it was a good idea for his loyal subjects to harbor stray thoughts or beliefs. Woe to them if they did! Heresy undermined the body politic. It always led to that tearing apart at the seams that, while inevitable given the cyclic nature of human affairs, had to be deferred at all costs. Well in that case, woe to a Protestant living within the Sun King's extensive domain. Food for thought!

How did such concepts square, Shen asked himself in one of his more reflective moments, with the ideal of love of neighbor that had so appealed to his kindly Christian grandmother back in

Nanjing? The short answer is that they didn't, but this wasn't the time to agonize yet again over such irreconcilable paradoxes.

It was by now becoming apparent to Shen that if a monarch such as the Sun King regarded himself as embodying a notion akin to that of the Mandate of Heaven, then it was understandable that he and the pope might not always see eye to eye. Weren't they in competition, he asked? Kangxi as the Son of Heaven faced no such dilemma. There were no popes among Buddhists, Daoists and Confucians to challenge him. The emperor of China was the undisputed arbiter of all things moral and religious.

Shen had raised an interesting point and all present agreed that such a situation would undoubtedly have appealed to Louis XIV. So, Shen, asked provocatively, could a Chinese emperor converted to Christianity be expected to show any more deference to Rome than did the most Catholic Sun King? Shen expressed the thought in Chinese and Couplet translated it. It was a question to which there was no convenient answer. The rector of the house in which the select advisory group had assembled thereupon gently chided Couplet by suggesting that Shen was imperiling his soul by asking too many questions. He did so with a smile. It was, of course, meant as a joke, but the smile was nonetheless a wry one.

So much for the Sun King's personality and political philosophy, but what about the pope? One of the problems was that there had recently been altogether far too many of them. No, the era of having one in Rome and another in Avignon was over. It was simply that they tended to be elected to their exalted office at rather too advanced an age and they therefore died off in quick succession. So far as Shen was concerned, they also had the unfortunate habit of choosing confusingly similar names. It was understandably difficult to keep track of them. The current pope went by the name of Innocent XI and, Couplet's advisors stressed, he was a welcome exception to the rule. He'd been elected in his sixties and was still in fair health. He was a man of modest origins who had made his way into the upper ranks of the Church's hierarchy largely thanks to his intellect and moral integrity. That also was unusual.

So, they elaborated, Innocent was, by nature, spiritually inclined and conducted the affairs of state in a manner that reflected his parsimonious personal habits. He did unusual things like balance the papal court's financial budget, enjoin sobriety on his courtiers and even express heartfelt sympathy for those who advocated a meditative approach to religious life. He couldn't help being emotionally at odds with those who, for political reasons, were intent on encroaching on the papacy's spiritual prerogatives. That went not just for Louis XIV's brand of absolutism but also for the Portuguese king's continuing insistence on meddling in Church affairs. Yes, the papacy had reluctantly given its assent to the Portuguese kings' oversight under the Padroado arrangement but that was over two centuries ago. The world had changed beyond recognition. Innocent was just as irked by the Spanish, who despite being increasingly at odds with their Portuguese cousins, had adopted the very same highhanded attitude and made a virtue out of treating their bishops and indeed the religious orders operating throughout the Americas as though their sole purpose was the spread of Hispanic cultural and political hegemony.

Up till this point in the conversation no mention had been made of it, but it was a looming, overshadowing presence and Couplet had known all along he would at some point have to deal with it. That was, of course, the Propaganda. Shen knew of it only too well. It had a way of insinuating itself into the many discussions he and Couplet had had during the course of their epic journeying. He even recalled it coming up while conversing during those simpler times when together with Dom João and Dona Inês they had gathered around a good meal evoking the challenges that lay ahead.

So, what did those who Couplet referred to in Louvain as his friendly advisors think of all this? Well, predictably enough they thought that in a perfect world, the Jesuits being the most international of organizations dedicated like none other to integrating Christianity into Confucian and traditional Chinese culture, should welcome the authority of a papal office such as the Propaganda. Shouldn't it be seen as a necessary and salutary counterweight to the nationalistically driven Portuguese Padroado? Wasn't it to be expected that Innocent XI by supporting the Rome-based Propaganda would be reasserting waning papal control over the worldwide missionary effort? Shouldn't the pope be seen as an ally of the Jesuits?

Yes, all this was obvious enough but there were complications that Couplet, and of course Shen, needed to be appraised of. The fact was that the Propaganda happened to be overseen by a group of overtly traditionally-minded Roman cardinals. These good people, Couplet's advisors stressed, were not exactly sympathetic to the thinking of pioneers such as Matteo Ricci. They tended to view practices such as Chinese ancestor worship as a dangerous invasion of rituals and beliefs that were deemed divinely ordained and therefore immutable. It was also obvious that competing religious orders, notably the Dominicans and Franciscans had, for reasons of their own, encouraged such thinking.

So, and here was the big question, where did Pope Innocent stand in all this? Might he be sympathetic to the Jesuit cause? And, as Couplet's sagacious advisors were quick to add, even if sympathetic, would he be willing to expend political capital to take on the powerful cardinals directing the Propaganda?

What everyone in the room seemed to like about Pope Innocent was that he felt neither beholden to nor cowered by the spirit of entitlement that seemed to so characterize contemporary power-hungry European monarchs. That made sense to Shen. Hadn't he been taught in Nanjing that the Christian God had bestowed upon the Church supreme authority over all matters spiritual? Didn't such authority therefore extend to the pope having the last word over selecting those deemed worthy and most capable of carrying out the practical aspects of its mission? Well, yes, and Shen was right to point out that this didn't exactly mesh with the squabbling over who had the right to appoint bishops and, of course, to the equally muddled politics surrounding the Padroado and the Propaganda. Couplet had transposed Shen's observations from Chinese to French. No one was speaking Latin and had Shen attempted to do so he would surely have tripped over the language's pesky declensions and tenses.

"Not only does your young Chinese scholar ask too many questions but he also thinks too much," observed the reverend rector. He still had that wry smile. All Couplet could do was to nod in meek agreement.

Here is how Couplet's notes summarized the advice he'd been given by his learned Louvain colleagues:

Louis XIV knows full well that Pope Innocent is less pliable than many if not all his immediate predecessors. The French had opposed his election.

Louis XIV has made it clear he considers it his God-given prerogative to have the last word over the appointment of French bishops.

Louis XIV claims it is his right to ensure that ecclesiastical affairs are conducted in conformity with his own political objectives. The man has a will of his own.

Louis XIV is prepared to dispatch French mathematicians to Beijing without consulting either Pope Innocent or the Propaganda in Rome…or the Padroado in Lisbon. The only mathematicians available happen to be both French and Jesuits! So, this is a way of satisfying both Emperor Kangxi and ensuring the continuity of our Jesuit Chinese missions. We run the risk of displeasing the Pope, the Propaganda, and the Portuguese, but we go along with it for the good reason that there are no other choices.

Most of the French clergy have, out of self-interest, been cowed into siding with the king's nationalistic and absolutist viewpoint. They are labeled as Gallicans. The others are Ultramontanes.

We Jesuits are caught between a Gallican rock and an Ultramontane hard place. Père la Chaise seems to be the only one in a position to keep this juggling act going. According to de Noyelle, I am to scrupulously heed his advice.

In our zeal to allow Chinese converts to worship their ancestors and practice traditional Confucian rites, we China Jesuits are up against the conservatism of the Propaganda and yet we need the Propaganda if we are to loosen the constricting grip the Portuguese Padroado seeks to exert over our Chinese missions.

Where does the Confucian Treatise that I am responsible for having published in Europe fit in this depressingly complex picture? I wish I knew.

Confucius says:

To rule a country of a thousand chariots, there must be reverent attention to business, and sincerity; economy in expenditure, and love for men; and the employment of the people at the proper seasons.

Analects I

What is called a great minister is one who serves his prince according to what is right, and when he finds he cannot do so, retires.

Analects XI

If the people are in want, their prince cannot enjoy plenty alone.

Analects XII

V
Versailles
Late summer of 1684 to December 1684

$\mathcal{C}$ouplet and Shen arrived in Paris on September 3rd of 1684. Paris held out the promise of great excitement. Charles de Noyelle had instructed Couplet in his letter from Rome that he and Shen were to go directly to Père la Chaise's residence where they were expected. It was a spacious and comfortably appointed property set on a wooded hillside with distant views of Paris' eastern residential quarters. Père la Chaise, as the king's confessor and confidant, could have resided in any of the royal palaces. An apartment in the Tuileries or the Louvre would have been the envy of the great bevy of courtiers that craved to be within earshot of the royal presence. Instead, he'd chosen to dwell a few miles away in the company of a handful of fellow Jesuits within a village that the locals referred to as Ménilmontant. There was speculation that, given the court's recent move to Versailles, Père la Chaise would at last forsake the apparent simplicity of village life and move to the rather more distant but magnificently appointed château. He had no such intention. He was a man who knew the value of maintaining a respectful measure of independence when dealing with those who seek to lord it over others.

Couplet and Shen were treated as honored guests and enjoined to rest after their journey. Despite Couplet's complement of camphor chests, they had made good time. The stagecoach ride from Brussels to Paris had nonetheless taken the best part of twelve days and included stays in flea-ridden inns. Following that short respite, Père la Chaise had generously arranged for them to visit Montmartre so they could pray at the church at which Ignatius, while still a student, had famously gathered his small band of companions, thereby giving expression to his desire to form a radically new religious order.

Père la Chaise, aware of de Noyelle's instructions that the two men make every effort to be in Rome by Christmas, promptly arranged for them to meet and work with the group of six he now referred to as the King's Mathematicians. They had, he assured his guests, been chosen with the utmost care. In addition to their mathematical competence, they represented a range of technical skills that would no doubt appeal to the Chinese emperor. Among them, for example, was an astronomer who, it was Père la Chaise's hope, had the potential to rise to the occasion and succeed Verbiest at the Beijing observatory. Père Joachim Bouvet was only 28, but a year older than Shen, as it happened. He showed great promise both as a teacher and as one committed to immersing himself in Chinese culture.

The work sessions were to be held in one of the spacious rooms of the recently renovated Louvre palace which, since the court's very recent transfer to Versailles, had become available to those involved in matters of state. Those arrangements had been made by one who Père la Chaise referred to as his friend Melchisédec and whom, given that he had just been appointed the King's Librarian, Couplet would have every reason to want to meet. He was no Jesuit, Père la Chaise had remarked, but nonetheless the most erudite and eccentric of men.

Shen was somewhat puzzled. Yes, he vaguely remembered a Biblical reference to a character bearing a similar name who was King of Salem and priest of the High God. Was this a common name among the French? Absolutely not, Père la Chaise reassured him. This man's family name was Thévenot, and he was admittedly a bit of an eccentric. He'd chosen Melchisédec at his confirmation in memory of some distant and apparently distinguished ancestor. The name had stuck.

La Maison de Mont Louis au R. Père de la Chaise, près de Ménilmontant.

Jesuit House on hill overlooking Menilmontant: 17th century French engraving

The man was already in his mid-sixties and had acquired considerable fame as a scholar and inventor for all seasons. He had, for instance, come up with a technique for building straighter walls by designing a spirit level. He'd also written a how-to guide with aerodynamic advice for those seeking to improve their swimming style and technique. All along he had been publishing papers on astronomy, physics, and medicine, thereby contributing to the latest craze—the proliferation of scientific journals throughout Europe. Above all, he had developed a fascination for collecting and publishing exotic materials brought back by intrepid travelers and explorers. It helped that he was an accomplished linguist, having mastered, in addition to Latin and Greek, Hebrew, Arabic and even Turkish.

Thévenot, Père la Chaise explained, had an encyclopedic turn of mind and was an avid collector of manuscripts. Furthermore, he was fascinated by China.

"Now, my dear Father Couplet, I must make you aware of something that is probably going to come to you as a shock. That said, I don't want you to worry about it. Thévenot is not going to get in your way. Quite the contrary—he'll see you as an ally. He'll want to be your collaborator. You may need him. Cultivate his friendship."

The matter at hand was that this man-for-all-seasons had compiled a monumental treatise consisting of almost 2,000 pages, generously illustrated and written mostly in French. Thévenot had published it over a nine-year time span and the last volume had appeared twelve years earlier. Its French title was the rough equivalent of Strange Tales from Faraway Lands. One of its more voluminous sections was devoted to China. Thévenot had incorporated into his text some of the maps and historical accounts published by Martini who of course was the man with the magic lantern who twenty-five years earlier at Louvain had so impressed Couplet and Verbiest. No harm in any of that, of course, but here was the startling, nay shocking, part. Thévenot had gone further and included within his Strange Tales not only a life of Confucius, but also a Latin translation of one of Confucius' Four Books, namely The Doctrine of the Mean.

Père la Chaise was right. Couplet reeled under the unexpectedness of this piece of unwelcome news. Weren't he and Shen on a mission to be the very first to bring to Europeans awareness of Confucius? How could they possibly have been upstaged by this man Melchisédec who knew no Chinese and had published this book of his in Paris twelve years earlier without so much as notifying anyone! Didn't he know that the Jesuits thought of themselves as having a monopoly over disseminating information pertaining to China? Couplet's head was spinning. He was of an age that caused him to be vulnerable to life-threatening apoplectics. Père la Chaise had him sit down and drink a draft of digitalis decocted from foxgloves grown on the hills of Ménilmontant. There is something of a physician lurking within every Jesuit.

What had happened? It turned out to be no great mystery. Ironically, it all went back to the indomitable Próspero Intorcetta, Couplet's superior and nemesis. It was he who, twenty years earlier, had found a way of evading house arrest in Canton and had spirited away a Life of Confucius written in Latin and a bi-lingual Chinese Latin manuscript of The Doctrine of the Mean. Couplet had contributed to both redactions. Of course, he had. He was one of the four translators who, reunited by the persecution that had followed the imprisonment of Adam Schall, had whiled away the days of their confinement by working on the project. Intorcetta, resourceful as ever, had managed to have half of these smuggled-out texts published and printed in Canton and then the other half in Portuguese Goa. Come to think of it, it was no great surprise that some of these printed editions had made their way to Europe. That was exactly what Intorcetta had intended. Still less that a set had ended up in Thévenot's possession. He was known to be an avid collector of such esoteric material and he corresponded actively with like-minded scholars throughout Europe. Thévenot had, in the most natural of ways, made use of what had come his way. He didn't need to know Chinese.

The digitalis broth did prove soothing. The projected Confucian Treatise was far more ambitious in scope than what Thévenot had cobbled together. So why fret? It was admittedly annoying that some Europeans might already be familiar with The Doctrine of the Mean. Arguably a distillation of Confucian thought, but hardly fatal to the success of the Confucian Treatise. Perhaps more galling to Couplet was the fact that even though he and Intorcetta were contemporaries, the resourceful Sicilian had been promoted and was now one of the senior missionaries in China. Intorcetta was the man to whom Couplet, on his return, would most likely have to give an account of his embassy. He'd be keen to assess how Couplet had acquitted himself in the final editing of the Confucian Treatise. Too bad!

Père la Chaise was right, though, about Thévenot. The fact that he was the King's Librarian meant that he had access to resources that would undoubtedly come in handy. He might take an invitation to be an active contributor to the editing of the Confucian Treatise as an opportunity to enhance his reputation as an orientalist. Make the man your ally, Père la Chaise had counseled. He has the king's ear, and the Sun King has his heart set on presiding over a Republic of Letters centered in Paris that could well encompass Confucian wisdom. Royal patronage was not to be sneezed at! Be guided by Père la Chaise, Charles de Noyelle had written from Rome.

When Shen did meet Thévenot he struck the young man as a cordially welcoming French aristocrat who in the mold of Père la Chaise displayed a refined manner betraying a mix of curiosity and restraint. He was tall with a broad forehead and deep set eyes that, so far as the young man could tell, were in these parts thought of as characteristic of one possessing a serious and all-encompassing mind. The sessions with the King's Mathematicians in the elegantly appointed apartments of the Louvre, presided over by Thévenot, were a resounding success. The mathematicians, faced with the daunting challenge of assimilating the essentials of Chinese culture, had studied his Strange Tales.

Couplet had brought gifts for everyone. Chinese language primers for the mathematicians and a selection of Chinese classical texts for Thévenot. Despite Couplet's initial concern about his work being upstaged, the two men became the best of friends. The contents of the camphor chest were coming in handy. Shen was, without doubt, the most popular man in the room. This was the mathematicians' first opportunity to meet a real Chinese scholar.

Père la Chaise had understandably excused himself from attending any of these sessions. His official duties required that most days he be present in Versailles. It happened, however, that one evening on their return to Ménilmontant, Couplet and Shen found him waiting for them. He wanted, he said, to talk about Siam.

The mere prospect of finding himself drawn into yet another entangled web of intrigue caused Couplet's heart to beat noticeably faster.

"Père la Chaise," he blurted out, "I know next to nothing about the Siamese."

"My dear Couplet, why don't you first listen to what I have to say?"

The Sun King and his advisors had recently been rather taken by the notion that Siam was a huge and powerful country, maybe even on a par with China. Some might have to be forgiven for thinking that the two countries formed the same big confusing blotch on an unfamiliar map. Few, alas, had even heard of Thévenot's Strange Tales, let alone referred to them for reliable information. The point was that the Siamese king had sent an embassy to France and preparations were under way for a formal reception. There was in Versailles, Père la Chaise explained, an anticipatory whiff of orientalism in the air. There was even talk of the Siamese king leaning toward the view that concluding an alliance with the highly civilized French might be preferable to one with the altogether overly aggressive and commercially minded Dutch. The Siamese king was thought to harbor similar feelings regarding the equally pushy and contentious English. In any event it was apparent that no expense was being spared. The Sun King planned to honor the Siamese dignitaries by allowing them into his presence while sitting on his jeweled throne in full regalia. The court had only recently moved to Versailles so that putting on such a show would be something of a trial run. It would be a test of just how impressive a reception within the now fully decorated hall of mirrors could really be.

"Now my dear Couplet, don't look so perplexed. Don't you see that this presents me with an opportunity to introduce you, and most particularly your engaging young friend, at court? The King has approved the mathematical mission to China. He's about to meet Siamese delegates. Some have whispered in his ear that the Siamese king is open to forsaking Buddhism and embracing Catholicism. I have my doubts about that, but that's not the point. Here's young Shen who, thanks to you, is a devout Catholic. When we have the time, I'll tell you why the King has recently become much more religious. Yes, it's a long and not altogether edifying story. Let me just say for now that Shen would make an excellent impression. No…no…my dear Couplet…no one is going to hold him out as being Siamese…and you certainly wouldn't pass for one. It's just that the timing of your presence here in Paris is fortuitous. That's right. Don't forget Confucius. I've talked this over with Melchisédec. Young Shen mirrors Confucian values. Has it occurred to you that printing this treatise of yours is going to be a very expensive and highly time-consuming affair? Well, I hate to be the bearer of bad news but if you think you're going to get anyone in Rome to pay for anything…well let's just say that it would be a good idea to explore other possibilities. Yes, my dear Couplet, we're off to Versailles. I've arranged for the carriage to be ready at dawn. Make sure Shen looks very Chinese…you've shown me some of those lovely gowns you've been carrying around in those chests of yours…that's right. Make sure you get a good night's sleep!"

Père la Chaise's official position entitled him to first class treatment when it came to traveling from Ménilmontant to Versailles. This consisted of a four-horse, comfortably appointed carriage and it bore the royal arms. The weather on that warm, late September morning was sunny and fair. The three passengers were in Versailles by ten o'clock, having made the five-league journey in just under two-and-a-half hours. Père la Chaise had arranged for an informal tour of the château's newly commissioned staterooms, magnificent to behold.

Palace of Versailles: 1682 French engraving

The party ran into some good luck. They were spotted by the King himself who, surrounded as he always was by a throng of courtiers, was on his way to Mass. The chapel was in the vicinity of the hall of mirrors, and it was by now around midday. There must have been something about Shen that caught the royal eye, because after attending Mass and then partaking of lunch, the king went out to meet his guests. The young man rose to the occasion. Not only did Shen and Couplet have at hand a set of gifts consisting of fetchingly artistic Chinese knick knacks, but Shen took it upon himself to initiate the elaborate nine-bow ritual that would have been expected of him had he been admitted within the walls of the Forbidden City. The Sun King obviously loved it but, feigning modesty, after three bows bid Shen rise and desist. Watching the young man enthusiastically hit the ground with his forehead caused quite a stir among the courtiers—a scene not easily forgotten.

Later in the day, a liveried crimson-clad messenger in a strikingly white powdered wig came up to Père la Chaise and, with a respectfully inclined forehead in the courtly French, rather than the imperial Chinese manner, presented him with a folded-over, sealed message. It was an invitation for Père la Chaise and his two guests to attend the following day's lunchtime royal audience. No, the king wasn't inviting them to lunch. Rather, they were being granted the inestimable privilege of watching the king partake of lunch! They spent the night in Versailles. The Royal Confessor had his own suite of apartments. The festooned moldings were gilded and smelt of fresh paint.

It couldn't have gone better. Shen put on his cyan-tinted gown. It was a blue-green admixture symbolic of peace and serenity. It was gloriously but discreetly embroidered with dragons. Candida Xu had had a hand in its design. It would have been customary for the King to have his queen sit beside him, but, as Père la Chaise whispered in Shen's ear in Latin, he was now a widower, and no such honor could be extended to a lady of which more would be said later. The lady in question was Madame de Maintenon. Instead, a Bavarian princess who was married to king's eldest son and heir was at his side. She was plain looking, but reputedly sharp-witted and of an enquiring mind. So, at her behest, Shen was granted the great honor of standing beside the King at the royal table so he could demonstrate the use of chopsticks. He obviously rose, literally, to the occasion. The chopsticks were made of ivory and appropriately sized morsels of an unspecified culinary delicacy were brought in from the royal kitchens on a gold platter. The King then asked Shen to recite prayers in Chinese. Shen did so, devoutly voicing out loud what the King and those in attendance were told was the Our Father, the Hail Mary and, for good measure, the Nicene Creed with all its trinitarian entangling subtlety.

To cap it all, the guests were invited into the gardens and the King gave orders for the fountains—his fountains—to be turned on. It's difficult to imagine a greater honor, although Père la Chaise did express the thought that it might really be a rehearsal in anticipation of the forthcoming Siamese reception.

The water for the King's Fountains was supplied by a set of gigantic water wheels that had been erected along the river Seine's left bank and therefore at some distance from Versailles. They were most ingeniously powered thanks to the river's mighty downstream flow. This most elaborate of contraptions had been designed to raise the water to the level of the higher ground on which Versailles had been built. The machine was a marvel to behold, and it was most likely the largest mechanical device to have ever been built anywhere in the world. If not, then certainly the most expensive, but that, according to Père la Chaise, can't have been of much concern to the Sun King since the expenditure was being met from the Royal Purse.

Shen thereupon remarked that things were no different in China when it came to grandiose imperial projects. The young man added that he had often heard his father, when in one of his more wistful moods, comment that excessively taxing the peasants had surely contributed to the demise of the Ming Dynasty. Did Père la Chaise think this was something that could possibly happen in France? The king's confessor chose to respond with an evasive shrug.

Couplet and Shen, with Père la Chaise's help and in accord with Charles de Noyelle's instructions, had arranged to leave Paris within days of the Versailles visitation. Why such haste? There was nothing easy about traveling by horse drawn coach from Paris due south into the Rhone Valley and then negotiating the foothills of the Alps. The need to make brief stopovers in Turin and Milan would surely add to the anticipated rigors of an already lengthy overland voyage. They had been further instructed, as they progressed toward Rome, to take in Parma, Modena, and Bologna. There were princes and dignitaries to meet in each of those powerful independent city-states on whose support the Jesuits depended for the furtherance of the Chinese missions. There was therefore some urgency to their undertaking so long a journey before the onset of heavy autumnal rains. They were, if possible, to reach the Eternal City in time for the Christmas festivities.

Melchisédec Thévenot had organized a farewell dinner. He'd shrieked with joy when told that Shen had tutored the Sun King in the use of chopsticks. This was something to be celebrated. The dinner was held in his favorite eatery in the Rue Neuve Saint Honoré. Chez Gaston was across the street from the Palais Royal, that elegant residence built some sixty years earlier by Cardinal Richelieu and within which the Sun King had lived the formative years of his early youth. Everyone had been invited: all six mathematicians, Thévenot's colleagues at the Librairie du Roi. Père la Chaise had regrettably been held back in Versailles. He would be missed.

How did the Burgundy compare to Chinese wine? Shen was surprisingly well informed and took evident pride at answering such questions. It would be a grave mistake, he kept saying, to think that the Chinese drank only rice wine.

"We Chinese," he proudly asserted, "just like you, long ago discovered the joys that come from learning how to coax magic out of the juice pressed from grapes. We write poetry about it and our physicians prescribe it as a means of banishing ills."

It then occurred to Shen that this was a good time to ask the assembled company about the lady who apparently was not allowed to sit at the king's table at the famous lunch at which the chopsticks had been demonstrated.

"Oh, you mean Madame de Maintenon!" Thévenot had joyfully exclaimed. "Are you ready for a long story?"

Thévenot was what the French call a raconteur and the excellence of the Burgundy had overcome much of his aristocratically bred reticence. He began his yarn by explaining that one of the Sun King's most enduring traits was that he took great pleasure in the companionship of women. Not, however, that of his queen. He'd been married off to her in his youth in one of those quintessentially politically motivated alliances. Maria Theresa was the daughter of the Spanish king. Thévenot, who claimed to be as well informed as Père la Chaise, asserted that while the Sun King had done right by her and made sure she bore him legitimate offspring, he'd also managed to have intermittent yet passionate relationships with no less than thirty mistresses. Thévenot claimed to have kept count. He had, he said impishly, noted it all down in a little black notebook.

It was now Thévenot's turn to ask a question of young Shen, whom he took pleasure in addressing as Sieur Michel Chinois. By imperial standards, wasn't thirty a rather puny number, given that emperors were encouraged to have several official wives in addition to an impressive household of concubines? Indeed, it was but Sieur Michel was quick to point out that Chinese emperors didn't hold themselves out as models of Christian virtue to their loyal citizens. Tradition had it in the Shen family that the ancestor whom Matteo Ricci had converted had caused much angst by having to dismiss his second wife and his three concubines before being baptized.

Couplet, who it appeared hadn't drunk quite as much of the excellent Château-Neuf-du-Pape as Thévenot, interjected that Père la Chaise had told him it would be quite wrong to regard the king as a philander. Arguably not, agreed Thévenot because there was the case of the Marquise de Montespan. She, in her time, had been the most famous and influential of the thirty mistresses and, yes, it was the Sun King who was without question responsible for all seven of her children. And because he was seriously minded to the point that Père la Chaise called him religiously devout, he'd taken responsibility for their wellbeing. They were illegitimate, admittedly, but of royal blood and thus entitled to be both well-educated and numbered among the aristocracy. And then Thévenot quoted a maxim that was often voiced at court by the king's obsequious courtiers, namely that it was a monarch's duty to do everything in his power to assure the continuity of his bloodline. Perhaps! To Shen, that sounded rather Chinese.

"Hold your comments," continued Thévenot with an engaging grin, "because I've left the most edifying part of my story for the last. I wouldn't want Sieur Michel to go back to China with the impression that we French are a bunch of savages and nor would you, my reverend friends."

At this, Thévenot raised his glass filled with the aptly named Château-Neuf-du-Pape to Couplet and to the six mathematicians.

Here's how the story went. A pious lady, who happened to be a widow, had been recruited to take care of the Montespan illegitimate but nonetheless royal children. She was, although three years older than the king, still relatively young and her deceased husband happened to have been an outstanding wit and playwright. He'd authored Le Roman Comique that Thévenot assured those present deserved to be translated into Chinese. It was an audaciously entertaining novelistic romp recounting the adventures of a troupe of actors. That said, it had been the oddest of marriages. He was considerably older than she and being debilitatingly deformed by a strange disease resistant to treatment, in much need of a kind and caring spouse. She possessed all those qualities together with an uncannily sharp and receptive mind. She had intelligently profited from what might have otherwise been the most dispiriting of marital arrangements. She had done so by engaging with her crippled husband's wit in such a manner as to further sharpen her own.

As to the Sun King, he took pleasure in regularly visiting his illegitimate brood and, well, Thévenot recounted with one of his sly grins, couldn't help noticing their rather attractive and intellectually vivacious governess. That's because she was fetchingly pretty but in other ways quite unlike the thirty others and not just because she coyly resisted the king's advances. A sequence of unrelated but consequential events resulted in this idyll having the most unexpected of outcomes.

Versailles

It all began with the Marquise de Montespan's fall from grace. The king, according to Thévenot, had tired of their ten-year relationship. Seven children had come of it and enough was enough. She hatched a plot involving his falling for a buxom young beauty in the hope that her youthful charms would distract the king from Madame de Maintenon's decidedly more mature appeal. It didn't work and the marquise found herself implicated, albeit obliquely, in a series of murky accusations and innuendos that had grown out of the presumed death by poisoning of members of the royal household. There was talk of black masses and of demonic possession.

Couplet was unpleasantly reminded of the accusations leveled against the unfortunate Adam Schall within the conspiracy-prone atmosphere that periodically resurfaced within the internecine politics of the Forbidden City. Would such thoughts, he asked himself, be also occurring to young, impressionable Shen?

The plot took the strangest of turns because at this point Queen Maria Theresa died of what the doctors pronounced was a cancerous tumor. It was an unexpected and sudden death. Louis XIV had by now reached the age of 45. It was a point in the story at which Père la Chaise had taken a lead part. Would Thévenot have proceeded with his yarn had the king's confessor been in the room? Probably not. The king and Père la Chaise had presumably had a heart-to-heart session. He'd sired a legitimate heir and given that he was now Europe's most powerful monarch felt no need for another of those unsatisfactory politically motivated marriages. He could manage perfectly well without a queen, and the fact was that he'd grown tired of mistresses, so why not marry Madame de Maintenon? It was common knowledge that within two months of Queen Maria Theresa's death, during the night hours and in the presence of the king's trusted butler and of the Archbishop of Paris, Père la Chaise had done the deed. The pious Lady was no queen, at least not in name, but she was now the king's legitimate wife and had made him a good Catholic. Yes, Shen must have been duly edified.

Thévenot told many other stories into the night hours, but they were of no relevance to the favorable outcome of Couplet's embassy and certainly less edifying.

Confucius says:

The Master said: To be fond of learning is to be near to knowledge.

In a high situation, he does not treat with contempt his inferiors. In a low situation, he does not court the favor of his superiors. He rectifies himself, and seeks for nothing from others, so that he has no dissatisfactions. He does not murmur against Heaven, nor grumble against men.

The Master said, "In archery we have something like the way of the superior man. When the archer misses the center of the target, he turns round and seeks for the cause of his failure in himself.

Doctrine of the Mean

VI
The Eternal City
1685

*C*ouplet and Shen did arrive in Rome before Christmas. Charles de Noyelle was there to welcome his Flemish compatriot, Philippe Couplet, together with his urbane young Chinese protégé. The superior general lived and worked in a building that, while modest in appearance, was impressively proportioned and abutted the Order's mother church. It was referred to as the Casa Professa and it was there that the two visitors were granted the singular honor of residing while in Rome. Shen was, on the very day of their arrival, shown around the rooms in which Ignatius had worked and had died more than a century earlier. It was a moving occasion. The Casa had been extensively remodeled and expanded since Ignatius' days but the suite of four cell-like rooms occupied by the saint had been preserved with much care and reverence.

The Casa abutted the Church of the Gesú. Shen was made aware that the construction of this magnificent church had begun a century earlier. Its most impressive feature was that it was based on plans conceived of by Ignatius himself and that he hoped would serve as a model for the churches the Order would build the world over. What distinguished it was that it had a single majestic nave with no aisles and no transept. Ignatius had wanted the congregation to

Shen's Unlikely Journey

be assembled as a single body with its attention focused on a high altar surmounted by an imposing dome. Shen was impressed by the richness of the interior. No expense had been spared when it came to the marble facing and the polychrome frescoed vaulting, most particularly that of the Triumph of the Name of Jesus to which, he was told, the finishing touches had only recently been added.

Church of the Gesù in Rome with (to the right) the Casa Professa: 17th century Italian engraving

The exterior façade was in the classical style. The main door was surmounted by a large medallion featuring the trigram of the name of Jesus (IHS) by which the Order identified itself. Matteo Ricci had included it on the title page of the first-ever book printed in China written by a European. To the left of the façade was a larger-than-life statue of Ignatius and to the right one of Francis Xavier. Shen couldn't help noting the striking differences from the Gothic churches he had visited over the past year during his travels through the Netherlands and then in Paris. Couplet observed that it would have been Ignatius' ardent wish that the small church Matteo Ricci had been allowed to construct in Beijing in the early part of the past century would one day be replaced by such magnificence.

There was more to see. The next day, Couplet and Shen were taken to the Collegio Romano. It was but a few of Rome's windy streets to the north and on their way, they passed walled-in gardens and small palazzos. Since its founding by Ignatius, the Order had grown exponentially and had become Rome's dominant educational institution. The Collegio, which Matteo Ricci had famously attended and at which he had been taught mathematics, had, since his day, been expanded beyond recognition. It was now housed in a palazzo with a hugely impressive classical façade and had been renamed the Gregorian University. The renaming was in honor of Gregory XIII, one of the previous century's most distinguished reformist popes who had convened the famous Council of Trent and lent his name to the updated Gregorian calendar that was now used throughout Catholic Europe. The Chinese emperors were not the only ones to be obsessive about calendars! Charles de Noyelle had arranged for Couplet and Shen to be allowed to study in one of the Collegio's several impressively wood-paneled libraries. It marked, the young man would later claim, the beginning of his fascination with European libraries.

Christmas came and went. Charles de Noyelle enjoined patience on his guests.

"In Rome," he counseled, "you need to be seen to want to see and to be seen. It takes time."

He suggested Shen begin with Queen Christina of Sweden.

Queen Christina! Well, yes, because she was possessed of a larger-than-life personality and was arguably Europe's foremost luminary. She was a six-year-old child at the time of her father's death in battle. He was King Gustavus Adolphus of Sweden. She had shown herself to be a remarkably precocious and gifted student. The French philosopher René Descartes had been among her many distinguished tutors in Stockholm. She had become Sweden's effective ruler on reaching her eighteenth birthday. The challenges facing the young woman were daunting. The climate in northern Europe was exceptionally harsh, and the Thirty Years War had visited unspeakable misery on the population not only of Germany where the Protestant and Catholic states were at each other's throats but also of the other nations that had been drawn into this most abject of religious conflicts. Sweden had been a major participant on the Protestant side.

Despite the momentous difficulties confronting her, Queen Christina had assumed her responsibilities with gusto and determination. Before long she was recognized as the wittiest and most learned woman of her era. Then suddenly, after reigning only ten years, she abdicated. It's not clear exactly why. The philosophically inclined young priest delegated by Charles de Noyelle to brief Shen on this woman's intriguing origins had commented that intellectual brilliance and the exercise of authority within established power structures seldom, if ever, coexist successfully. So, she apparently had spent lavishly on the things that pleased her and shocked her courtiers by announcing that, following the example of Elizabeth, the erstwhile Virgin Queen of England, she had no intention of marrying. Besides she'd secretly become a Catholic in what was a strictly Lutheran society. So, assured of a source of income from her extensive Swedish landholdings, she had moved to Rome where she had been warmly welcomed by the then pope. Despite being neither a great beauty nor a strict conformist in either the religious or social sense, she had in short order became Rome's undisputed powerhouse personality.

It didn't, however, always go smoothly, Shen's informant explained. Her popularity had ebbed and waned. A couple of times she fell for dubious schemes designed to enthrone her as queen of Naples and then later of Poland. Then while on a visit to France she'd been involved in a murky incident that had culminated in having her equerry, who was a respected Roman nobleman, executed for alleged treason. It was also rumored that she'd had an affair with one of the Roman Curia's younger cardinals. No matter, she had remained extraordinarily active socially and expended great energy and enthusiasm on promoting the arts and advocating food, clothing and shelter for those at society's margins.

Queen Christina of Sweden: 18th century French engraving

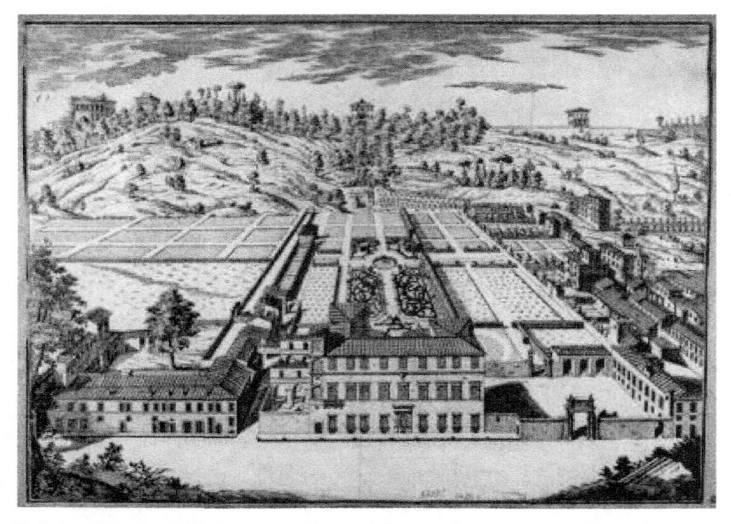

Palazzo Riario Nella Longara, Queen Christina's residence in Rome from 1659 to 1689: 18th century Italian engraving

When the invitation eventually came, it was for Shen to present himself at the Palazzo Riario. He was in for a treat. This imposing residence had been built in the 15th century and was at the foot of the Janiculum, one of Rome's loveliest and most peaceful hills. Queen Christina had lavished care on the palazzo's delightful gardens. The hill afforded breathtaking views over the city. It was beyond the Tiber and a mere half-hour walk from Saint Peter's square. Shen was told that it was there that, under her aegis, Rome's leading artists and scientists met regularly. She had created an academy. It included luminaries such as Alessandro Scarlatti, and Arcangelo Corelli. Who were these people?

Scarlatti was a precocious Neapolitan musician. He was still in his twenties. He'd composed operas and oratorios. His latest operatic production Il Pompeo had brought him considerable fame.

"The Queen is the most generous person". Shen's guide had told him. "Make sure she invites you to one of Scarlatti's performances."

Couplet had added that Shen would find it rather different from Peking Opera. "It'll broaden your artistic horizons!" he quipped.

And Corelli? He was, as Shen soon learned, another musician. This one from Ravenna in the north. He was a composer of tuneful sonatas with a gift for playing the violin. Did Shen know about violins? Yes and no. The Chinese, he explained, had for the longest time played folk tunes with a bow on a double-stringed instrument. It wasn't so much that the instruments were different but that the music he was hearing in Europe sounded to his ears as though it were from another planetary sphere. He'd by now learned about scales and how in his native China they were divided into five rather than seven intervals. That was something Queen Christina would be interested to hear about. Shen should also tell her, Couplet suggested, about how Matteo Ricci had been the first to bring a western instrument into China. It was, famously, a harpsichord presented to the recluse Ming emperor Wanli. It had been treated with reverential curiosity in much the same way as the intriguing clocks with which Ricci has drawn respectful attention to himself in Beijing.

Queen Christina, now aged 58, began Shen's artistic education by showing him around her impressive collection of Venetian paintings. She recognized in Shen a shy and overly deferential, clerically mannered young man and set out to emancipate him by smothering him with attention. Some of it was almost embarrassingly over-the-top. She drew out of him all kinds of insights concerning the pursuit of artistic excellence in his native China. She also turned out to be the one person he met in Rome with a genuine desire to learn about the influence that newly fashionable Manchu customs were having on traditional Ming society. She even succeeded in wheedling out of him salacious tidbits. She couldn't help being interested in the conduct of imperial affairs in a Forbidden City populated with eunuchs, concubines, and a bevy of fawning hangers-on. Shen marveled at her curiosity.

On one of his visits to the Palazzo Riario, Shen demonstrated the blue-green silken robes he'd worn in Versailles, and she even persuaded him to wear them at several of the musical soirées to which she was in the habit of inviting guests drawn from her large circle of artistically inclined friends and would-be courtiers. Among the most memorable was a private performance of Scarlatti's first major opera, A Comedy of Mistaken Identities. It was no longer the young composer's most famous work, but it was as charming as ever a portrayal of young love and it had a special place in Queen Christina's heart. Scarlatti had composed it thanks to her patronage, and it had launched his remarkably successful musical career. She told Shen that it was the first opera to feature women on a Roman stage and that she'd insisted on it being performed in public despite Church opposition. No one, not even the Pope, could risk displeasing Queen Christina.

On another evening Arcangelo Corelli appeared in person and led a trio that included a second violin and a viola. They performed, to the extravagant praise of everyone present, a rousing rendition of his latest sonata together with a selection of country dances.

Shen was interested in books and hers was one of the largest private collections to be found anywhere in Europe. Couplet had wisely thrust into his young protégé's hands a few of the precious woodblock printed volumes he had lovingly packed in the famous camphor chests rescued from the Banten shipwreck. At Couplet's urging, Shen had spoken of Candida Xu, and how it was thanks to this remarkable woman that it had been possible to bring these books all the way from China. Couplet had expressed the thought that had fate conspired to bring the two women together, they would surely have seen reflected in each other the God given qualities with which they had been so generously endowed.

"Father Couplet," Shen assured Queen Christina, "will, of course, see to it that you are among the very first to receive a copy of the book he fondly hopes to publish and that will be dedicated to extolling the life of Candida Xu."

Queen Christina expressed her heartfelt gratitude and went on to say that she would be only too pleased to add all these volumes to her splendid collection which, incidentally, already included a copy of Ricci's famous diary as edited by Trigault.

"When I die," she'd exclaimed, "all these books will go to the pope's library."

So, for Shen, this was a coming-of-age kind of experience and certainly an exciting one, even if being in the presence of such an overwhelming personality, a woman most especially, was disconcerting. It would turn out to be a welcome diversion from all those protocolary visits he would inevitably be subjected to that involved soft-spoken, black-robed Jesuit fathers, purple-clad monsignors, and red-hatted eminences.

Shen came to the gradual realization that in Rome he was something of a curiosity. The way it was put to him was that Rome thought of itself as the center of the world and was enamored with the idea that it was a magnet for all things curious and exotic. Well, Shen commented, wasn't that also true of the Middle Kingdom from whence he had come? It also thought of itself as the center of the world. Yes, but he further reflected, its ancient culture had never developed a sense of curiosity for what might lie beyond it. Barbarians might be useful, but they were to be treated with caution and when in doubt, walled off. Romans, in contrast, were intensely curious people. They worshiped the exotic. So, he, the young scholar from exotic China was on show. He was an object of curiosity.

Couplet felt somewhat responsible for not having put Shen on guard. The Jesuits were partly to blame for his notoriety. One of theirs, a German by name of Athanasius Kircher, had made a virtue out of titillating the growing ranks of those throughout Europe who were beset by wanderlust. Kircher had died just a few years previously, but his presence was still felt within the Eternal City. He'd been interested in absolutely everything. He was an avid reader of the detailed reports that Jesuits assigned to distant Asian and

New World outposts were required to remit annually to Rome. He had a particular affinity for China and almost twenty years before had published a highly successful tome titled China Illustrata. In Latin, of course, and spiced with all kinds of wondrous facts, many of which were outright fanciful but did wonders in terms of getting Europeans to pay at least some attention to China in all its vastness. Kircher had worked hard to ensure it was lavishly and imaginatively illustrated. It was the kind of book that was now regarded as an essential addition to the libraries of those indulging in the increasingly popular fad of book collecting. Couplet told Shen he didn't think it was all that bad a development. It should help create demand for their intellectually highbrow Confucian Treatise—even by those whose Latin wasn't up to the challenge.

Kircher had gone so far as to set up a museum within the Collegio Romano and house within it all manner of exotica. It had become a repository for a great variety of mechanical contraptions. Even Queen Christina, who had known Kircher, had encouraged this extravagantly conceived project. She'd told Shen she'd thought of the man as just one more of those brilliant oddballs the Jesuits seemed to have a knack for attracting into their ranks. He had what it took to teach such diverse disciplines as mathematics and oriental languages and did so with the flamboyance that was expected of him. He'd speculated extravagantly on what he took to be the mystical underpinnings of Egyptian hieroglyphs and was fascinated by Chinese ideographs. If alive, Athanasius Kircher would have peppered Shen with questions and, as Queen Christina put it with a broad smile, no doubt found a way of putting him on show in his museum. That's for sure!

It took all of six months of soliciting, negotiating, and persuading for Couplet and Shen to be granted an actual audience with Pope Innocent. It didn't happen until June of 1685. That was a long wait even by Roman standards. The best explanation Couplet's Jesuit backers could come up with was that the pope was very busy.

Well, of course he was. Shen hadn't been told this in Nanjing, but it was a fact that the pope was the political head of one of the larger Italian states that included not just Rome but also key cities such as Ravenna and Bologna. The man, in addition to his spiritual responsibilities, was therefore expected to oversee the civil administration of several provinces, concern himself with a standing army, and involve himself in the maelstrom of European politics.

Pope Innocent XI: memorial coin

A crisis was in the offing. The centuries-long animosity that repeatedly brought the Turks into conflict with Christian Europe had once again reached boiling point. The Ottoman Turks had been pushing their luck and for several years had focused their military efforts on taking over large areas of Central Europe. They had, while Couplet and Shen were still in the Spanish Netherlands, gone so far as to threateningly lay siege to Vienna. It wasn't the first time. A century-and-a-half before, Suleiman the Magnificent had mustered one-hundred-thousand janissaries and likewise attempted to overwhelm this most Christian of cities.

Shen was shown a map of Central Europe and told about the Austrian-Hapsburg Empire and how the imperial dynasty ruling it had established itself in Vienna. The Turks, if victorious, would also have overwhelmed nearby Christian Hungary. Disaster had been averted thanks to a counterattack by a Polish-led force. Pope Innocent, however, was convinced of the mounting importance of forming an alliance as a means of countering Ottoman territorial expansion. Largely at his urging, one such alliance had been cobbled together the year before Shen and Couplet's arrival in Rome and was referred to rather bombastically as a Holy League. It included Hapsburg-ruled Austria and Hungary, Poland, some of the German States, and eventually the perennially independently-minded Venetians and even Moscow. Papal involvement and support of the League was clearly a subject of intense interest and preoccupation at the papal court.

The French, most significantly, had not joined. There were rumors to the effect that the Sun King, the opinionated contrarian that he was, prided himself on being on cordial terms with the Ottoman Sultan. That was one more reason for relations between Paris and Rome being at a low ebb. Couplet asked Charles de Noyelle whether he thought that Pope Innocent might be showing his displeasure at he and Shen having spent time in Paris and been introduced by Père la Chaise to the Sun King. The superior general was non-committal. He had his own concerns regarding Père la Chaise's desire to be seen by the Sun King as supportive of the Gallican position. It was a precarious balancing act. Jesuits took a solemn vow of loyalty to the pope.

When Couplet and Shen were eventually ushered into Pope Innocent's presence, he showed himself to be both benevolent and open minded. Shen put on his green silken dragon-embroidered finery for the occasion and this time, rather than attempt a ninefold-bow-with-forehead-touching-the-ground, simply kissed the Holy Father's feet.

Innocent was aware of the perils facing those attempting the journey to and from China and wanted to know more. Couplet told him that it wasn't unusual for ships on the Lisbon-Goa leg to spend many months without seeing land. Innocent lamented the high mortality rate that such journeys entailed. There must have been a sense of poignancy, even foreboding, permeating that part of the meeting. Couplet and Shen would, after all, be affronting those very dangers on their return to China. Pope Innocent was indeed both compassionate and open to listening.

Couplet needed to seize the moment. He spoke as insistently as he felt he could in the Holy Father's presence of the two issues that were foremost on his mind, namely the celebration of the liturgy in Chinese and, of course, the ongoing and still unresolved strongly held differences of opinion surrounding the celebration of ancestral rituals. Innocent couldn't help being sympathetic and it was in his nature to be encouraging of those he knew to be sincere. He voiced words of encouragement but that was as far as he was prepared to go.

In concluding the audience, Innocent thanked Couplet with genuine sincerity for the trouble he and his China-based companions had gone to in shipping books to Rome. Couplet had, of course included in the camphor chests a trove of Chinese texts with the intention of impressing not just the pope but also the members of the Roman curia overseeing the Propaganda. The books would surely demonstrate just how sincere and foresighted the Jesuits were in their desire to integrate the Chinese and their venerable culture into a truly universal and therefore Catholic worldview. Couplet even mentioned Candida Xu as the generous procurer of these books and in a flight of mystical fancy imagined her eternal soul basking in the knowledge that the Holy Father had now heard of her by name. The texts had been deposited in the Vatican

Library. Pope Innocent's expression of gratitude must have been heartfelt. These men had a reverence for books even when written in languages they were incapable of comprehending.

Shen had kissed the pope's feet. It was a moving gesture, and Couplet had given in to the temptation of imagining that the young man had done so in the name of Emperor Kangxi. It was yet another dream, that of China paying homage to the Holy Father. Hadn't the wise men come from the East? In any event hadn't Innocent been a most attentive listener?

"Perhaps!" Charles de Noyelle had mused, before tactfully reminding his guests that popes were but nominal overseers of a sprawling bureaucracy whose actual managers were typically imbued with institutional conservatism.

"So, all we can do is wait. Now, my dear Couplet, tell me how your Confucian Treatise is progressing?"

It was an embarrassing question. If there was a Melchisédec in Rome, Couplet hadn't yet come across him. He'd spoken to Roman printers, but none seemed willing to undertake such an intricate project. Couplet had hoped to include illustrations and a sampling of Chinese characters. It was a fact that Kircher's ambitious China Illustrata had been printed in Amsterdam. Worse, Couplet hadn't yet found a deep-pocketed patron. Even Queen Christina had proved elusive. So, to quote the superior general, all the two men could really do was wait.

They made the best of Rome's libraries. Shen was flattered to have been asked to help classify the small but growing number of Chinese books in the Vatican. Virtually all had been contributed by Jesuits beginning with Matteo Ricci and his emissary, the gentle Michele Ruggieri who had lived out his final years composing Chinese poetry as he gazed across the Bay of Salerno. It was a further opportunity for Shen to make practical use of the Latin he was still studying. Popes, he learned, had always collected books, but it was only during the 1400s that Rome, after centuries of cultural and economic decline, had re-emerged as one of the bright lights of the Italian Renaissance. By then the papacy had returned from its Avignonese exile. In those early days the papal collection would have consisted of little more than a thousand manuscripts. It would, however, have included not only scriptural and patristic texts, many in their original Hebrew and Greek, but also an impressive number of Greek and Latin classics. The collection had grown rapidly so that it was eventually housed in a suite of ornate rooms within the newly rebuilt Vatican palace. By the end of the preceding century, the rate of expansion, thanks largely to the increasing use of the printing press in Europe, had progressed to the point that it had become necessary to move the collection into a fully dedicated building.

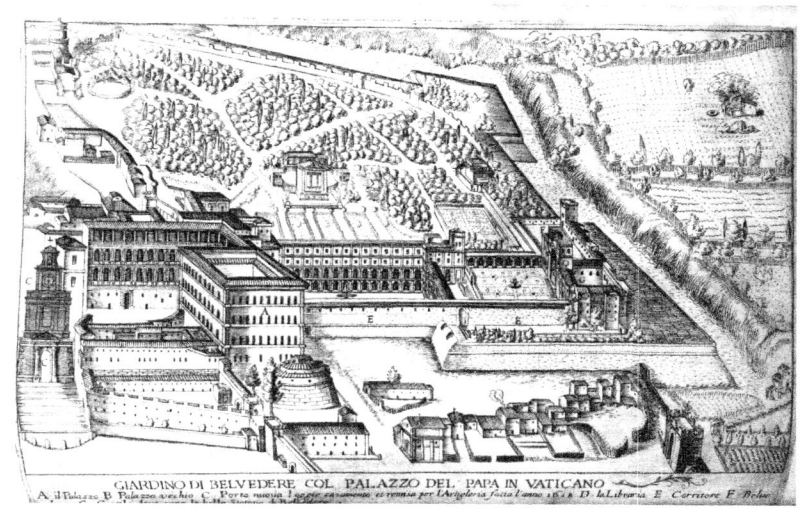

Belvedere Courtyard linking the Vatican Palace (left) to the Villa Belvedere (right) with the Sistine Library (center, dark and narrow) named after Pope Sixtus V (1521-1590): 1618 Italian etching

This was the building into which Shen had been invited. It was a rare honor. It had been made part of the greatly expanded Vatican palace complex and was a two-storied marvel. The architect had allowed for an upper room that was known as the Salone Sistino. The Sistino part had to do with Pope Sixtus who'd had a hand in its conception. Its barreled ceiling, its walls, and a series of deftly constructed interior panels had been decorated with lavishly colored frescoes. Shen was told that this frescoed brilliance had no equal anywhere else in Italy and if not in Italy, then surely nowhere within the civilized world. Well, Shen took the liberty of pointing out, the Tang dynasty had produced some rather impressive frescoes of Buddhist deities. They were, however, admittedly rather different because here the Roman artists had been inspired to include imagined scenes depicting themes as varied as the invention of the alphabet, the conception of magical Egyptian hieroglyphs and the burning of heretics. The heretics, Shen was told, were people who had clearly made abusive use of the God-given gift of written expression and richly deserved to burn in hell. Their punishment was a mere anticipation of what awaited them in eternity. Well, perhaps! Shen was aware of painful episodes in Chinese history when intellectuals had been hunted down and they and their books consumed in officially sanctioned bonfires.

Shen noted that the library's more popular books were securely chained to tables fitted with wooden benches. Fine woodblock-printed Chinese volumes, he observed, didn't lend themselves to be chained. While Shen's guides treated this particular insight with a mere shrug they were nonetheless only too happy to tell him how the papal collection had, two centuries ago, been enriched by the books dispersed following the fall of Constantinople to the Turks. More recently, and during the early phase of the Thirty Years War, the Catholic Emperor Maximilian had captured the Protestant stronghold of Heidelberg and taken as booty the contents of its fabled university library. Out of gratitude to the papacy for supporting his election as Holy Roman Emperor, he had the booty carted to Rome. It was a donation, as it were, and would surely earn the

Emperor a shorter stay in purgatory. It had been, without doubt, the richest library of any of the German states and included numerous priceless ancient manuscripts. It was all very impressive and Shen had the good sense not to ask whether the inhabitants of Heidelberg had ever thought of chaining their books to keep them from being plundered.

Sistine Hall (Salone Sistino) of Vatican Library

As he helped classify and explain the contents of the Chinese books, Shen was asked whether any should be placed in the inaccessible shelves or boxes to which it was customary to consign material that was judged theologically subversive. No, Shen didn't think any deserved to be included in the Index Librorum Prohibitorum and in any event, there couldn't be too many heretics around capable of reading Chinese. A comforting thought, no doubt.

Charles de Noyelle was right. Couplet and Shen had little choice but to stay put in Rome and wait things out. Given the pope's favorable comments, there was reason for optimism, but the more sobering reality was that the matter regarding the use of Chinese in the liturgy had been referred to the Propaganda for ultimate resolution. Roman summers are notoriously hot and uncomfortable, but the time spent in the company of books turned out to be for Shen the happiest of interludes.

The bad news came in October. The cardinals overseeing the Propaganda and those advising them heartbreakingly upheld the primacy of Latin, and Couplet's request was formally rejected. Worse, the decision was a clear indication that the far weightier issue relating to the Chinese rites surrounding ancestor worship faced an uncertain future. Worse still, after two years in Europe, Couplet hadn't even found a publisher for the Confucian Treatise. What to do next?

Charles de Noyelle didn't say so in so many words, but it was clear that he and Père la Chaise had corresponded. He'd secured an invitation for Couplet and Shen to return to Paris. Thévenot must have spoken with Père la Chaise who had then whispered in the Sun King's ears thereby laying the groundwork for royal patronage. The glory of the Republic of Letters radiating out of Paris would be enhanced by its association with Confucian wisdom. Money, and this was no minor consideration, would be forthcoming from the Royal Purse. How would Pope Innocent, the Propaganda cardinals and the Padroado authorities in Lisbon react to this unforeseen turn of events? Wasn't Couplet expected to just bow his head, forget about Confucius, and obediently return to China? Of course, he was, and Charles de Noyelle was aware that he'd stepped into a hornet's nest. Jesuits, however, were used to dealing with hornets and the risk was worth taking.

The fact was that the Sun King's credentials as champion of the Catholic cause were unequaled. That was because, animated by a newfound streak of religious absolutism, perhaps abetted by Madame de Maintenon's piety, news had just reached Rome that he had revoked the Edict of Nantes. It was the edict thanks to which Louis XIV's grandfather, the wily and pragmatic Henri IV of 'Paris is worth a mass' renown had, barely a century earlier, granted the kingdom's industrious and influential Protestant minority the absolute right to practice their faith. All that was history. The time for religious pluralism had run its course. Rather expel the Huguenots and Calvinists than risk jeopardizing France's Catholic identity.

No matter that Pope Innocent saw the situation somewhat differently. He would have advised the Sun King that rather than risking chaos and national impoverishment by expelling many of his law-abiding and productive citizens, he would have done better to go easy on religious zeal. He would have suggested that instead, the Sun King focus his religious energies on supporting the Holy League against the Turks and, while he was about it, stop injecting identity politics into the appointment of French bishops.

So, now Couplet and Shen were resolved to leave Rome and planned to do so in time to reach Paris early in the spring of 1686. They would have spent a full year in the Eternal City. They were granted a second audience with Pope Innocent. Shen kissed the Holy Father's feet a second time. Couplet made his case one more time and Innocent again, as was his wont, listened sympathetically. Faint hope indeed. Couplet had little choice but to come to terms with the reality that his mission in Rome had been a failure. Worse, he felt obligated to subscribe to what was somewhat threateningly described as an oath of subjugation to the Roman Propaganda. He did so, fully realizing that it would anger the Portuguese on whose goodwill he depended for a passage back to China.

Shen was arguably more fortunate. Charles de Noyelle confirmed his acceptance as a novice into the Order and agreed to Couplet's request that the young man accompany him to Paris. That way he'd contribute his expertise to the publication of the Confucian Treatise. He would, however, have to join the Order's Lisbon novitiate and not any other. Otherwise, the Portuguese would step in and make his life miserable. It was the most politically predictable of outcomes. When Couplet asked Shen whether being accepted into the Order as a novice was the culmination of a lifelong ambition, the young man replied that indeed it was but that he was also enough of a realist to realize that it was the only way that he could ever hope to return to his homeland.

"Yes, the die is cast," exclaimed Couplet wistfully. "When we get a chance I'll tell you about a Roman by the name of Caesar whose journey led him to cross a rather insignificant little river in northern Italy called the Rubicon."

It was de Noyelle's idea and yes, Couplet was touched. It was the superior general's way of expressing his gratitude and putting a good face on what had clearly been a trying episode with more than its fair share of disappointments. It would not only be an evening to be enjoyed among friends, but it would also be one spent a world away from the institutional constraints of time and place that so characterized the ponderous inner workings of protocolary Rome. There would be no discussion of eternally vexing issues and instead Couplet would set the tone by reminiscing about his childhood in Mechlin. He and de Noyelle were proud of their shared Flemish ancestry. And then Shen could be relied on to tell edifying stories about being raised in a Christian family within the four walls of a Nanjing ancestral compound. He would add telling and evocatively picturesque details by referring to the glazed ceramic dragons gracing the ridges of the tiled roof of its great hall and its proximity to the mighty Yangtze, abuzz day and night with the unceasing traffic of junks and sampans.

The osteria chosen was La Campana or The Bell. It was aptly named since it was in the vicolo della Campana halfway between the Piazza di Trevi and the bend in the Tiber guarded by the Castel Sant'Angelo. Also, this being Rome, there were plenty of church bells in the neighborhood. It was an eatery de Noyelle had frequented in the more relaxed years that had preceded his election as superior-general of the Order. It was a happy place suggestive of earlier and simpler times. Despite his austere appearance—he was not only tall and thin but also possessed of a narrowly drawn face with piercing eyes and a strikingly long nose—he enjoyed hearty food and was known to take even greater pleasure in talking about it. He did so in the professorial and scholarly manner of the Jesuit tradition.

"Polenta, my dear young friend," he declared addressing Shen, "is the most Roman of dishes. Its vigor-inducing qualities have been known since antiquity. Polenta is the Latin word for crushed grain. You knew that? Good! Your teachers are to be congratulated. I'm prepared to wager that a pot of lovingly prepared polenta gruel is as precious to a Roman as might be to you a bowl of steaming delicately spiced rice. Do you agree? Good! So let me tell you, a skilled polenta cook will choose and mix her grains with the utmost care—spelt, wheat and even the soft, sweet-tasting corn Columbus brought back with him from the New World. This evening you're going to try out all of my favorite combinations. Some of our polenta will be fried and some of it will be baked. Then I want you to try it together with shrimp, with fish both fresh and salted and even pork. This might not be as elaborate a meal as one of those ten-course Chinese banquets Father Couplet has told me about, but we'll do our best to leave you with a good impression to carry back to Nanjing."

And then, inevitably no doubt, the question of noodles had come up.

"Noodles!" exclaimed de Noyelle joyfully. "Yes, of course you'll be eating noodles this evening. Romans feast on them when they're not eating polenta. I've ordered a dish of them cooked together with those intriguing little golden apples from the New World that have become all the rage. That's something else we can thank Columbus for. Add some pepper and a smattering of olives and you have a nice little dish. No wonder it's catching on! That's right Father Couplet, some people call them tomatoes—a Mexican word I believe. Excellent! I hear they can be grown out of Roman and Neapolitan flowerpots. When you get back to China, young man, talk up Columbus' tomatoes—they go well with noodles, and don't you Chinese eat an abundance of rice noodles?"

Shen nodded enthusiastically, at which point de Noyelle laughed contentedly and raised his glass. It had been filled by the attentive proprietor who had chosen this very moment to hover busily over his distinguished guests. It wasn't every day that he had the opportunity to welcome the Black Pope into what he self-deprecatingly referred to as his lowly establishment. It was, the man declared, his very best Tuscan chianti. He had a hearty laugh, a protruding belly and the easy avuncular manner befitting the owner of one of Rome's most frequented osterias. De Noyelle, in a laudable show of magnanimous inclusiveness, had invited him to join in the merriment and so he stood there beside the table beaming and fussing.

"You've no doubt heard the story about Marco Polo bringing back noodles from China." exclaimed de Noyelle.

Guffaws all around. Even Shen knew that the inhabitants of the Eternal City had never taken Marco Polo at face value. Besides, the jovial proprietor took it upon himself to point out the self-evident truth that Romans were smart enough to have figured out how to make their own noodles, and even if they hadn't, they certainly wouldn't have taken kindly to being told what to do by a Venetian!

More mirth. In vino veritas! Shen's dogeared Latin grammar included a list of proverbs. Dum Romae…While in Rome do as the Romans do.

Then, as the evening drew to a close, much was made of the serving of a generous dish of tiramisu. This would be a first for Shen. The Chinese, despite their reputation as fiercely competitive master cooks, had never wholeheartedly pursued the art of preparing sweetened dishes. His ancestors, Shen reflected, had instead turned their minds to mixing the sweet with the sour…the yin and the yang…the three sages sampling the big pot full of vinegar… that was the Chinese way…the eternal Dao!

The jovial proprietor was back hovering over his guests as he poured shots of fortified, cloyingly sweet vino santo into silver goblets. There he was reciting, as though he were declaiming a poem, the ingredients that had gone into the making of his tiramisu—biscuit, egg yolks, mascarpone cream cheese, sugar, coffee and yes, chocolate: the chocolate that was yet more God-given powdery magic the Romans could thank Columbus for.

"Tiramisu!" he continued. "A strange name no doubt to Chinese ears. We name it thus because it has a reputation of picking a man up…infusing him with vigor."

So far so good, but then the exuberant proprietario bent over and, in a stage whisper directed into Shen's left ear, offered a further explanation. Now, it should be noted that while Shen had been quite successful at familiarizing himself with rudiments of Italian during his extended stay in Rome, he still relied on Latin for the clarification of finer points and his informant was no Latinist. Shen did gather that this had something to do with the Greek goddess Aphrodite, Venus by another name. Enough said. Superior General de Noyelle was, ostensibly at least, not privy to these particular elucidations.

Shen would look back on the evening spent in the vicolo della campana with a mixture of fondness and nostalgia. He'd gone to bed that night unusually late and quite unsteady but also as a man enriched by an increasing understanding of the complexity of the human journey.

Confucius says:

When you do not know a thing, to allow that you do not know it; this is knowledge.
Analects II

I am not one who was born in the possession of knowledge; I am one who is fond of antiquity, and earnest in seeking it there.
Analects VII

To go beyond is as wrong as to fall short.
Analects XI

The scholar who cherishes the love of comfort is not fit to be deemed a scholar.
Analects XIV

VII
Confucius in Paris
1686 TO THE SPRING OF 1687

To Couplet's surprise and Shen's befuddlement Charles de Noyelle had made a last minute request. One of the residents of the Casa Professa was a man who went by the aristocratic-sounding name of Francesco-Maria Spinola. He was to accompany them all the way to Paris. He'd be assisting Père la Chaise in connection with a diplomatic mission which de Noyelle referred to only in the vaguest terms. The further surprise was that Spinola was destined for the China missions. So, on the journey to Paris, Shen was to teach him the rudiments of Chinese and, as de Noyelle had described the arrangement, it would be a mutually enriching experience since the tutoring would obviously be conducted in Latin.

Spinola was from Genoa and it was rumored that he counted among his ancestors not one but several of the doges who over the centuries had contributed to the city-state's success as a maritime and commercial power vying with the Republic of Venice for dominance of the Mediterranean. More recently a member of the Spinola clan had been among the Jesuits tragically martyred in Nagasaki. Although only a few years older than Shen he was already a priest and would soon be taking his fourth and final vow as a Jesuit.

De Noyelle assured his departing guests that Spinola would be a congenial and usefully well connected travel companion. To Shen, and from the outset, he had indeed come across as unusually cordial.

"Yes", Couplet had remarked, "effusively so!"

The three men left Rome just before Christmas and, despite the winter weather, arrived in Paris in the early spring of 1686. That wasn't bad, especially since they managed to take in visits to two of Tuscany's most historic cities, namely Florence and Lucca.

Bibliothèque Du Roi in the Rue Vivienne: detail (medallion second from the right) from The Glory of the Might of Arms

Paris was almost familiar. Père la Chaise had once again extended the hospitality of his residence. It was the famous house perched on the hill above the village of Ménilmontant. This time, though, there would be for Shen and Couplet a daily back-and-forth to the very heart of Paris, where the Bibliothèque du Roi was housed. It was the book-filled domain over which Thévenot exercised his mastery and to which he had summoned his honored guests.

Père la Chaise had thought it wise to provide Couplet and Shen with a preview of what to expect. He'd sent to Rome, in the care of Charles de Noyelle, a copy of a handsomely engraved calendar for a recent year that with recourse to rich allegorical imagery extolled the military might, the scientific prominence and the artistic prominence of Louis XIV's reign. In one of the decorative medallions appearing above the magnificently costumed Sun King surrounded by his deferential courtiers was pictured one of the rooms of the Bibliothèque du Roi. It depicted five broad-rim-hatted gentlemen in formal doublets sitting around a table surmounted by a globe and a bookstand. They appeared to be carrying on an animated conversation. Bookshelves lined the walls, two turbaned assistants were bringing in more books, a window looked out onto a city street, and in a corner stood an impressively large clock worthy of comment. The clock was animated by a pendulum connected to an escapement mechanism. It was a prestigious, state-of-the-art contraption capable of hitherto unimaginable accuracy and it was all due to the creative genius of a Dutchman by the name of Christiaan Huygens who happened to be a very good friend of Thévenot.

The horse-drawn carriage that each morning ferried Couplet and Shen from Ménilmontant let them off at a stop on the right bank of the Seine in the vicinity of the Louvre Palace. It did so for a small fee. The Louvre had, of course, been the Sun King's principal residence before his move to Versailles. The Bibliothèque du Roi was but a short, and in fair weather, pleasurable walk to the north. The walkers, after crossing the gardens abutting the Tuileries, made their way along the Palais Royal and thence to the rue Vivienne. The Palais Royal had been built some sixty years earlier by the immensely wealthy Cardinal Richelieu who had been the Sun King's father's all-powerful chief minister. The Palais Royal was known for its perfectly lovely cloister-like columned galleries.

Just west of the rue Vivienne was another palais, smaller, but just as opulent. This one had been acquired and enlarged by Richelieu's successor, Mazarin. He was also a cardinal and an equally astute, powerful, and wealthy first minister.

So, Shen asked, were these men much like the grand chancellors of the Ming dynasty? Didn't they resemble the fearfully powerful regents and chief ministers of the Qing dynasty's imperial Grand

Council? These great men had likewise built themselves spacious and magnificent pavilions. Most had also collected books and precious manuscripts, many of which had been handed down the generations from as early as the Tang dynasty.

The Glory of the Might of Arms, Science, and the Arts *under the auspicious reign of Louis the Great: 1676 French engraved almanac. The medallion second from right features the Bibliothèque du Roi.*

The thing about Mazarin, Thévenot had hastened to add, was that he was an avid bibliophile and, given that he had the means, had accumulated within his palais one of Europe's greatest libraries. Mazarin died relatively young and so great was his wealth that he provided in his will that it be applied to building a prestigious educational institution on the Left Bank of the Seine. It was to be surmounted by a magnificent dome and what he wanted above all else was that room be made within it for his beloved books.

Couplet voiced the stray thought that this was perhaps Mazarin's way of seeking immortality. Thévenot agreed that it was no doubt his wish to live on through the books he had lovingly collected. Shen should make a point of visiting it. All he had to do was take a break from his academic duties and head south past the Palais Royal and the Louvre, cross over the Seine at the Pont Royal that was so named because of its closeness to the Louvre, and then walk along the Left Bank toward the twin towers of Notre Dame. That way he'd see for himself what Mazarin had dreamt of on his deathbed. He could watch the workers atop scaffoldings heaving up the stones being used to erect the most impressive of domes. Yes, it was all about the quest for immortality and the love of books.

Thévenot further recounted that at Mazarin's untimely death, Louis XIV had appointed as his successor a man named Colbert. In those early days, the young monarch was not yet referred to as the Sun King. It was Colbert who had turned out to be the principal architect of his meteoric rise to power. Was Colbert a cardinal, Shen asked? No, there was no requirement that the king's chief minister wear a red hat. It was just that men like Richelieu and Mazarin had coveted one and that the popes had readily obliged. France was, after all, the Church's eldest daughter. Mazarin's successor had been variously referred to as Le Grand Colbert and most tellingly as the king's Éminence grise. So, Shen had a point, he was a lay cardinal of sorts!

Colbert also loved books and particularly the learning encompassed within them. He was also very much aware of his inordinately ambitious young master's desire to reign over the best of everything. So, Colbert had arranged for the foundation of the Académie des Sciences. He then went one significant step further. French kings had long been the proud possessors of fine book collections, but the time had come to find a worthy home for the Bibliothèque du Roi. The need was urgent because the royal collection, while maybe not as extensive as Mazarin's, was nonetheless bursting at the seams.

The situation in Paris was therefore no different, observed Shen, to that which he and Couplet had observed in Rome. Indeed, not, commented Thévenot. Private libraries had taken off during the Renaissance. Book collections were no longer the exclusive preserve of wealthy monasteries. For those who could afford them, they bore witness not only to the extent of their owners' material wealth, but also to their commitment to the higher things of life such as the pursuit of wisdom and the cultivation of erudition. So, naturally the same went for monarchs and popes, only more so. Given the expense and rarity of manuscript books, early Renaissance European collections, despite the general increase in wealth that characterized the period, were still small. It took a while for Guttenberg's revolutionary innovation to take hold, but when it did, combined with the availability of affordable paper, there was no stopping the proliferation of printed books. So, the issue of where to store and how to catalog them came to the fore. A library was no longer a word used to refer to a mere collection of books. It had become a building. A proper library needed a capacious home built not just to meet current needs but to also provide for its inevitable and exponential future expansion.

It had therefore fallen to Colbert to accommodate the Bibliothèque de Roi within an elegantly remodeled townhouse or hôtel particulier he had acquired in the rue Vivienne. Being famously shrewd, he had known all along that the royal collection would soon enough again run out of space. Libraries always did. He'd figured out that the now vacant palais built by Mazarin would become available. Mazarin's erstwhile palais was literally across the street and its bookshelves were now empty. That, Thévenot explained, was exactly what was going to happen. In the meantime, though they would be working in the rue Vivienne.

Room was made at the rue Vivienne for the many manuscripts and translations in Couplet's famous camphor chests. It was right here that their extended circuitous journey was destined to come to an end. Over the past four-and-a-half years these chests had traveled halfway around the world. From China to the rue Vivienne by way of Batavia and Enkhuizen.

Initially, Thévenot and the scholars in his entourage were fascinated by the intricacies of the Chinese language and kept Shen hard at work. He obligingly provided them with numerous calligraphic samples. Thévenot was also working on the publication of a French edition of a summary of Chinese history and culture compiled by yet another gifted Jesuit. The author was Portuguese and a distant relative of Magellan whose expedition had famously been the first to circumnavigate the globe. The author had spent over a quarter of a century in China and, following his death, Couplet had managed to gather his voluminous workpapers. They were in Portuguese, and he had fortuitously included them in one of the camphor boxes. Some of the documents were charred. Not during the shipwreck, obviously, but some other mishap must have befallen them. Fortunately, they were for the most part still readable and Thévenot had arranged for one of his many scholarly acquaintances to translate them from Portuguese into French. Shen, together with Thévenot and his scholarly associate huddled over them. The book would eventually be published and be known as the Nouvelle Relation de la Chine. Sieur Michel Chinois was paid 400 livres or pounds-worth-of-silver out of the Royal Purse for his troubles.

As to Couplet, his first order of business was to find a publisher willing to take on the Confucian Treatise. Thévenot had it all worked out. It was to be a prestigious project sponsored by the Sun

King and therefore carried out by the Bibliothèque du Roi using the good offices of a Parisian-based publisher and printer. The name Daniel Horthemels came up. Although it was an instantly recognizable Dutch name, Horthemels did business at the most Parisian of addresses, namely the rue Saint-Jacques. It was one of the principal north-south thoroughfares of the Latin Quarter. Why Latin, Shen wanted to know. It went back to the founding of the city's famed medieval university on the left bank of the Seine. It had been customary for the students to practice their Latin by speaking it whether in or out of class. As to the rue Saint-Jacques, it was so named for the good reason that it had once been the starting point for pilgrims making the awesomely long journey on foot across the Pyrenees and along the Camino de Santiago that eventually led to Compostela. Horthemels had apparently moved to Paris from Amsterdam following his conversion to Catholicism. In any event, he had an excellent reputation and the Sun King's ministers were only too happy to promote the culturally prestigious book business. Horthemels had obviously found a ready market for his skills.

Shen was invited to visit Horthemels' print shop on the rue Saint-Jacques. It was, for him, a fascinating experience. He'd never seen a book being printed using movable type. The first step in the process involved an operator deftly selecting individual metal cast letters and lining them up, one by one, in a temporary holder or stick. The letters were taken from two large boxes divided into compartments, one for each letter of the alphabet. Capital letters were stored in the upper box or "case" and standard ones in the lower case. Chinese calligraphers and printers made no such distinction. The compartments allocated to common letters were understandably more capacious than those used to store others. Skill was required because, as Shen knew from his experience in China, printing involves dealing with mirror images. The letters in the stick faced backwards and the words they formed were lined up counterintuitively from right to left.

Sticks of set words were then assembled in another part of

Horthemels' shop into a column of continuous, properly justified text that matched the width of a page. It was a painstaking business because individual letters, together with the necessary spaces, had to be precisely lined up and placed atop a perfectly flat tray called a galley. No one seemed to know why French printers likened the tray to the flat oar-powered boats that plied the Mediterranean. Perhaps because, given that it was the width of a page, a tray was relatively narrow and oblong.

Shen was made aware of an interim step in the process that over the next months would involve him, together with Couplet and Thévenot, in many hours of mentally demanding work. It was customary to give the type assembled within each galley tray a quick preliminary inking and then press against it a continuous roll of cheap paper. The purpose was to produce a rough but accurate image or proof of the text. Given the complexity of the process and its many moving parts, mistakes were unavoidable. This was an opportunity to correct them and make last minute changes. Shen would be among the proofreaders. These rough sheets were referred to as galley proofs.

The next step was to remove from the galley trays the page-wide proofed assemblies of type and arrange them within a large frame, often referred to as a forme. This frame was destined to be affixed to the bed of the press for the final printing. The dimensions of the frame were fixed and corresponded to the standard size of the sheets of paper used by printers. The number of pages arranged on each frame was, however, dependent on the dimensions of the book being printed. The smaller the book's format, the larger the number of pages assembled on the standard-sized frame. The frame was made of wood and fitted with a special tightening mechanism, thanks to which all the moving parts within it were secured into place. The frame was then affixed to the bed of the press. The remaining steps were familiar to Shen because they also applied to woodblock printing. These involved inking the raised type, applying blank sheets of paper to the print face and, of course, manually lowering the press.

Another aspect of the printing process that was strange to Shen was the way in which European books were assembled. Since most presses produced standard-sized printed paper sheets, the dimensions of the pages of a given book were therefore determined by the number of times a sheet was folded after printing. It had been decided early on that the Confucian Treatise would be an in-quarto volume. Each sheet coming off Horthemels' press would therefore be formatted to have four pages (hence in quarto) appearing both front and back. Two folds would then be required to produce a unit of eight pages of readable text. These units, or signatures as they were technically referred to, would then be trimmed, and sewn together at the spine to form the book. In quarto, due to its generous size, was thought to be the ideal format for scholarly reading and study.

Horthemels had heard that it was the Chinese who had pioneered and then perfected woodblock printing. After the tour of his shop, he sat Shen down to a cup of coffee in his back office. Coffee was an expensive new-fangled drink, thought to energize the blood - just like tea, only more so. It was becoming increasingly popular among aristocratic Parisians. Horthemels liked to impress his clients.

"So just when did the Chinese start printing?" Horthemels asked.

It was a long story. The Chinese, confirmed Shen, had very early been enamored not just with woodblocks but also with seals. Printing went back a long way because the Chinese were the first to produce large quantities of high-quality affordable paper. Horthemels knew that and readily admitted that without paper, printing, even with movable type, didn't make a whole lot of sense. Guttenberg had found that out the hard way: he'd printed his first bible on parchment. It was beautiful, but hardly a commercial success.

Well, Shen explained, printing in China came into its own during the Tang dynasty, a time when Buddhism created a mass market for printed sutras and other religious texts. It made sense to use woodblocks.

"The Tang dynasty?" Asked Horthemels.

"A period in our history we look back to as a golden age of refinement. It lasted, one way or another, for three long centuries just about a thousand years ago. Father Couplet told me it corresponded very roughly to the Islamic expansion here in Europe… Charlemagne…Viking raids. For you Europeans, that's a long time ago…for us Chinese it still feels quite recent…we feel connected to it."

"You know," continued Shen with an uncharacteristic lack of modesty, "we could have been the first to use movable type on a grand scale. We were, in fact, the first to pioneer it. It's simply that woodblock printing works far better for us since our venerable writing tradition has given rise to thousands of distinct characters. Here's what we do. A skilled calligrapher using brush and ink writes out a full page of text on a sheet of fine paper. The paper is then coated with a specially prepared rice paste. The ink sticks to the paste, and the paper is then spread face down on a flat woodblock."

"Incredible!" exclaimed Horthemels. "You're telling me that the paper is peeled off and that the paste stays behind, stuck to the wood."

"That's it. We Chinese can do almost everything with rice. It doesn't just feed us. It sustains our culture. You've guessed correctly. What's left on the woodblock is therefore a perfect mirror image of the finely calligraphed text. An engraver then goes to work and using delicate scooping tools, carves out the areas that are ink-free. It's a skilled and time-consuming process, but it's surprisingly efficient. A carved-out block of text can be used to make large numbers of prints. We can keep it indefinitely, which allows us to produce cheap subsequent editions. That explains why we Chinese have produced more books than any other nation and why our libraries are so extensive."

"We couldn't afford to keep our type permanently set," explained Horthemels, "It's far too expensive. Each piece must be used repeatedly…otherwise I'd go bankrupt. After every print run, my men disassemble everything and return each piece to its proper box for reuse."

Thévenot had joined the conversation. What kinds of books, he asked Shen, did the Chinese place in their libraries? Chinese libraries, Shen explained, were often attached to official buildings and temples. He remembered one in his native Nanjing that had imbued him as a child with a love and respect for books. It was a temple-like structure with a sloping roof in the classical hip-and-gable style. It was set in a garden with reflecting pools. What kinds of books did the Chinese collect? Well, Buddhists had an affinity for printed texts and especially sutras, but the most revered texts were the ones educated Chinese liked to call the Four Books and Five Classics. They formed the basis of any self-respecting book collection. They'd been available in printed form many…many centuries before Gutenberg.

"We also value poetry and historical annals," exclaimed Shen. "Libraries and books are important to us because we tend to think of culture as consisting of a body of knowledge and shared principles capable of being comprehensively committed to writing. Writing is important to us. If you visited China you'd be impressed by how much we like to display our culture-laden characters in our streets, in our temples, in our homes and even in our shops. This may strike you as odd, but the officials of many of our past dynasties attempted to produce comprehensive lists of approved texts and commentaries. They were codifications in the sense that they were often attempts to produce updated and corrected versions of what Chinese culture should be, but as interpreted by those currently entrusted with the Mandate of Heaven. That might necessitate censoring past interpretations and producing revised commentaries. Some of our emperors were known to have forcibly rounded up old books reflecting outdated views and replaced them with new ones that were more to their liking."

Shen's explanation put Thévenot in a reflective mood.

❖

Thévenot, Couplet and Shen sat in their manuscript-littered high-ceilinged but otherwise exiguous room in the rue Vivienne. The one window overlooked the Palais Mazarin but, unlike the vignette from the elaborately engraved calendar of a few years back, there were no turbaned flunkies in attendance. Nor was there a grandfather clock in sight. Couplet had reason, though, to be satisfied. A willing and enthusiastic printer had come forward with a financially acceptable proposal. The allocation from the Royal Purse, while not overly generous, was sufficient to see the project through, and the Latin translations and Chinese originals had been taken out of their camphor chests never to be returned to them. It had taken the best part of five years to reach this point. It was time to put the finishing touches on the Confucian Treatise.

Well, almost. Key decisions had yet to be made. Couplet had originally been charged with publishing all Four Books and not only the texts of those hallowed books, but also certain commentaries whose antiquity had likewise endowed them with an aura of sacredness. That was the dream. He'd been told to see to it that the translations were in impeccably precise Latin and that they also be accompanied by the Chinese originals. Why the originals if no one, absolutely no one, in Europe would be capable of making sense of them? It all went back to what Shen had talked about while visiting Horthemels' print shop. There was a mysterious quality attached to those characters. So much so, Couplet argued, that seeing them would surely help impress on European readers that the time had come to recognize the overarching cultural importance of what the Jesuits were single-handedly and wholeheartedly seeking to achieve in China. Namely that there was a universal dimension to the human experience and that it could only be fully appreciated by those who were open to the ways in which other cultures had expressed it.

That was a thought to which Thévenot had reacted not just with a heavenward glance, but also by stating in his native tongue that Couplet was turning into a "philosophe" and that it was a trend that seemed to be increasingly "à la mode". In Paris, anyway.

Well, maybe, but did Couplet realize that Horthemels could only cope with Chinese text by having it engraved on copper plates? The time and expense involved in doing so would be prohibitive and it would necessitate a second volume. So, including the Chinese originals was regrettably out of the question. That was a pity, since Couplet and Shen had devised a clever system according to which numbers would be used to cross reference Chinese characters to their Latin equivalents. Some of the Latin texts typeset in Horthemels' shop already included those numbers.

Couplet was crestfallen, but Thévenot stood his ground. The King's purse was impressively large, but it was no mythical horn of plenty. So, yes it was a pity but still out of the question.

There was yet another snag. Couplet was planning on a very long introduction. He was still working on it. It was growing longer by the day, and it included a wordy section written by Próspero Intorcetta. Given the man's growing influence within the Order's hierarchy, Couplet was understandably reluctant to shorten it. Then, and on this point all agreed, a Life of Confucius would have to be included otherwise the book wouldn't deserve to be referred to as a Confucian Treatise.

And then there was another issue about which Couplet had demonstrably strong feelings. The Chinese, given their propensity to document everything, prided themselves on having handed down the generations a historically credible chronology of their rulers and dynasties. It extended back to days that by the reckoning of European Biblical scholars were those of the Great Flood and arguably to an even earlier time. That, admittedly, raised some ticklish questions regarding the accuracy of the Biblical record. Couplet had distilled all this within the covers of a 125-page treatise and had made it clear to Thévenot that this was his brainchild and that he hadn't come all the way from China just to see it cast off as superfluous.

Thévenot was once more puzzled. Wasn't this altogether far too arcane a subject, and why did the Jesuits care? They cared, Couplet explained, because they were out to demonstrate that Confucian ethical and philosophical traditions were rooted in and true to the practices of Noah's immediate descendants. The irrefutable logic was that if the waters of the Great Flood had purged the world of sin, and if the beliefs and practices that had inspired Confucius had been handed down from Noah's progeny directly to the Chinese, then surely, they were in a pristine unadulterated state and thus fully consistent with the Christian message. That, Couplet emphasized, was what the Confucian Treatise was out to demonstrate. Not to the Chinese, of course, who couldn't read Latin, but to the Europeans. Europeans would then come around to unreservedly supporting the Jesuits in their quest to demonstrate to the Chinese scholarly class that a true Confucian couldn't help recognizing that the Christian religion embodied the fulfillment of his ideals.

Had Couplet's passionately expressed reasoning dispelled Thévenot's puzzlement? No, it hadn't. He asked Couplet whether, in the final analysis, that was what the long preface to the Confucian Treatise was all about. The reluctant answer was a tentative yes. And then what did Shen think of all this? That wasn't, of course, a fair question to ask of a young man who had been accepted as a novice by the Order's superior general. What Shen did say was that the Chinese tended to think of the universe as without beginning or end. There were popular creation stories, of course, but they weren't quite as explicit as the Bible.

"So," asked Thévenot, "did that mean that the Chinese might be more inclined to think of creation as something that was ongoing? Was it more like the opposite forces of the Yin and the Yang continually interacting?"

TABULA CHRONOLOGICA
Monarchiæ Sinicæ
JUXTA CYCLOS ANNORUM LX.
Ab anno ante Christum 2952. ad annum post Christum 1683.
Auctore R. P. PHILIPPO COUPLET Belgâ, Soc. Jesu,
Sinensis Missionis in Urbem Procuratore.
Nunc primùm in lucem prodit
è BIBLIOTHECA REGIA.

PARISIIS,
M. DC. LXXXVI.
CVM PRIVILEGIO REGIS.

Chronology of Chinese monarchs: title page to Couplet's 125-page brainchild that he wanted to include in the Confucian Treatise

Confucius in Paris

Couplet winced. This, he said, a tad exasperated, was not the time and place to get into such an argument.

All well and good, but the issue at hand was really a practical one, namely just what could be reasonably fitted within the covers of the Confucian Treatise Horthemels had taken on. If Couplet was hellbent on including his 125-page chronology, there was no way all Four Books were going to fit within one volume. Neither Horthemels' skills nor the Royal Purse could cope with a volume much longer than six-hundred pages. Too bad! The venerable Four would have to be reduced to three. The obvious one to be dispensed with was Mencius (Meng Zi, 孟子). It was the longest, and even Shen agreed that it was overly discursive. It was the one most likely to be off-putting to European readers. So that left the Great Learning (Da Xue, 大学), the Doctrine of the Mean (Zhong Yong, 中庸), and, best known of all in China namely the Analects (Lun Yu, 論語).

Then there was the matter of a dedicatory letter. Thévenot was quite insistent about it. When it came to literary endeavors, patrons expected dedicatory letters. Great men felt entitled to some return on their money. Had there not been funds available from the Royal Purse, the contents of Couplet's precious camphor chests would be rotting away gently in some Ménilmontant cellar or gathering dust in a Roman garret!

"Don't, my dear Father Couplet assume for one moment that the Sun King will so much as peruse your book, but he'll without a doubt be shown a copy. He'll delight in seeing his royal emblem on the title page and someone, it might turn out to be your humble servant, may well be called upon to read to him some of the more exaggerated and laudatory phrases from the dedication. Yes, the money comes out of the Royal Purse, but he considers it to be his and to be spent in ways that contribute to his personal aggrandizement. L'État, c'est moi. So, my dear Father Couplet, stoop as low as you feel able to. Grovel as would our friend Shen before his emperor. Make sure your forehead hits the ground no less than nine times. Cast all your inhibitions aside. Go to work."

Couplet outdid himself. It was an epistola addressed to the Most Christian of Kings. It analogized the book's publication to Confucius visiting Paris in person. It was as though this wisest of Chinese philosophers, having heard of Louis XIV's unrivaled reputation as the most prudent and virtuous of sovereigns, had come over two millennia ago all the way from the Orient to France just to pay his respects. The Confucian texts, the letter pointed out, mirrored the prudence and good sense exercised by the emperors of antiquity. These writings were reflective of a Golden Age during which the Chinese had been aware of the existence of the one true God and had therefore named him Supreme Emperor. Were Confucius, by God's grace, to come back to life, he would surely see in the Sun king the perfect sovereign and recognize that, despite his own reputation for wisdom, he would be no more than a humble star yielding to the radiance of the sun.

Confucius would be the first to recognize that since religion plays an overwhelmingly dominant role in the proper governance of nations, it is clearly incumbent on a wise and prudent sovereign to preserve its integrity. Confucius would encourage him to do so by eradicating any trace of heresy. Couplet then went on to state that he was personally comforted in the knowledge that on his return to China, the effectiveness of his own labors as a humble missionary would be enhanced by his being able to recount what the Sun King, inspired by Confucius' words, had been able to achieve in France. Imagine then, added Couplet in a final flourish, the thrill the Chinese will experience when they find out that the words of their great sage have been committed to a book that will be part of the Bibliothèque du Roi. Couplet proposed to sign the Epistola as Philippus Couplet and declare himself His Majesty, Devotissimus and Addictissimus, servant.

Thévenot was impressed. "I couldn't have done better myself. The reference to the Revocation of the Edict of Nantes is over the top but it will please Madame de Maintenon. Let's leave it in."

Thévenot did suggest an improvement. "Add a reference to the recent visit to Versailles by the Siamese ambassadors. The king sat on his high throne and the ambassadors doffed their pointy hats. He loved every moment of it, and it has whipped up enormous enthusiasm at Versailles for all things oriental. Add some wording to the effect that, just like Confucius, the Siamese had come to Versailles attracted by the Sun King's radiance. He'll like that and so will Madame de Maintenon. It'll cause some of the courtiers to want to be seen reading our book."

Speaking of the Siamese, were Couplet and Shen aware of the mystery surrounding the King's Mathematicians and how their fate had become entwined with that of the Siamese? No, all that Couplet remembered was that before leaving for Rome almost two years earlier, he and Père la Chaise had talked over a troubling question. How were the mathematicians going to secure a passage to Beijing? Certainly not via Lisbon, Goa, and Macao. The Portuguese authorities were dead against the French involving themselves in the China missions. Nor were the mathematicians going to get any sympathy or help from the Propaganda in Rome. What about the Dutch? Questionable at best. The Dutch weren't exactly on speaking terms with the French. Not after the Sun King's latest attempt to send his dragoons into their watery polders and take them over.

What Couplet hadn't known at the time was that the French had been planning a high-level mission to Siam. It consisted of two French ships that had in fact sailed out of the port of Brest several months after Couplet's and Shen's arrival in Rome. The expedition included high-ranking French aristocratic worthies handpicked by the Sun King based on their presumed ability to impress the Siamese. The expectation was that the Siamese were about to abandon Buddhism for Catholicism. The thinking was that their conversion would favorably dispose the Siamese king to pledging undying allegiance to the French. This would do wonders for the commercial prospects of the not-so-recently incorporated Compagnie royale des Indes orientales. It needed a boost. The Dutch VOC and the English EIC were running rings around it.

Siamese Delegation received by Louis XIV at Versailles' Hall of Mirrors in 1686: 1687 French engraving

All this, according to the well informed Thévenot, had turned out to be delusional. What Couplet and Shen also couldn't have known, due to their being in Rome, was that at the last moment a decision had been made at the highest level to have the mathematicians join the Siamese expedition. It wasn't so much that their efforts were now to be redirected to converting the Siamese king, but rather that it would be a means of getting them on their way without attracting the unwanted attention of the papacy or of the Portuguese. They'd be smart enough to figure out a way of getting to Beijing from Siam. Seen from Versailles, Beijing was probably no more than a skip and a hop from the Siamese capital. It wouldn't have occurred to anyone to look at a map. So, as far as anyone knew, instead of being on their way to Beijing, where the emperor Kangxi was apparently anticipating their arrival, the King's Mathematicians were most likely stranded somewhere between Siam and God-only-knew-where. Neither Père La Chaise nor Charles de Noyelle in Rome were any the wiser. So much for relying on the glib assurances doled out by the high and mighty.

"What would Confucius have made of this mess?" Asked Thévenot of Couplet in jest.

"Oh! It would simply have confirmed his jaundiced view of how the princes of this world run roughshod over their poor defenseless subjects. In disgust, he'd probably have moved on to a neighboring kingdom in the hope of encountering a more forthright and principled monarch."

"Good luck with that!" exclaimed Thévenot. "Incidentally, despite what I made you write in your dedicatory letter, I don't think Confucius would have approved of the revocation of the Edict of Nantes. He would, as I do, have considered it to be both ethically reprehensible and economically suicidal."

"Should we revise the dedicatory letter before sending it on to Horthemels for typesetting?" asked Shen with more than a touch of irony.

"I can tell that you're joking, Sieur Michel Chinois!"

The upshot of it all was that while the King of Siam had absolutely no intention of abandoning Buddhism, he nonetheless felt obligated to reciprocate the Sun King's expedition by sending his own lavish embassy to Versailles. The good news was that while the previous Siamese embassy to Paris had literally ended on the rocks, this one had managed to avoid shipwreck and had arrived in Brest in reasonably good shape, baggage, and all. It was reported that in Versailles the Siamese ambassadors wore strikingly tall pointy hats, prostrated themselves multiple times before the royal presence, and were allowed to raise their heads just high enough to gaze upon its radiance. They were then treated to an exclusive tour of the royal apartments and, of course, of the gardens, together with the fountains turned up full blast. There were apparently 1,500 guests present and it turned out to be a grand party. That was reason enough for Couplet to refer, in his dedicatory letter, to their having been drawn into the Sun King's presence, thanks to his irresistible radiance.

Then there was the issue of selecting illustrations for the Confucian Treatise. Artistic renderings did not come cheaply in Paris. Furthermore, producing the kind of high-quality copperplate engravings that Horthemels deemed worthy of being included in books published under his imprint was a skilled and time-consuming business. So naturally, Couplet and Thévenot fell to arguing over how many illustrations could reasonably be commissioned. It was decided at least one illustration should be dedicated to Confucius, the man himself. That was challenging given that he'd lived a good five centuries before the Christian era, and no one had the faintest idea what he might have looked like. It was important though because of the earlier decision that the Confucian Treatise include a biography of the great sage. The choice fell on Jean-Baptiste Nolin, one of Paris' best-known engravers and mapmakers. No expense should be spared on this aspect of the project. It was also agreed that Nolin should have the opportunity to learn something about the life Confucius had led before getting down to work. Thévenot, therefore, had one of his assistants rough out a French translation of the Latin text Couplet was about to send to Horthemels for typesetting. Here was the gist of it.

Confucius was said to have once met Laozi, the reputed founder of Daoism, so his dates probably correspond very roughly to those of Socrates and possibly of Gautama Siddhartha, the historical Buddha. In China, the long-lasting Zhou dynasty was in decline and power had devolved into the hands of regional kingdoms. Chinese historians, Couplet had learned, referred to it as the Spring and Autumn era and it eventually degenerated into the more realistically named Warring States period.

Confucius was born in Shandong, an area bordering the East China Sea. His birthplace was within the state of Lu, which in his time was just one of the many fractious regional kingdoms. Confucius had the bad luck of being born to an elderly father who'd made a career out of soldiering, and although educated, was both a commoner and impoverished. Young Confucius was precocious and had little difficulty mastering the skills expected of one who aspired to one of the higher ranks into which Chinese society was rigorously stratified. He was expected to achieve competence in archery, charioteering, music, and computing with an abacus. Then there was the art of writing that depended on mastering a respectable number of characters, and then there was knowledge of ritual. Ritual in China revolved primarily around honoring ancestors and those in authority. Ritual, according to Confucius, usefully trained the mind by inducing it to follow predetermined patterns of thought.

Confucius was determined to work his way up in a world dominated by wealth and social status. He had neither, but made up for it by being patient and industrious. He rose to the rank of junior minister within the State of Lu bureaucracy. He had a way with words and was a good judge of character. He could fathom people's strengths and weaknesses and sense whether they were sincere or mere bluffers. The problem was that he neither suffered fools gladly nor showed any willingness to do the bidding of those who were self-servingly opportunistic, politically devious, and generally manipulative. That meant he was virtually unemployable. So, Confucius, out of growing disillusionment, abandoned the King of Lu to his corrupt and devious ways and went in search of a more principled ruler. He reasoned that to act in accord with the mandate of Heaven, a ruler should care for his subjects as would a father for his children, an elder brother for younger kin, a teacher for his students, and a seasoned friend for those who might profit from his wisdom. Such relationships, rather than any rule of law, were the only ones capable of truly binding a subject to his sovereign.

So, Confucius exiled himself to a neighboring state. There he found employment but shortly thereafter, disillusionment once more set in. So, he yet again packed his bags. His was the most noble of quests, but it condemned him to a peripatetic way of life. It wasn't so much a question of going from village to village as from warring state to warring state. He spoke to kings, ministers, and courtiers rather than to villagers. His musings on the qualities that make a true ruler out of a prince took on a prophetic dimension and he attracted disciples. He dialogued with those who followed him and that is how the text of the Analects came to be. Those inspired reflections became a record of the life he led. It was a difficult life with more than its fair share of apparent failures and disappointments. He had condemned himself to being an eternal wanderer. Only in his waning years did he come to be reconciled with those who ruled over the state of Lu. They invited him back and it was a homecoming of sorts. He was fortunate to be left to die in peace rather than be done away with as a troublemaker voicing unwelcome truths. Prophets are rarely left alone, Couplet had mused. Their teachings come to be recognized only after their deaths or, as in the case of Confucius, after he'd become old and harmless.

Here, as described by Thévenot in his private journal, is what the celebrated Jean-Baptiste Nolin came up with.

"Confucius has the most benign of expressions and his impressively large portly body is enfolded within generously flowing robes. His hands are clasped around a tablet. He's bearded and swarthy but otherwise doesn't strike me as having particularly Chinese features. Shen agrees with me. He's wearing what Nolin must have assumed was an ancient scholar's headdress. I don't know where Nolin got the idea. It's curiously leafy and to me looks more like an artichoke head than an academic cap. Such impressions, I'll freely admit, are subjective. The setting is reminiscent of an Italianate painting and evocative of the great hall of a Greco-Roman temple. What Nolin does well is perspective, but the overall impression is frankly Renaissance Tuscan rather than Chinese. No matter. He's made it look as though Confucius is holding forth in a library. That's apparent from the book-lined shelves and from the diminutive figures at the great man's feet. They're pygmy-like and shown busily inscribing manuscripts. It wouldn't have done to place Confucius in a temple—that would have brought Father Couplet all kinds of grief. The Jesuits argue that what the Confucians do in front of their altars has nothing to do with religion. Good luck! Nolin has included Chinese characters here and there. They're well drawn thanks to Sieur Michel Chinois spending time in Nolin's workshop and lending a helping hand. Thank God for Sieur Michel! The titles of Confucius' Four Books are inscribed in Chinese characters along bookshelves arranged on either side of the central figure. That was a good idea, and it was done at Sieur Michel's suggestion. Another of Sieur Michel's ideas was to get

Nolin to prominently display on the so-called library's pediment two characters that apparently convey that the building's purpose is to foster reverence for imperial authority. That young man is turning into quite a politician. He has a future. The important thing is that Couplet is happy about it. When we showed it to Père la Chaise, he grinned. He can be enigmatically cat-like at times. We all agree, though, that Nolin's illustration has absolutely nothing to do with how Confucius might have lived or appeared to his contemporaries but that it will contribute to the book's success. Incidentally, what Couplet wrote in the dedicatory letter about Confucius coming back to life and seeing in Louis XIV the very embodiment of political wisdom is, if anything, even more egregious and fanciful. It's the illusion that counts!"

There wasn't that much residual work to be done on the Latin translations of the three of the Four Books that were to be the mainstay of the Confucian Treatise. These were texts that had been worked on and then repeatedly reworked, not only in China by the Four Translators, but also by Couplet during the idle months spent in Rome. What was exercising Couplet was the final editing of the lengthy preface. He'd asked Thévenot to review it. Shen, by force of circumstances, had also become familiar with an earlier draft. Because it was in Latin, he'd treated it as a school exercise to be mastered, not so much for its content but for its grammatical intricacies. That didn't mean that he hadn't also reflected on what the authors were out to demonstrate.

Thévenot had made no bones about it. Had it been up to him, which it obviously wasn't, he would have written something rather different. European readers couldn't be expected to know very much about China's culture and history. He would have focused his efforts on helping readers situate the Confucian writings within their historical context and then commented on why they were still thought of as the bedrock on which the Chinese based their worldview. That, he observed, is what he'd attempted to do by publishing his Strange Tales from faraway lands.

Confucius: engraving by Jean-Baptiste Nolin (1657-1708); facing: Life of Confucius

Wouldn't it have made sense, for example, to explain that the Four Books and the Five Classics were to this day the basis on which young men seeking to enter the imperial civil service were examined? Thévenot stressed that he wasn't trying to be critical, but he did feel that the preface was overly polemical. He had come away with the impression that the authors, instead of seeking to explain, had gone out of their way to criticize how over the centuries the various Chinese schools of thought and religious traditions had coped with interpreting and adapting the Confucian texts. Was it that the Jesuits were seeking to impose their own interpretation?

Thévenot had hit a nerve. Couplet found himself unwittingly on the defensive. He reminded Thévenot that it was Próspero Intorcetta who had written the first draft of the Preface. He, Couplet, didn't feel at liberty to run roughshod over it. Intorcetta would almost certainly consider himself to be its principal author. Of course, Thévenot had a point, but the reality was the Confucian Treatise hadn't been conceived of as an altruistic effort to educate Europeans. No, like it or not, it was part of a thoughtfully orchestrated campaign designed to make those critical of the Order aware that the Jesuits were facing major challenges in China and that the approach they had adopted was the only one that made sense. So, yes, there was an argumentative tone to the Preface. Couplet was sorry about that but wasn't the present state of the world such that kings, princes, popes and even ordinary people were being put in the uncomfortable position of having to take sides on all kinds of issues that were seen as fundamental to those advocating them? Why had the Sun King decided to revoke the Edict? Why, Couplet lamented, had the Propaganda forced him to subscribe to an oath of subjugation potentially complicating his already conflicted life? Couplet, in that moment, felt sorry for himself.

Thévenot then turned to Shen and asked him what he thought about the Preface. He was, after all, Chinese and this long commentary had been written by men who had come from afar and had presumed to interpret texts that were quintessentially Chinese. Thévenot had a habit of asking difficult questions. It wasn't fair to put Shen on the spot. Not again! This further upset Couplet. Thévenot was being too direct. He should know it wasn't a good idea to put people at risk of losing face.

Shen sensed the moment had come for conciliation. He had

taken notes of the discussion, he said. It was still possible to make changes to the Preface. Going through his notes, he suggested, might help suggest last minute changes. A softening, perhaps, of the odd word might be in order. There was no need for anyone to get upset over this. Shen put his shuffled papers in order, smiled broadly, and went ahead.

The Preface started off by evoking Matteo Ricci's seminal work. He was the pioneer: the first to reflect on Chinese culture through European eyes. His interpretation was that the ancient Chinese were imbued with a God-given understanding of what Christian theologians referred to as the natural law. There was, of course, talk of Noah and of the Great Flood. It was a way of introducing the idea that Confucian ancestor worship had its origins in a pristine God-inspired state. Didn't Catholics offer masses in memory of the deceased? Since the would-be readers of the Confucian Treatise were Europeans they would therefore be familiar with theological terms and the likes of Noah. So, that was just fine. Let them argue among themselves. Ricci's inestimable merit was that he'd engaged in Chinese culture. He was an Italian and might not have gotten everything right but at least he'd tried. He'd paid attention to China. He'd listened. He was a hero. All present agreed. Good!

"Next point. The Preface refers to sects. According to the Preface there were three; Buddhists, Daoists and Neo-Confucians."

Shen offered the thought that referring to these good people as followers of sects was rather unfair if not darn right disrespectful. Yes, the wording was unfortunate. Yes, but it probably didn't matter because only Chinese readers would take offense and since no Chinese, other than Shen, knew Latin and the Preface was in Latin no great harm would come of it. Let it pass!

Now here's what was unduly harsh. Wording like: The Buddha is an impostor, his words give rise to the poison of atheism, monks are charlatans who go about preying on simple folk, they encourage idol worship and mouth and chant meaningless sacrilegious prayers.

"Tone it down," suggested Thévenot.

"You can't," Couplet shot back, "Intorcetta wouldn't approve, and most educated Confucians would agree with that statement."

"Sieur Michel, what do you think," Interjected Thévenot.

The young man wasn't so sure. The Shen family in Nanjing counted among its esteemed acquaintances urbane, sagacious, and highly principled Buddhists who were known for their erudition. Thévenot and Couplet argued back and forth, but a consensus emerged that there was a highly spiritual and altogether admirable form of Buddhist spirituality and that what was being referred to here was a popular form that had corrupted the original teaching.

"Doesn't that apply to all religions?" Quipped Thévenot.

Couplet winced and ultimately, it was decided to leave the text just the way it was. The observations would please the religious conservatives in Rome and in Paris and like it or not there were plenty of them. There always are! Anyway, Couplet didn't want to run the risk of being blamed by Intorcetta for changing the thrust of the Preface.

Shen added the following comment to his notes: animated discussion regarding Buddhism. No changes recommended.

The Daoists didn't come off any better. At least Laozi, their presumed founding father, had intuited, although apparently imperfectly, the reality of a supreme being. That had spared him the ultimate putdown in the Preface which was to be accused of atheism. The Daoists were nonetheless taken to task for encouraging the practice of alchemy and witchcraft and bestowing lavish privileges on their clergy.

"That," Thévenot observed, "is something you could never accuse the Roman Curia of. Look at Richelieu and Mazarin. They were cardinals and lived like impoverished hermits."

Shen looked in Couplet's direction and, noting his frown, decided that bursting out in raucous laughter would not be the correct response to Thévenot's observation.

Shen added to his notes the following laconic comment: same discussion for Daoism as for Buddhism and same conclusion. No changes recommended.

Then there were the Neo-Confucians. Who were these people and why such antagonism?

Thévenot voiced the thought that before addressing that particularly thorny question some historical background might be in order. He prided himself on his knowledge of Eastern religions. At sixty-six he was the oldest man in the room and had spent his whole life collecting everything oriental he could get his hands on. Much of what he'd collected had come from India and of course China. He therefore spoke with authority when reminding everyone that while Buddhism had taken root in northern India at roughly the same time as Confucius was leading his peripatetic existence, it took a while to get to China. A good five centuries! When it did, wasn't it a fact that its spirituality and ascetic practices had proved immensely popular with the Chinese?

Couplet reluctantly agreed. And continued Thévenot: "Didn't Buddhism's openness to coexisting with Daoism contribute to its success? Didn't it endow with spiritual legitimacy many of the popular beliefs and traditions that were so characteristic of Chinese culture? Wasn't it also a fact that it never set out to challenge or diminish the influence of Confucianism? Nothing surely wrong with any of that!"

"No, not really," Couplet agreed grudgingly, "but the problem was that all this had led to a long-term decline in traditional Confucianism. What you're failing to appreciate is that when, centuries later, scholars went back to paying attention to China's neglected Confucian inheritance, they compromised. They introduced into Confucianism a spiritual and religious dimension that even if not explicitly attributed to Buddhism and Daoism was clearly inspired by those two traditions."

"Aha! So, those are the ones you refer to as neo-Confucians. I'm beginning to see why they upset you. Their version of Confucianism no longer mirrored the pristine ethics and principles handed down from Noah. You see that as a problem because you base your missionary strategy on arguing that only Christianity is capable of satisfactorily fulfilling that spiritual and religious dimension. Buddhists and Daoists are competitors and so are these re-interpreters of older forms of Confucianism. Am I right?"

"You put it all rather crudely. You lack subtlety, my dear Thévenot."

"Of course, I do. We can't all be Jesuits!"

The three men confined in their rue Vivienne cell had been working diligently that entire week. Horthemels was pressing them for more finalized text so he could keep his compositors busy. Silence ensued. They were tired. Their workday was coming to an end. Shen added to his notes: interesting but heated discussion regarding neo-Confucians. No changes.

Rather than Couplet and Shen returning promptly to Ménilmontant, Thévenot suggested a lighthearted meal at Chez Gaston. The table d'hôte that evening offered a rabbit stew aux fines herbes. It was within this rather more relaxed setting that Thévenot, the ever-curious linguist, asked Shen about two Chinese characters he'd come across. He'd done so in his proofreading of the Preface's segment referring to Neo-Confucians. One was Tai and the other was Chi. Did they have philosophical meaning? Shen was happy to oblige. He liked to be asked such questions.

The two characters, he explained, had an architectural origin. They were used to refer to the sturdy master beam that is locked into place at the pinnacle of the roof of a formal structure such as a temple or palace pavilion. The question reminded Shen of the great hall around which his ancestors had built the family's ancestral compound in Nanjing. It made him feel, he admitted, quite nostalgic. It was the beam that was key to securely holding together the skillfully assembled wooden framework that gave Chinese structures their innate balance and resilience. There was an analogy with the structure of the heavens above.

Thévenot was intrigued.

"You're telling me that the Tai Chi beam is reflective of your ancient culture."

"That's a good way of putting it. As you have correctly surmised, it has also taken on what you Europeans generally refer to as a philosophical meaning. Yes, the Neo Confucians came to use the term symbolically. Understandably so. It evokes the tension arising from the counteracting and complementary forces that keep a structure standing. There's a dynamic and creative dimension to it."

"So, it's another way of expressing the primal tension out of which emerges the duality of the Yin and the Yang? I see. So be good enough to explain to me why you Jesuits find it troubling."

"I'm too young and inexperienced to answer that question, Sieur Thévenot, but it's probably because we Chinese tend to think of the universe we are part of as being not only in constant flux but also as being continuous. We don't think of it as having begun at a specific point in time. It just all holds together. Some might therefore think of that master beam as godlike. It's not easy for me to describe this in Latin. Forgive me."

At this Thévenot whispered in Shen's ear: "Your Latin is perfectly good enough. I get it. There's the Yin and the Yang, then the Tai and the Chi and of course the Yi Jing. The world is seen as continuous and yet in constant change. It's not very Biblical and that, I suppose, is why the Preface speaks of the abyss of atheism. Enough said. Let me give you another serving of rabbit stew. C'est une spécialité de la maison and you wouldn't get anything like it in Nanjing. You'd have a hard time eating it with chopsticks!"

The evening went by most pleasantly. Shen had also mentioned to an ever-curious Thévenot that a form of martial arts had recently become all the rage in China. It consisted of a carefully coordinated set of movements designed to bring opposing bodily forces into dynamic balance. It was being referred to as Tai Chi. He'd seen it practiced in Nanjing. There were spiritual and Buddhist meditative overtones to it.

❖

The Preface included a significant section taken up with describing the Yi Jing (易經) or, as Couplet described it, the Book of Changes. That section of the Preface came up for review two days later. Thévenot, ever critical, thought it was interesting but rather long.

"The Yi Jing comes across as a mysterious and opaque divination manual. Won't most readers question why so much of the Preface has been devoted to it? Aren't we publishing a book of Confucian wisdom literature consisting of morally and politically engaging sayings and aphorisms? I don't see the connection. The Yi Jing is admittedly very Chinese, but I'm puzzled."

"Well, yes," agreed Couplet, "it certainly isn't one of the Four Books, but it's one of the Five Classics, and is so much part of the Chinese tradition that Confucius has been credited with authoring the most inspired of its many commentaries. It's evocatively titled the Ten Wings. We obviously have room neither for the commentary nor for the Yi Jing itself. Before leaving China, I had this very conversation with Intorcetta. He thought it belonged in our preface because of its antiquity. It's said to have been born of a mystical vision dreamt of by a venerated king by the name of Fu Xi."

"Aha! So, it shouldn't be ignored. Are you suggesting, Father Couplet, that Fu Xi's antiquity might be such as to associate him with Noah's early descendants…that his dreaming might therefore be inspired?"

"Perhaps! Let's just say that the Yi Jing is worthy of mention, that its symbols may well be inspired, that some pre-figure the Christian message or could be interpreted as such. Why don't you ask Shen about it? He's quite a devotee."

It relieved Shen's homesickness to talk about such things.

"My grandmother was a devout Christian, but she was familiar with the Yi Jing. When faced with a difficult decision, she knew just who to consult. Everyone around our ancestral home did so. As a child I was taught about hexagrams. They involved writing and numbers. It was part of my education. My grandmother was always willing to answer my many questions about the Yi Jing. Those arrayed signs fascinated me. I remember her telling me that what she liked about the Yi Jing was that it helped her come to terms with the disquieting truth that nothing lasts forever. She'd tell me, for instance, that I was going to grow up and leave her. Perhaps travel to strange lands. It would break her heart, but the Yi Jing, she reflected, had taught her that it would somehow all be to the good. She'd enjoyed a long life but many of the events she'd lived through reminded her of the apparent role of chance and conflict in human affairs. She'd seen the Manchus storm into Nanjing and trample over much of what we held sacred. You throw the dice you're given, she liked to say, and you do the best you can. She taught me that for all we knew there was a mysterious, unseen hand guiding the dice. She suggested we might even have it within us to nudge them ever so slightly—to where we'd like to see them land. She'd also tell me about the spirits that dwelt in our hills, mountains, streams, and valleys. They played games with each other, she would say jokingly, and that's what helped keep the dice rolling. My most vivid childhood memories of the Yi Jing were visual ones—the arrayed hexagrams, the elegantly calligraphed characters associated with the arrays. I vividly remember my grandmother allowing me to accompany her when she visited those skilled in the art throwing the dice. They were the ones who knew how to interpret the hexagrams to which the thrown dice pointed. Sometimes instead of dice or coins, the diviners threw slender arrow-like sticks encoded with signs. There was much rattling to all that throwing, and I remember the sounds and also the pungency of the clouds of incense that hung around the temples. Yes, I dare admit it, we sometimes went into temples. My grandmother did so discreetly because we were Christians. So, for me, there was something particularly mysterious and exciting about sneaking into a Daoist or Buddhist temple."

Couplet wanted to include in the Preface a copper engraving of a table showing all sixty-four hexagrams—in their proper traditional order and under their eight columns and along their eight rows. The Chinese characters labeling the upper and lower segments of each hexagram had been replaced with Latin renderings. Couplet and Shen had labored mightily on producing this elaborate visual. It had added to the cost of the project, but Horthemels had obliged and Thévenot had not objected. Couplet had insisted because he believed that the task of explaining what a hexagram was defied description in any language: not just in Latin.

"Well, just what is a hexagram," Thévenot had exclaimed. "I know you're referring to those puny darkened squares made up of six little bars stacked neatly and horizontally above each other but, you're using a Greek word to describe something quintessentially Chinese. Sieur Michel Chinois, pray tell me how you say hexagram in Chinese?"

"We use a character that is pronounced gua. It has nothing to do with the number six. We write it thus: 卦" Shen sketched it out on a sheet he then handed to Thévenot. "On the left you will note a doubling of the sign that stands for the earth and on the right a sign many of our scholars suggest evokes the oracle bones our distant ancestors once used for divination. Those were the bones on which we believe characters were first written. Our ancestors heated them over hot embers and watched the way the cracks went. Much skill went into the interpretation of the cracks. So, you see, Sieur Melchisédec, we Chinese are very visual."

There was more to those so-called hexagrams than met an untrained eye. Each hexagram, Shen went on to explain, consisted of a different combination of continuous and non-continuous bars.

Continuity…discontinuity…a reflection of reality! The continuous bars had a Yang quality to them and the discontinuous ones, well that was obvious, were the Yin. It all came back to the conversation of the other night at Chez Gaston over the rabbit stew. The gist of which had been that the Tai Chi and the Yi Jing were all part of an intricate web of Yin and Yang symbolism. The cosmos, nature, and the vagaries of human life were all interconnected in one glorious unending flow of boundless energy. It was by combining a fathomless multitude of those continuous and discontinuous signs that nature had conjured up the richness of the world within which we live. That was the visual and conceptual universe within which Confucius had given expression to his political and moral musings.

The sixty-four hexagrams underlying the Philosophy of the Yi Jing included in the Preface

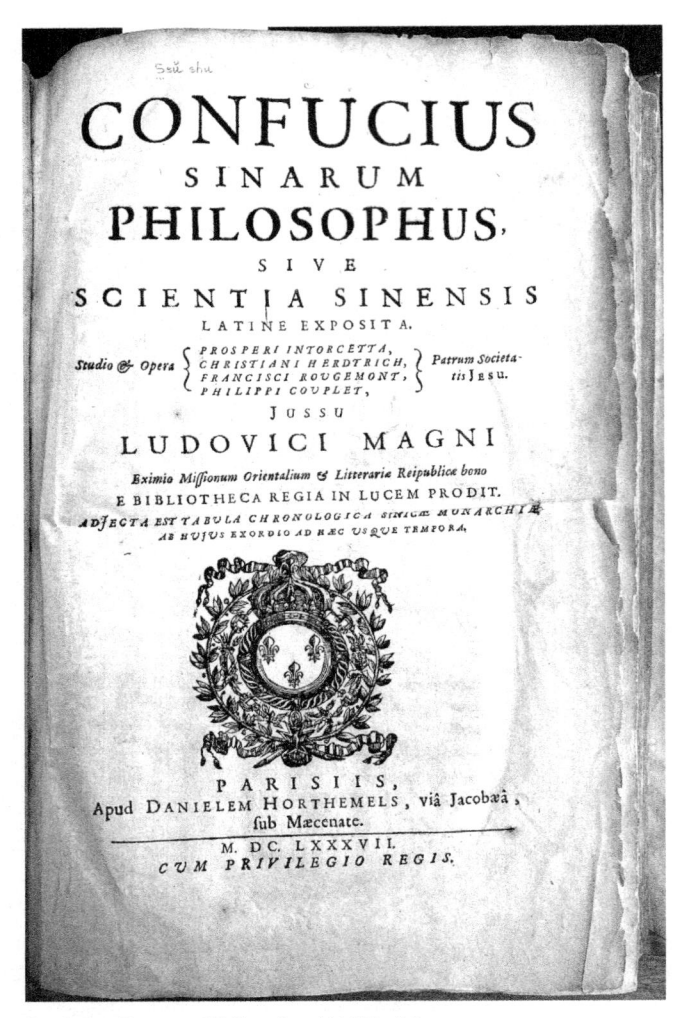

Confucius Sinarum Philosophus (1687): title page

"C'est compliqué, Sieur Melchisédec, et veuillez m'excuser mais c'est la Chine!" Shen had picked up a few words of the local language. It wasn't straightforward but it wasn't anything as tricky as Latin.

The final act was approving the Confucian Treatise's title page. It had been commissioned by Horthemels. He had given the job to one of his best engravers. Visually there was nothing Chinese about it. A good third of it was taken up by an admirably executed rendering of the Sun King's regal coat of arms which, as everyone knew, was made up of three fleurs-de-lis surmounted by a crown with the whole entwined and garlanded by a profusion of lilies. Voilà! The Confucian Treatise would henceforth be known as:

Confucius sinarum philosophus sive scientia sinensis latine exposita

The names of the four editors-translators were displayed in significantly smaller type below that most impressive of titles. Couplet had not hesitated. He had placed Próspero Intorcetta's name on the top line and his own on the bottom rung. Modesty and political expediency, he had quipped, have their place in human affairs. Sadly, the two other men were no longer alive. Rougemont, another of Couplet's Flemish compatriots, had died in Shanghai ten years earlier and news had just reached Paris that Herdtrich, the mathematically gifted Austrian whose brilliance had come to Emperor Kangxi's attention had died just two years earlier. They had both died short of their sixtieth birthdays.

Shouldn't Thévenot's name have appeared on the title page? None of this would have been possible without him. He'd thanked Couplet profusely for the offer but insisted that his name be left off. He gave as a stated reason his strongly felt view that it would have been quite wrong to draw attention away from the translators. Then, he added, that when in presence of the Sun King, he made a virtue of maintaining a respectful distance. That said the Sun King was unquestionably very present on the title page. It proclaimed not only that the Confucius Sinarum Philosophus had been published by order of Ludovicus Magnus, but it also made much of the fact that the book would be part of the Bibliotheca Regia.

What about Shen's name? No, no, such an inclusion would have been dreadfully out of place for a mere aspiring scholar who was expected to show humility and profound respect for his teachers.

There were meritorious finishing touches to be made such as references to Couplet's 125-page long tabulation of the names of those who had ruled China from the beginning of this era to the present, and to the fact that Horthemels had benefited from the Sun King's patronage.

❖

The year was 1687. Parisians were looking out for glimmerings of spring in the hope that it would bring an end to a long and harsh winter, the King's Censor had given his approval and the ecclesiastical authorities had failed to detect any trace of heresy. So, all was in order. Horthemels' pressmen at the rue Saint-Jacques were ready. They would soon be working day and night printing one-by-one and both front and back each of the seventy-five sheets configured in the in-quarto format that were required to produce the book's six-hundred-pages. It was an energy and time-consuming business requiring concentration and dedication.

Now that the work was done, and the die was cast, Shen's thoughts turned to the question of how he was going to embark on the last leg of his European journey. He'd after all been instructed by Charles de Noyelle to begin his novitiate in Lisbon. Couplet, given that he was resolved to return to China as soon as practicable, would also be headed for Lisbon. Would they be traveling together and if so how? Couplet, however, was undecided when it came to timing. He'd discussed his concerns with Père la Chaise who in addition to having the king's ear was in frequent communication with Charles de Noyelle in Rome. A letter entrusted to a reliable courier service might with luck reach Rome in less than a month. For Couplet, remaining in Paris a while longer made a good deal of sense. Shouldn't he be around to promote awareness of the Confucius Sinarum Philosophus among those likely to support the China missions? He'd also hoped to publish his biography of Candida Xu, the pious lady from Shanghai. He had a title in mind: Histoire d'une dame chrétienne de la Chine and Horthemels had even suggested the name of a fellow printer, also established on the rue Saint-Jacques, who specialized in religious books and would be in a better position to handle Couplet's project.

Couplet's Histoire D'une Dame Chrétienne de la Chine (1688) depicting Candida Xu: Engraved Frontispiece

The news, when it came through, took Couplet quite by surprise. It must have been, he reflected, an idea conjured up by both Père la Chaise and Charles de Noyelle. There were obviously political overtones. It was indeed startling. Shen was to leave Paris for London. There was no objection to Couplet remaining in Paris a while longer, but Shen was to go to England and do so as soon as practicable. Couplet would join Shen but later, perhaps several months later. Yes, it made sense to sail from London to Lisbon in a Portuguese ship but that wasn't why Shen was being instructed to board a ship in Calais and cross the Channel now rather than later. Would he travel on his own? By no means. It had been decided that Spinola would act as Shen's guide and mentor. It was a decision that on the face of it made some sense. Spinola and Shen had developed a close enough relationship. They had after all not only traveled together all the way from Rome to Paris but also over the past year they had lived in close proximity to each other at the Ménilmontant residence, shared meals and yes Shen, following de Noyelle's request, had done his best to introduce Spinola to conversational Chinese. All the while, however, the young priest had been at Père la Chaise's beck and call. He'd obviously acted as his confidential go-between in affairs that involved frequent visits to Versailles. Was this part of a diplomatic rapprochement with the English that involved not only the French but also Pope Innocent? Possibly. The fact was that Spinola had let on that he'd acquired an English phrase book and even found himself a tutor among the many English expatriates living in Paris. Spinola was indeed a busy man.

If there were, to put it mildly, political overtones to this business of being shipped off so unexpectedly to London, then Shen needed to be subjected to a crash course designed to familiarize him with the political intricacies of a nation about which he knew next to nothing. Père la Chaise decided that, given the importance of the matter at hand, he would be the one to conduct Shen's briefing. It would indeed be a crash course since the king's confessor, taken up as he was by his official duties, had little time to spare. That said, Shen was arguably a lucky man. He would be tutored by one of the Sun King's most prominent advisors.

Couplet was anxious to know how Shen had withstood the ordeal. Had Spinola been in attendance?

"He certainly was, Father Philippe. The three of us met in Père la Chaise's private apartments at Versailles, the ceiling was gilded, and we were ushered in by a costumed flunky in a powdered wig. Father Spinola told me that he would be acting as my interpreter."

"Interpreter?"

"Yes, because as you know Père la Chaise speaks rather fast and uses refined expressions that bring out the inherent elegance of the French language. The concern was that despite my having spent the last year in Paris, I'd fail to fully appreciate the import of his remarks. So, there was Spinola taking notes in Latin and whispering in my ear…in Latin. It was rather confusing, but I'd like to think that I held my own."

"It sounds rather theatrical. Were you allowed to ask questions? I'm curious. What were you told?"

"At the beginning a lot was said about the English, or rather the British, being an island people. With examples drawn from history Père la Chaise made the point that this accounted for their being both difficult to deal with and different—at times aggressively so. They didn't, for example, always appreciate the superiority of French culture. Did I grasp the subtlety of what I was being told? Of course, I did. Don't we Chinese harbor similar feelings toward the Japanese…another island people. They've adopted the best of our culture, even our Confucian ideals, and yet they ever so often give in to the delusion that they can invade us and reduce us to being a vassal state. So, yes, I mentioned the Japanese."

"Père la Chaise has to be painfully aware of the heart-rending difficulties we Jesuits have encountered in Japan."

"He was but that's not a subject he wanted to dwell on, so he moved on to the English language, explaining that it was akin to Dutch, and that it would sound strange to my Chinese ears. I shouldn't worry too much about that though because English wasn't a language anyone had reason to want to learn and in any case I'd be meeting educated people who knew Latin. The thing he really stressed about the English, or British I should say, is that they are aggressively Protestant and in the past have been notoriously ill-disposed toward Jesuits. That doesn't, however, mean they always see eye-to-eye with other Protestants. Until recently the British and the Dutch have been cannonading each other's ships and the British have been busy dislodging them from wherever opportunities present themselves to do so including from northern regions of the Americas. That said, they still think of each other as cousins, albeit distant ones and they are both against what they refer to as political absolutism. That's why the English are suspicious of the Sun King's motives. They associate political absolutism with Catholicism."

"Hadn't our year in Batavia made you aware of a lot of this?"

"Of course, it had. I did mention that I knew about the Anglo-Dutch rivalry in the Spice Islands. All this made me think nostalgically of our good friend João Atayde and most especially Dona Inês for whom, remembering her kindness, I pray every day. It also occurred to me that the British were probably of the opinion that the revocation of the Edict of Nantes was an example of religious absolutism."

"I hope you had the good sense not to mention that in front of Père la Chaise."

"Knowing me as you do, Father Philippe, do you really think I would be so foolish? No, no, I just sat there listening respectfully while Spinola scribbled his Latin notes, making himself look both scholarly and busily useful."

"You were, I hope, told about the history underlying this hatred that the English have of Catholics."

"Yes. You're referring, I take it, to the religious schism that arose a century-and-a-half ago. It had to do with the unfortunate fact that the English queen who was, in fact, Spanish, hadn't given birth to a male heir. So, the king decided to solve the problem by marrying another woman, but the pope didn't agree. It was admittedly a ticklish situation because, as we all know, divorce isn't exactly a Catholic thing, but the real problem was that she was the Spanish king's aunt. The pope didn't want to offend him. Hence the schism. The trouble was that things didn't work out as hoped and the English king kept on trying his luck with different wives and wasn't very gracious about it. To move things along he had two of them beheaded."

"Graphically put, my dear Michael, but yes that's the gist of it."

"I did mention that in China such beheadings would have been unnecessary, since concubines and second and third and even fourth wives are allowed to produce heirs to the imperial throne. Père la Chaise looked at me disapprovingly, and yes, I should have been more careful. I risked giving the impression that we Chinese lack subtlety. That wasn't the end of the story, because from what I gather, one of the English king's wives did eventually produce a male heir, but the boy didn't live long and in the end, it was his daughter Elizabeth who inherited his kingdom."

"Did you find that surprising?"

"That the mandate of heaven should pass to a woman? Yes, because although some might argue that this is what happened to Empress Wu in the seventh century, that's a very un-Chinese outcome. But Père la Chaise did stress that she was a formidable lady and saw fit to transform what she had inherited quite by chance into an aggressively Protestant fiefdom. She was hellbent on extending her domain to wherever her sailors steered their ships. So, for those and other reasons, this queen had taken an intense dislike to the Jesuits. She had them hunted down and executed. It was dangerous to be a Catholic. You risked being accused of promoting treasonable thoughts and were slapped into jail."

"You're a fast learner, my dear Michael, and I think that you've successfully summarized what is a very complicated story. Did Père la Chaise go on to tell you about more recent events? If anything, the story gets even more complicated."

"The part about a king called Charles who believed kings were divinely inspired and therefore had absolute authority over their subjects? Yes, he wanted, in other words, to be like the Sun King in France. As a result, he ran into this business about the English being exceedingly independently minded and therefore proudly contentious. They have a parliament and use it to keep their kings' power in check. It didn't end well. Charles was beheaded. The English do seem to go in for a lot of beheading—more so than us Chinese, but then we do have plenty of other ways of getting rid of people who need to be disposed of."

"That you do by, for example, flaying them alive or confining them to bamboo cages. Did Père la Chaise explain what a parliament was?"

"He tried. I still find it rather confusing. It's something like a scholarly council whose members are somehow empowered to prevent the king from doing what he wants to do…but only sometimes. I asked whether members of parliament have to pass some kind of examination based on English philosophical texts? He demurred on that point. I told Père la Chaise we didn't have parliaments in China. It wasn't something Confucius, the wisest of sages, had ever even considered. The point, I think, of all this is that Charles believed in the mandate of heaven and would have wanted to be treated like a Chinese emperor."

"You're right, Michael, he would have liked that, but it was not to be and I'm sure Père la Chaise told you about the militaristically inclined general who, having told the English they'd be better off without a king, had himself proclaimed supreme ruler."

"He did. He described him as a rather unsavory character who was both puritanically inclined and extreme in his Protestant inspired religious views. I gather that after a while the independently minded English grew tired of the man and a decade later went back to wanting to be ruled by a king. He was also called Charles. Am I remembering all this correctly?"

"You are. He was Charles II and at first he was very popular. The English indulged themselves by dancing, singing, drinking, watching cleverly written plays and writing poetry."

"Sounds very Chinese to me. We also grow tired of tyrannical regents who usurp imperial power. Deep down, when given a chance, we also like composing poetry. We dream our problems away by imaging nature-loving hermits seeking enlightenment. We also enjoy watching plays accompanied by dancing and clanging gongs. But the good times never last, do they? I was reminded of the story you once told me about the frogs who got bored and thought they'd be better off with a colorful and bossy king."

"You're referring, Michael, to one of Aesop's fables that we Jesuits translated into Chinese to prove that we weren't ignorant barbarians. So, I suppose you could say that the English decided to restore the mandate of heaven by handing it over to the elder son of the king they had beheaded. I know it sounds complicated, but people are known to do that kind of thing…even you Chinese."

"Yes, and to make the point that good times don't last forever, Père la Chaise explained that although Charles II, thanks to his many concubines, had sired plenty of children, none of the sons born of his Portuguese wife survived. That wouldn't have troubled us Chinese but for the English that was, once again, a problem. I was relieved when told that this time around there was no beheading of wives. The English are apparently more civilized than they used to be."

"No beheadings, Michael but it didn't go smoothly. Were you told why?"

"The problem, I was told, was that Charles II died almost exactly two years ago…totally unexpectedly because he was still young. He suffered from gout. We Chinese also know about gout. My grandfather suffered from it. What everyone in England had assumed was that his queen would eventually bear him a son. So, in the absence of a son, it was his younger brother James who succeeded him. Isn't he a Catholic and isn't that something that troubles the English? Yes…and yet…well Père la Chaise went into a long explanation, the details of which escape me…even Spinola's Latin notes are garbled. It's because James is a Catholic that it's possible and, in fact, desirable for us to visit England."

"Yes, Michael, it's fiendishly complicated. Years ago, James, who as you correctly state is now king, had married a woman who convinced him to convert to Catholicism. No one in staunchly Protestant England liked the idea, not even his elder brother Charles II. His Catholic wife then gave birth to two daughters. The elder was called Mary and the younger Anne. At his older brother's insistence, James reluctantly agreed to bring up both Mary and Anne as Protestants. It was, I suppose, just possible that one day one or even both of them might inherit the throne. James was otherwise left in peace. No one expected him to become king. When his wife died of cancer he remarried. He was still relatively young. His second wife was an Italian princess who, obviously enough, was also a Catholic. Again, no one in Protestant England liked the idea of his marrying yet another Catholic but then he wasn't expected to become king."

"At last, I'm beginning to understand what this is all about… your Chinese, Father Philippe, is a whole lot easier to understand than Père la Chaise's French, and Spinola's Latin. I get it. So, even though James wasn't expected to become king, he now is and is reigning as James II. The fact that he's Catholic and married to an Italian princess is now of deep concern to the Protestant English. She hasn't yet borne him any children but is likely to do so and she'd raise them Catholic."

"Good summary, Michael. I suggest you add marginal notes in Chinese to the papers Spinola gave you. That way you can refer back to them when you meet these confusing English people. And wait…it gets even more complicated. This James has an autocratic nature."

"Yes, that came up in the discussion with Père la Chaise… he likes to think he's inherited the mandate of heaven…like our emperor Kangxi…like his beheaded father Charles I and his now deceased brother Charles II…very human if you ask me… Confucius could see that power corrupts irresistibly…too bad that we've never discovered an antidote…."

"You're turning into a philosopher, Michael, be careful. It's dangerous; just look at poor old Confucius. But yes, it doesn't help that James and the Sun King are first cousins. The independently minded Protestant English are highly suspicious of the French and, most of all, of their king."

"Père la Chaise didn't say so, but the fact that less than two years ago the Sun King revoked the Edict of Nantes and is still ridding France of its Protestants can't be very reassuring to the English."

"You're on to something there, Michael and you should also know that James has set his heart on promulgating a decree referred to as the Declaration of Indulgence. It would lift restrictions imposed on those who are not members of England's Protestant official church. He wants to enshrine the principle of freedom of worship. It wouldn't just be welcomed by the few but influential Catholics still living in Britain. It would also give greater freedom to the minority of English Protestants who disagree with the official church."

"I'm constantly being reminded that not all Protestants think alike. I see now why the conservative upholders of the official Protestant church who are in the majority have even more reason to be wary of James."

"Yes, and Catholics get blamed for all of this…especially we Jesuits. We're seen as instigating what the English refer to as Popish plots. It's terribly unfair because most of us think James is making a big mistake. He shouldn't flaunt his Catholic faith. He should just do things like quietly encouraging us Jesuits to return to England. In fact, he's already done that. If he hadn't you and Father Spinola wouldn't be going to London. They'd instead slap you in jail. Do you realize why Charles de Noyelle and Père la Chaise think it's a good idea for you to visit England?"

"I've been giving that question a lot of thought, Father Philippe. Here's what I think. I'm on show. Precious few Europeans have had occasion to meet someone from my homeland. I'm the first. I was chosen to accompany you to help dispel the commonly held assumption in Europe that we Chinese are all savages. I'm to go to London because the English need to be reminded that China is the largest and wealthiest of all kingdoms, that its culture is impressively ancient and sophisticated and, above all, that you Jesuits know more about China than anyone else and are therefore useful…even to Protestants."

"Bluntly but correctly put, my dear Michael. There's money to be made by trading with you Chinese and Jesuit intelligence might come in handy…even to the Protestant English. I'm becoming, I know, overly cynical in my old age."

"So, the hope is that the English can be persuaded to be more tolerant to Catholics. Religious tolerance is what we are also hoping for in China…that we will continue to enjoy emperor Kangxi's favor."

"Long may it last!"

"I asked Père la Chaise why it was that the Sun King was expelling Protestants from France? Wasn't that the very opposite to what we were hoping for in England and in China? I should, I know, have been more discrete. He sighed and said that there were questions best left unanswered. It reminded me of our Chinese expression: There are mysteries know to heaven alone; 天機—Tian ji."

"Let's leave it at that, Michael. It's getting late and I'm even more tired than usual."

❖

Shen and Couplet took emotional leave of each other. They had been together continuously since their departure from Macao just before Christmas of 1681. Over six years had elapsed. Shen was about to celebrate his twenty-ninth birthday. The six letters he had received in as many years from his family in Nanjing had been forwarded to him from the Casa Professa in Rome. The most recent had taken over eighteen months to reach him. It had erratically hopscotched from Canton to Goa, to Malindi on the East Africa coast, to the Cape Verde Islands, to Lisbon, to Marseilles along the Mediterranean and then finally to Rome. Shen had learned to his great sadness of his beloved grandmother's death. Through the first letters to reach him he'd also learned to his chagrin that his parents, having heard of the shipwreck of the Santo António, had mourned his passing only to find out later that he had in fact survived it. He'd, however, been happy to hear that the younger brother he missed the most had successfully negotiated the first grade of the imperial exams and was looking forward to an official posting in nearby Anhui province. For Shen this was a time for nostalgia. The excitement of being invited to contribute his linguistic skills to Confucius Sinarum Philosophus in Paris had run its course. It had given way to the much anticipated and but also unsettling prospect of at last entering the Order's novitiate. Why, he asked himself, did it have to happen in yet another unfamiliar and distant city.

Confucius says:

Riches and honors are what men desire. If they cannot be obtained in the proper way, they should not be held. Poverty and meanness are what men dislike. If they cannot be avoided in the proper way, they should not be avoided.
Analects III

We should be apprehensive and cautious, as if on the brink of a deep gulf, as if treading on thin ice.
Analects VIII

Men of principle are sure to be bold, but those who are bold may not always be men of principle.
Analects XIV

VIII
An English Summer
1687

The journey from Paris to London took no more than ten days. Shen and Spinola had been lucky. The sixty-league ride in a horse-drawn chaise post from Paris to Calais was by far the longest and most tiring stage of the journey. At Calais, they boarded an English-operated packet boat and reached Dover a day later. The winds were favorable, and they were thankful to have avoided the worst of the rough tidal waters that often made it difficult to cross the Channel at this point which is its narrowest.

Père la Chaise, most likely at Charles de Noyelle's behest, had sent advance notice of their planned arrival in London thereby insuring them of a warm welcome. There was a Jesuit house in London. In Enkhuizen, the fathers had described their establishment as clandestine. If not clandestine, the London residence certainly struck Shen as discrete. It was, however, sited at the very center of the now fashionable part of the capital that had expanded westward in the two decades that had followed what was still referred to as the Great Fire of 1666. It was comfortably furnished and had been graciously made available to the Jesuits by one of the aristocratic English families that, despite persecution and threats of banishment, had over the last century-and-a-half held firm in its loyalty to what they referred to as the faith of their Fathers.

Only a few days following their arrival in London, Shen was notified that he and Spinola had been granted the exceptional honor of attending an episcopal ordination in none other than the king's presence. The ceremony concerned one who had been recently named an archbishop by Pope Innocent. The very pope into whose presence Shen had been ushered together with Couplet not once but twice and whose feet he had kissed on both occasions.

Archbishop of London? Shen had asked. It had turned out to be an embarrassing question. Absolutely not! Only Protestants could aspire to such a position and even then London ranked no higher than a plain bishopric. No, no...this man happened to be one of Pope Innocent's Italian relatives. His diplomatic skills had earned him the highest respect and the Holy Father had appointed him nuncio to the English court. This required further elaboration. Nuncios were the pope's ambassadors. Ambassadors? In a spiritual sense, of course, but Shen had also come to realize from the year he'd spent in the Eternal City that the papacy was no stranger to the world of politics. Besides, didn't the pope have a standing army and reign over his possessions as would a temporal prince? He did indeed but there was more to this nuncio business than met the uninformed eye.

The very idea of a nuncio was, so far as the Protestant English were concerned, suspiciously and dangerously Popish. There hadn't been a nuncio at the English court since the days of Mary Tudor and that was well over a century ago. She, of course, in the eyes of James II's right minded courtiers, was the Bloody Mary who, during her brief and ill-starred reign had seen to having good Protestants burned at the stake. Was this nuncio business yet another of James II's ideas? It was and perhaps, in the circumstances, not the wisest.

So, if not archbishop of London archbishop then of where? Shen had asked somewhat ingenuously. It was simply that the pope had wanted to confer an honor on his nuncio and that the idea had appealed to James II.

King James II: detail of 1686 portrait by Nicolas de Larguillière (1656-1746)

Spinola took Shen aside and summoning his considerable Latin linguistic skills initiated his protégé in the mysteries of titular episcopal sees.

There was a string of ancient bishoprics throughout the Near East that had long ago been overrun by the Ottoman Turks. Once flourishing Christian communities had over the past centuries, and even more so since the Fall of Constantinople, been thoroughly Islamized. So, the nuncio was to be consecrated as archbishop of some remote long-forgotten region overlooking the Black Sea. Shen wondered what would happen if the man were ever to visit his see and inform the local Turks that he was their archbishop. Spinola expressed the hope that they'd have the good sense to do no more than politely roll out their prayer mats and regard the whole business as harmless and just quaintly Catholic. Hopefully, so would James II's devotedly Protestant nobility although that wasn't an altogether foregone conclusion.

James II did indeed seize on the opportunity to make a great big show of consecrating the nuncio. It was a means of showcasing the reintroduction of an official Catholic presence in England. James II had consecrating bishops brought in from Catholic Ireland and chose as a venue the chapel of St James's Palace. It was a late Gothic gem built in a typically English perpendicular style. The chapel was part of an elegant palace of modest proportions built of fine weathered bricks in the earlier decades of the 16th century. It was the brainchild of none other than Henry VIII who Shen now remembered from his notes was the king who had caused the schism by divorcing and beheading wives who had failed to provide him with a legitimate male heir. The sanctuary was oak paneled, the floor was set in marble, and the ornately carved dark stained pews were arranged choir-style at right angles to the altar.

Shen had been warned that grumblings of dissatisfaction had come to the fore. In the eyes of many if not most of James II's courtiers, the chapel was quintessentially characteristic of the Established Church and was therefore thought of as the most Protestant of places of worship. Be that as it may on the day of the ceremony some two hundred dignitaries of the realm had been squeezed into the little chapel. It was beyond Shen's comprehension why he, a humble visitor from a distant land, had been numbered among those so honored.

He had been very specifically instructed to appear in his fulsome silken robes and wear a cross. This he did. He felt honored but self-conscious. He knew full well that the dragon-embroidered robes confected by Candida Xu implied that he was a member of the Chinese high nobility. He took comfort in the thought that through his mere presence, he was doing his Confucian duty by honoring both his emperor and the ancestry of his humble but much respected Nanjing family clan.

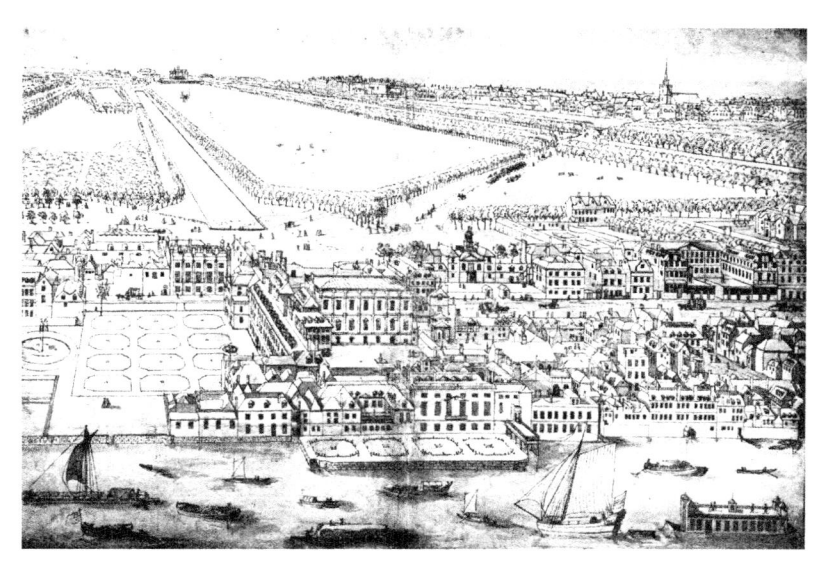

Palace of Whitehall: 1696 Anglo-Dutch engraving

What is clear is that James II, notwithstanding the solemnity of the occasion, did become aware of Shen's presence among the throng of those in attendance. The newly installed and consecrated nuncio had, after the ceremony, whispered in the royal ear that it had been at Charles de Noyelle's suggestion that the one he described as the young Chinese convert had been summoned to London and invited. Was this not a way of reminding those present of the admirable universality of the Catholic religion? The king, duly intrigued, made known his desire to meet Shen so that he was, and in short order summoned to present himself at court.

James II took pleasure in receiving dignitaries and holding court in Windsor. The castle was a mere six leagues from London and its stately apartments had been enlarged and decorated by none other than his father, Charles II. When in London, however, James II had several palatial residences at his disposal. While he had a special affection for St. James since it was there that he was born to his French mother Henrietta Maria, he had nonetheless established his official London residence at the Palace of Whitehall. It was far larger, included a magnificent banqueting house of classical design and was attractively sited in the vicinity of both Westminster Abbey and the River Thames.

Shen had therefore been summoned to Whitehall. He'd been informed that until recently it had unquestionably been Europe's largest palace. Rumor, however, had it that the Sun King's Versailles had now eclipsed its splendor. Shen was ushered into the royal presence by none other than the newly installed nuncio. It was a great honor. The king conversed engagingly, desirous of setting his young Chinese guest at ease. James II's Latin was scholarly and fluent, and he was curious. How many Catholics were there in China? How did the Forbidden City compare to the Palace of Whitehall? How many Chinese characters did a scholar have to learn to reach the higher rungs of the imperial administration? The king had been told about the publication of the Confucius Sinarum Philosophus. Would copies soon be available in England? Indeed, they would, and Shen was able to say that he'd brought with him one of the very first to have come off the Horthemels press. It would soon be in the hands of one of Melchisédec Thévenot's scholarly English colleagues.

Shen made the best of impressions. The king on the spur of the moment, and with the enthusiasm that was characteristic of his oft criticized habit of making hasty decisions, gave very specific instructions that the court painter be summoned forthwith and enjoined to execute a full-length portrait of the young Chinese convert. Shen bowed deeply. He'd been advised when in England to avoid any kind of prostration. It wasn't an English thing. The kissing of feet was equally discouraged. It would be regarded as distinctly Popish. Then, as though in a dream, it was all over.

Shen would reflect later that he'd been presented to two reigning monarchs, a queen in splendid exile, and a relatively long-lived pope.

❧

Thévenot's scholarly correspondent who was anxious to have in hand one of the first copies of the Confucius Sinarum Philosophus went by the name of Thomas Hyde. Hearing of the fine impression Shen had made at court and knowing from his correspondence with Thévenot that he was in possession of the coveted volume, Hyde lost no time in issuing the young man with an invitation. Would Shen be his guest and plan on spending several weeks with him at Oxford? It was, Shen gathered, an academy akin to that in Beijing to which those among the well-born who aspired to the highest rungs of the imperial bureaucracy hoped to be admitted.

Who exactly was Hyde?

Hyde, Shen was told, had achieved eminence in Hebrew and Arabic at Oxford and had, for the past twenty years, held the prestigious position of chief librarian of the Bodleian library. Hyde wasn't just interested in Semitic languages. He was also fascinated by Persian and had made it known that was anxious to add an understanding of Chinese to his remarkable mastery of linguistics. What, Shen had asked, might he be expected to see and do at Oxford? Well, since Hyde was a librarian, he'd get to see and perhaps work in yet another library. That, surely, was an attractive prospect to one who in his youth had not only fallen in love with the temple-like libraries of his native China but had also been privileged to encounter the sacredness of the Vaticana and then that of the Bibliothèque du Roi.

So, whyever not go to Oxford? By stagecoach it was a journey that took but a day. So, on a bright sunny early June morning, Shen with appropriate guidance made his way to the Oxford Arms. It was an inn and busy coaching establishment within a short walk of London's St. Paul's Cathedral. There, holding on to a tightly packed bag that included a copy of the precious Confucius Sinarum Philosophus, he boarded a westward bound horse-drawn coach. It would, he was told, make but one stop before reaching Oxford and that would be at the market town of Wycombe. He was apprehensive, conscious of being a strange sight on this most local of English conveyances. What if he were to run into some kind of trouble? Would he be able to converse with the coachman in Latin?

When, by early evening on the same day, the coach finally reached Oxford it did so on the High Street at the Angel Inn. All Shen could do was join the crowd milling noisily around amid the shouts of porters, lackeys, and coachmen. There he stood, anxious and bemused, holding a card bearing Thomas Hyde's name. Not for long, mercifully because out of the chaos emerged Hyde's most trusted manservant. The Queen's College, where Hyde resided, was but a short walk from the Angel Inn. There he was welcomed by the great man himself, invited to share an evening collation, and before dusk accompanied to the lodgings he was to occupy during his Oxford sojourn. They were close by and within easy reach of Hyde's library.

The very next day, Hyde asked Shen whether he would be interested in learning of the library's history? How could he not be? While still in Paris Thévenot had spoken of Hyde's dedication to books in elegiac terms. For men such as Hyde, libraries had near legendary origins and Shen's Confucian upbringing had taught him that it behooved disciples to listen reverentially to the utterances of their teachers.

An introductory tour was in order and there could be no better qualified guide than Hyde. It was, he assured Shen, one of the finest libraries in Europe but hadn't always been so. It owed its beginnings to a wealthy Duke of Gloucester whose name was Humfrey. He'd collected books well before anyone had heard of Gutenberg's press. They were therefore handwritten and made up of carefully bound costly parchment sheets. On his deathbed he had bequeathed all three hundred of his lovingly collected manuscripts to the scholars at Oxford. They, it so happened, were at the time busy erecting an airy high-ceilinged great hall that was to serve as the university's divinity school. Impressed by the size and value of Duke Humfrey's magnanimous legacy, they took it upon themselves to give it a worthy home by adding an upper floor to what turned out to be a gloriously ornate perpendicular late Gothic building.

Then, more than a century later, disaster struck. Religion had become a source of divisiveness that had disastrously degenerated into mindless violence. There was no easy way of recounting this part of the narrative and here was Hyde a Protestant divine with a doctorate in divinity attempting to do so for the benefit of an aspiring Jesuit who had come to Oxford all the way from China.

Père la Chaise had made Shen aware of Henry VIII's rejection of papal authority. Of course, he had. But there was a yet darker side to the story. Three of Henry VIII's children, each from a different wife, had succeeded him on the throne of England. The first, a son raised as a Protestant, had died before reaching adulthood. The second was Mary who in her intransigent ardor to return England to its Catholic past had ill-advisedly ordered the summary imprisonment and even execution of numerous Protestants. Plagued by ill-health she reigned for only five years. The third was Mary's younger half-sister Elizabeth. She, in an environment rendered toxic by religious extremism and intolerance, abruptly reversed course and appointed commissioners charged with expurgating the realm of anything remotely smacking of Catholicism. Libraries were prime targets. Of the three-hundred manuscripts collected by Humfrey only three escaped being summarily tossed into a raging bonfire. It was a way of visiting righteous revenge. Three years before the Protestant Archbishop of Canterbury, together with two other bishops deemed heretical, had been burnt at a stake erected on a broad thoroughfare within shouting distance of Humfrey's library. The purging was thorough to the point that even the library's shelves were removed. Soon enough the handsome building fell into disrepair.

Shen had his own story to tell. Chinese emperors were known to have committed similar desecrations. Among them was a certain Chin who had reigned some two-thousand years earlier. Being a diehard autocrat brooking no opposition, he had taken an intense and quasi-religious dislike of anything smacking of Confucianism. He'd had Confucian texts rounded up and burnt. For good measure he had likewise done away with uncooperative scholars. He'd reputedly built himself a vast army of life-sized terracotta warriors. His hope was that they'd be available to defend him should those he had persecuted attempt revenge in the hereafter. Hyde, the linguist that he was, was grateful to Shen for informing him that this was the very Chin who was responsible for foreigners erroneously referring to the Middle Kingdom as a country called Chin-a.

So, how did Oxford's library, like a mighty phoenix, rise out of the ashes of Duke Humfrey's ill-fated collection? Hyde, the explainer extraordinaire that he was, couldn't help, in an irrelevant aside, telling Shen about Greek and Egyptian phoenixes. This gratuitous explanation inevitably led to the question of whether the Chinese had equivalent legendary beasts. Well, yes they did but they were more like birds of prophecy encompassing creatively conflicting yin and yang tendencies. All that to say that it had taken next to no time for Hyde and Shen to discover that they both took inordinate pleasure in the recounting of linguistic trivia.

The name of the man who had coaxed the phoenix back to life was Thomas Bodley. He was no duke. His father was a well-to-do Cornish merchant who so abhorred Mary Tudor's Catholicism that he exiled himself together with his family to Protestant Europe. In Geneva, young Thomas came across Protestant luminaries such as Knox and Calvin and being linguistically precocious was taught Latin, Greek, and Hebrew. Following Queen Mary's untimely death, the Bodley family returned to England by which time Thomas was of age to further his studies at Oxford. It was there that he developed a lifelong love affair with books and with the place in which he had been given the opportunity to read them.

That was something Shen had little difficulty relating to. Did Hyde appreciate the extent to which the Chinese formed a deep cultural and emotional attachment to the image-rich characters thanks to which they gave written expression to the wealth of their ancient culture? Well, yes, because Hyde possessed that kind of mind.

Young Bodley was too bright and talented not to have attracted Queen Elizabeth's attention. She entrusted him with delicate diplomatic missions thanks to which he had occasion to travel throughout the European continent within which he had been raised as a child. He made a point of visiting libraries and collections. They were, thanks to Gutenberg's innovation, growing at an unprecedented rate. The queen solicited his advice on matters of state, and he was inevitably drawn to politics. He married late in life and when he did so, it was to a rich widow. On reaching his fiftieth birthday, he decided to withdraw from courtly and political concerns and, accompanied by his monied wife, returned to Oxford.

Why not dedicate his waning years to rebuilding the abandoned library? He did so with gusto. Elizabethans, Hyde explained, were notorious for having made a virtue out of the aggressive pursuit of wealth. When well spent, wealth had a way of bringing to the fore the finer things of life and that included books rare and ancient as well as modern and usefully instructive. The Elizabethans had also set their sights on exploring the wider world and that dovetailed with Bodley's other love which was the art of practicing languages. The more the better! That was not all. What about an aesthetically pleasing building to house all this finery? So, soon enough Bodley was hard at work doing what he'd always wanted to do. Visions, though, in the absence of money are but empty dreams. Well, Bodley had married a rich widow and he and his wife happened to be childless. That helped, no doubt about it, but he also had many friends. His persuasiveness was such that they took pleasure in parting with their money knowing that, in Bodley's care, it would be used to foster elegance and erudition. Those were qualities, they knew instinctively, that would in some measure endure beyond their own rather exiguous and fragile lifespan.

"That", Hyde remarked wistfully to Shen, "is why we love books. We harbor the happy illusion that they prolong our earth-bound existence."

The building of Oxford's new library went ahead and continued after Bodley's death. James I, the grandfather of James II who had welcomed Shen to his court, had by now succeeded Elizabeth as sovereign. The English now referred to themselves as Jacobeans and were even more committed to the finer things of life. Humfrey's venerable but neglected library had by now been meticulously refurbished. Wings were built at both its ends and the one to the East had been designed to blend harmoniously into a new and impressively spacious two-story-high quadrangle. Hyde proudly informed Shen that Bodley had built all this in the hope that it would one day house reading rooms and accommodate one of the most impressive book collections in all of Europe. By the time of Shen's visit all this was solidly in place.

Following the introductory tour and over a lunch of smoked kipper and braised cabbage at the nearby Bear Tavern, Hyde broached the ticklish subject of why he'd invited Shen to Oxford. It was, of course, at Melchisédec Thévenot's suggestion. While in Paris, Shen's command of the subtleties of Chinese and his willingness to be of service to scholars had made a lasting impression. Hyde was one of those librarians who really cared about books and went to great lengths to ensure they were appropriately cataloged

An English Summer

and stacked for easy retrieval. Here was what was of concern to Hyde. He'd gone to considerable trouble gathering the Bodley's Chinese volumes in one place. He'd counted well over a hundred and had not the slightest idea regarding their subject-matter or scholarly value.

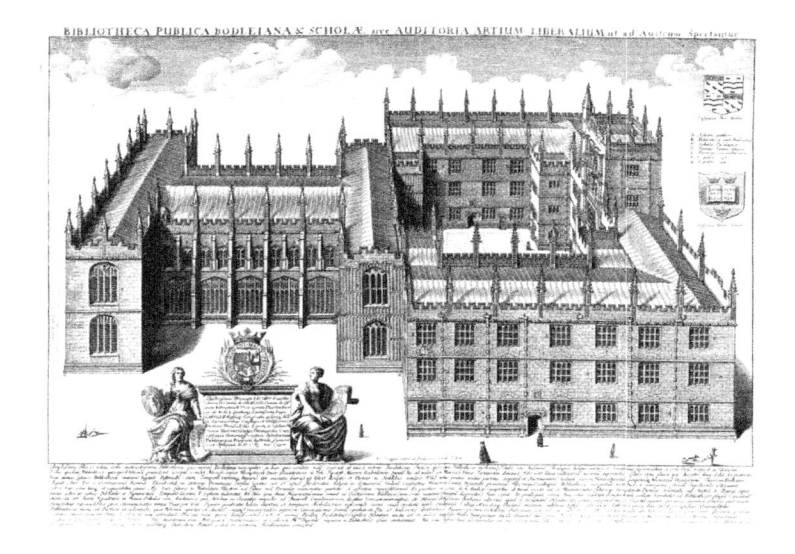

Bodleian with Duke Humfrey's Library above the Divinity School (left facing) and the Schools Quadrangle (right): 1675 English engraving

"What," asked Shen, "was their likely provenance?"

Thomas Bodley had been a builder rather than a cataloger. He'd been only too happy to welcome into his rapidly expanding collection whatever books or book-like objects came his way even if their subject matter was a complete mystery. Hyde commented that the East India Company had received its charter on the last day of 1600 and that since then, British merchants venturing East often brought back all manner of exotic curios including, of course, handsome woodblock printed volumes inscribed in enigmatic Chinese characters.

Would Shen be willing to read through each of those volumes? A time-consuming task, admittedly, but an important one because what Hyde had in mind was to ask Shen to briefly summarize the content of each volume.

"In Latin?" asked Shen.

It needs to be said that during all this time the two men had been conversing in Latin. With lapses into French, that is, and frequent recourse to gesticulation and to jotting down words on a notebook. On arriving in England, Shen had been struck by the fact that the English had their own way of pronouncing Latin.

"Yes and no," had been Hyde's response. What he really wanted Shen to do was to write out a summary of each book's subject matter in carefully calligraphed Chinese characters, then show how each of those characters was voiced in Chinese. Could he please render an approximation of the voicing by using letters of the Latin alphabet? Then, yes, it would be necessary to translate the Chinese summary word for word into Latin. He and Hyde would then decide how to catalog the book. Yes, there were over a hundred volumes. Yes, Shen should plan on spending more than a month in Oxford. Summers were lovely on the river and the English countryside was worth exploring. The pubs would be open, and Shen would get used to the beer. Shen's rooms were in a nearby college and being Catholic he'd appreciate the pre-Reformation monastic-like intimacy of its two rather lovely quadrangles and chapel. It had been founded a few decades before the Fall of Constantinople by the erudite bishop of a northern English city made wealthy by the wool trade.

Hyde was more than a librarian he was also a linguist and to cap it all a taskmaster. Did Hyde realize that Shen was unlikely to know all the characters in each of the hundred volumes? He was only an aspiring scholar. The mastery of Chinese was a lifetime endeavor, and he was still young.

An English Summer

Hyde was not one to take no for an answer. He brushed aside Shen's concerns and as an added incentive mentioned he'd arranged for him to work in one of the carrels of the exquisitely restored Duke Humfrey library. Had he noticed its magnificently decorated coffered high ceiling? It was a setting fit for an emperor. A studious one, that is. Wasn't Kangxi studious? He had to be if the Jesuit Verbiest had been his tutor. Hyde was fiendishly well informed. He must have gathered all this by corresponding with his friend Thévenot. Thévenot had, of course, made it his business to extract as much information as he could from Couplet during the time spent in Paris mutating the Confucian Treatise into the Confucius Sinarum Philosophus.

Hyde had held out yet another incentive, namely lunches at the Bear Tavern. A hefty daily portion of cabbage and kipper with a mug of beer would surely help Shen make light of the task ahead of him. The young man took it all in good part. While still in Paris, he'd been told about English food. It wasn't one of their cultural aspirations, was the way Melchisédec Thévenot had put it. Indeed not, but that didn't mean that Hyde didn't have an intellectual interest in the subject matter. So, he made a point of bringing along a sheaf of paper together with quill and inkpot.

"How do you write 'breakfast' in Chinese? Good! And how about the characters for 'lunch' and 'dinner'…for 'drink'… and could you write out 'snack'? Ah! so the two characters for a snack imply that a tasty morsel 'touches the heart'. How do you say that… 'dim sum'… I like that. Don't forget to write next to each character how it is pronounced. Good! And then add in the Latin translation. Excellent! You'll go down in history as the first person to have taught Chinese at Oxford…at the Bearn Tavern. I'm honored to be the first student!"

Hyde had a hobby-like interest in games such as chess. Within days, Hyde let on that he was writing a treatise exploring the historical and strategic aspects of board games all of which, he asserted,

Shen's Unlikely Journey

were of Persian, Indian or Chinese origins. He'd found a printer in Oxford open to publishing it and given that the subject was of growing interest throughout Europe, he was planning to write the book in Latin. That, Hyde admitted, was yet another reason why he'd invited Shen to Oxford. Hyde was in luck. Shen was an experienced player both of what he referred to as the encirclement game and of traditional Chinese chess. Not a master of the first rank, by any means, but an expert, nonetheless.

Breakfast, lunch, dinner, drink and a snack (dim sum) in Shen's handwriting while at Oxford

An English Summer

Shen was only too happy to oblige. It was generally known that the Japanese Samurai class had become fiendishly addicted to the military aspects of the encirclement game. They called it Go. It was, however, a game so quintessentially reflective of Chinese culture that it was thought to have had legendary origins. Because it was strategically challenging it was regarded as a worthy Confucian and scholarly pursuit and, according to Shen, was even referred to in the Analects. Shen, for Hyde's benefit, jotted down the number of intersecting lines necessary to form a traditional Go board and mentioned what Hyde already knew, namely that the game was played with stubby rounded tokens referred to as stones. Stones, unlike chess pieces, were undifferentiated and therefore of equal value. The white stones were played against the black. Players set out to encircle each other's stones in the hope of capturing them. The size of the board was such that the number of possible moves was virtually infinite, hence the strategic and intellectual challenges involved.

What particularly intrigued Hyde was the concept of an eye. Hard to explain! Players tended to array their stones in groups thereby staking out strategically valuable territory. Groups, however, were vulnerable to being encircled by stones of the opposite color. So long as at least one of the stones in a group had next to it a vacant space, the group itself couldn't be treated as encircled and all its stones remained alive! So, players were challenged to include a vacant space inside each of their groups. That space was the eye that titillated Hyde's curiosity. Shen's explanation was a eureka moment for Hyde. He couldn't contain his excitement as he feverishly wrote up his notes—in Latin, of course!

So much for Go. How about a game or two of Chinese chess? Less time consuming and far more linguistically intriguing. Of course! Hyde warmed to the idea. It assured him of yet another chapter in his book. Shen, however, would have to produce a board and the necessary tokens. Making a board was the easiest part. It was almost square consisting of nine lines across and ten lengthways. A river ran down the middle separating the warring camps. Shen drew two short diagonal lines at each end thereby designating the four squares that were the symbolic palaces wherein dwelt the generals.

The difficulty lay in producing the wooden circular tokens. They were no mere stones. Hyde suggested a visit to the Bodleian's carpentry shop. This was an unusual request given that the head carpenter was more attuned to supplying Hyde with ever larger quantities of shelves. That said he was only too happy to meet the challenge.

"There are sixteen to a side," Shen specified, "so, that's a total of thirty-two but we'll need a few extra just in case."

The carpenter didn't speak Latin, so Hyde served as interpreter. To Hyde's delight Shen then went to work with brush and ink carefully inscribing in his best calligraphic style each little circular wood token with a character. Specific Chinese characters, he explained, were used to designate generals, chariots, cannons, horses, soldiers, scholarly advisors and, of course, elephants. Elephants were the heavy-duty pieces that, according to Shen, had given the game its Chinese name of Elephant Chess. Shen used black ink for one set of opposing armies and red for the other. To Hyde this was linguistic heaven. He took copious notes peppering Shen with questions. How was this character pronounced? Which strokes represented its radical?

The two men, England's foremost authority on Oriental languages and librarian extraordinaire and the young aspiring Chinese scholar from Nanjing, then spent the long evenings that so characterized English summers playing the game. They did so in Hyde's commodious rooms overlooking the fellows' quad of The Queen's College. At first Shen let Hyde win but since his opponent was no slouch and aspired to be a consummate puzzle master and strategist, the games in no time at all took on genuine competitive ardor.

"By the way," Shen remarked one evening, "there's a reason why we Chinese refer to the piece that by rights should be a king as a general. Just like Buddhism, chess came to us from India, and Indians always had plenty of kingdoms and kings. It's just that our emperors have never taken kindly to competitors. So, our forebears were instructed by imperial decree to play with generals rather than kings."

"Sounds strangely familiar," Hyde exclaimed. "Did this inspire Confucius to formulate any of his pithy aphorisms?" The chess players burst out laughing.

On his arrival in Oxford, Shen had dutifully handed over to Hyde the copy of the Confucius Sinarum Philosophus he had brought with him from Paris. Hyde was already halfway through the Preface.

"Is there a reason," Hyde asked, "why so much space has been devoted to the Yi Jing?"

"Well," replied Shen, "isn't the Yi Jing all about constant change, chance, and the mysterious interplay of opposing forces? Aren't those the very aspects of our existence that we encounter symbolically when playing games such as Go and chess?"

"Beware," exclaimed Hyde, "you're turning into a philosopher. It's a dangerous calling but it will make you into a good Jesuit."

"You're not the first one, Master Thomas, to have made me aware of the dangers that confront those who dare voice their inner thoughts."

Hyde wasn't only interested in games. He had another academic publication in mind. What units of measure did the Chinese use when dealing with dimensions and weights? Yes, it would also be in Latin, but why such an interest in ferreting out how different cultures had dealt with the serious business of weighing and measuring the goods they were increasingly exchanging with each other?

It was Hyde's turn to give a philosophically tinged answer." They are simply another form of communication. So, we linguists shouldn't ignore them."

Hyde was once more in luck. Shen knew a good deal about how Nanjing peasants and street hawkers weighed out their cabbages and measured swigs of rice wine. In his youth he'd taken great pleasure in accompanying his grandmother and her following of servants as she bargained and wended her way through the city's many markets.

<hr />

By the end of July Shen was almost done with working his way through the intimidatingly large stack of woodblock printed Chinese volumes Hyde had charged him with annotating and classifying. So, he'd soon be returning to London. Hyde, one evening and after the two men had supped at the Bear Tavern, mentioned that he'd written to a friend who lived in London suggesting he invite Shen to pay him a visit. The friend's name was Robert Boyle. Shen might not have heard of him, but he was a well-known physicist. This would be an opportunity for him to meet one of the founding members of The Royal Society which, together with the even more recently instituted French Académie Royale des Sciences of which Thévenot was a member, were among Europe's leading scientific societies.

Hyde went on to comment that these emerging learned societies bore witness to the fact that scientific knowledge was increasingly seen as making a significant and essential contribution to the progress of nations. It was no accident that this awareness had stimulated interest in China. It was a sobering fact that Europeans had only very recently become aware not only of China's geographic importance but also that its population far outstripped that of any other kingdom. Then there were thorny questions raised by the realization that its culture and linguistic tradition stretched farther back than had hitherto been thought possible.

"Just how compatible is the biblical narrative with the remarkable antiquity of China's recorded history?" exclaimed Hyde.

By this time the two men had arrived at Hyde's rooms in college. As they sat in commodious armchairs before an unlit fireplace stacked with logs—it was a warm July evening—an elderly and slightly hunched-over manservant came by with a silver tray bearing a cut crystal flask of decanted port wine.

This was, Shen fully realized, a subject of consuming interest to men such as Hyde and Thévenot. No wonder Couplet had insisted on having his chronology added to the Confucius Sinarum Philosophus. It raised a question in his own mind and he thought fit to ask it.

"There's something I don't understand that perhaps you could help explain. While in London, I was asked several times to say something in Chinese…not recite a prayer which is what was often expected of me in Rome and even in Paris. No, I was asked to say out loud something that is ancient and traditionally Chinese. I like to oblige, and it so happens that I've composed a little poem that is based on Emperor Fuxi's evocation of the eight principles underlying the Yi Jing. It refers to heaven for inspiration…to a lake that encompasses the placid quietness of joy…to fire since warmth sustains our bodies and encourages us to act…to thunder that otherworldly energy that arouses our senses…to the wind that encircles us…to water that symbolizes all that is deep and life-giving…to mountains thanks to which we can aspire to stillness and meditation…and lastly to the earth that feeds and comforts us. That's it. People just listen, and I smile. I'm puzzled."

"Your response Master Michael has much to commend it. My guess is that you were asked to do this because you are the only Chinese person these people have ever met and most likely will ever meet. They've also heard that your mother tongue, being tonal and monosyllabic and relying on a highly imaged script, is startlingly and provocatively different…perhaps even otherworldly. So, naturally, they want to listen to its sounds. It's important to them because there's a theory going around that there was once a single divinely inspired universal language from which all others are derived."

"That, I suppose, raises the question of how Chinese fits into that picture? Yes, now I recall that Father Philippe and your friend Sieur Thévenot often talked about this in Paris. They said, if I remember correctly, that some people believe that with the right key, the Chinese language, despite its apparent complexity, could become intelligible to everyone and therefore reveal itself to be universal."

"You're highly perceptive, Master Michael. Yes, that's an idea that's also floating around these parts and it gets to be even stranger. There's a fellow I've met who, despite being trained as an architect and knowing virtually no Chinese, argues that Chinese was the language universally spoken…until the linguistic chaos that followed when we humans foolishly imagined we could build a tower reaching into the heavens. There are people who want to believe those kinds of fancifully extravagant stories…stories that help them escape from the drudgery of daily living… and because he's vocal and persuasive, he's built up quite a following. He's even suggested that Noah visited China before the Great Flood and that the arc itself might have been made in China."

"Ah! So, some people want to hear Chinese spoken in the hope of discerning a glimmer of what a pre-Babel world might have been like."

"I advise Master Michael a hefty dose of skepticism. We librarians, being by trade collectors of diverse opinions, would do well to be followers of the Greek philosopher Pyrrhus and he, for your information, made a point of avoiding rash judgments. Need I say more? I'm going to enjoy a little more port wine. May I replenish your glass?"

Hyde went on to mention the startling fact that there was no record of any Chinese having traveled as extensively within Europe as Shen had? That's why he couldn't help being an object of intense curiosity. Of course, people wanted to hear him speak his native language. His very presence was a sign of just how much the world was changing.

Hyde's comments put Shen in a reflective mood. Yes, of course, change was in the air. His own emperor Kangxi had taken Father Verbiest as a tutor. He was an ambitious ruler who wanted to pursue expansionary policies. He wanted to see China's influence expand beyond its present borders. He had the foresight to recognize the relevance of technical knowledge in achieving that goal. There was good reason to believe that the young emperor's interest in mathematics went far beyond the traditional Chinese concern with Confucian-inspired astronomy. Hadn't the emperor made a point of requesting the presence of a group of mathematicians trained in diverse aspects of western science? Wasn't this reflective of a growing awareness in China of the very same trend of which Hyde spoke and which had led to the recent founding of those scientific academies? So, naturally, Shen wanted to know about Robert Boyle and what he had done to make him so famous.

Boyle, the way Hyde put it, was part of an emerging movement that placed great emphasis on understanding the fundamental principles that gave rise to observable natural phenomena. Unlike sages of the past, scientists like Boyle didn't believe in sitting in their studies and theorizing. They had developed a motto that, roughly translated from Latin, was "don't take anyone's word for it". In other words "go out and observe for yourself." They treated mathematics as though it were a language thanks to which they could precisely describe what they had personally observed through experimentation. So, Hyde explained, this man Boyle wanted to know more about the nature of air. Sages had been speculating about it since early antiquity and had developed all kinds of fancy theories they took pleasure in arguing about.

That approach wasn't good enough for Boyle so he, together with a friend who was a high-class tinkerer, devised a machine the sole purpose of which was to carry out an experiment. It was a precisely engineered pump.

"Hard to believe," said Hyde, "but here we are drinking my best Portuguese imported port wine in my comfortable rooms in The Queen's College and these two men did their experiment in a shabby lodging they had rented literally across the street from where we are sitting."

They figured they could use the pump to compress a given volume of air into a smaller space. So, they reckoned that the more they pressed down on the pump the smaller the space occupied by the air and the greater the pressure it was capable of exerting. They wanted to know whether they could use a mathematical formula to describe that relationship with great precision and thereby establish a fundamental rule of nature that would be universally applicable. The pump was only the beginning. They linked it to a specially shaped glass tube partly filled with mercury. Because mercury is a weighty metal that has the unique characteristic of also being a liquid they used it to devise a way of measuring the changing pressure of the air as they varied the space it occupied.

"These two men are geniuses," Hyde exclaimed enthusiastically, "but the greater significance of their story is that they belong to a group of similarly motivated scientists. The others instantly recognized the usefulness of knowing this mathematically formulated natural law and began to apply the very same methodology to other areas of scientific inquiry. They were motivated to write each other letters and publish articles in the scientific journals that are today proliferating all over Europe. Thévenot, by the way, as a member of the Académie des Sciences is very much part of that new way of exchanging ideas. So is a Dutch friend of his who by experimenting with mechanical devices has revolutionized timekeeping by perfecting a pendulum clock."

Shen interrupted. He knew all about that clock. He'd seen one in Paris. Thévenot was indeed proud of his friendship with the inventor and had one ticking away in the rue Vivienne. His name, Shen recalled, was Christiaan Huygens. Another of those clever Dutchmen he kept meeting.

"The great thing about Boyle's experiment," Hyde continued, "is that it established the principle that experimentation is fundamental to scientific progress. If you can't devise an experiment to validate a theory, it can't be relied on. Not everyone agrees, mind you. Many still cling to the brilliantly devised theoretical framework derived by the Greek sage Aristotle. It's hard to admit that someone can be both brilliant and wrong. Especially if what is held out as truth has been revered as such over centuries. Time has a sacralizing effect on assumed truths. It makes it hard to let go of them."

"So, we Chinese have work to do," Shen observed wistfully.

"Oh! We all do. Just give it time. Your Confucius was no slouch. Besides while we were still worshiping Aristotle, you were doing far more useful things such as inventing papermaking and developing mass woodblock printing. I don't think we should thank you for discovering the chemical formula for gunpowder but that's something else, I suppose, you can take credit for. I heard it said only the other day that it was you Chinese who invented the compass and that it was thanks to the compass that we Europeans found a way of steering our ships in your direction. There's irony to that, surely. You never know who is going to benefit from what you invent. It may well one day be used against you."

Shen was an eager listener, so Hyde thought fit to mention that Boyle's experimenter went by the name of Hooke.

"This Hooke went on to use his tinkering ability in other areas. He discovered that optical lenses could be assembled to magnify imaginably small objects. He used them to make the startling discovery that living things were made up of a mysterious agglomeration of tiny blobs. He called them cells because he thought of them as diminutive walled-in spaces. Odd, isn't it, that this man Hooke made his discovery by experimenting with much the same lenses that Galileo had used to make telescopes? It's just that Galileo looked heavenward and observed the moons of the planet Jupiter. Many, including your pope, wished he hadn't or at the very least kept his thoughts to himself. It was upsetting to those God-Fearing geocentric traditionalists. Inertia they say is a powerful force. Too bad! Have you Jesuits told Emperor Kangxi about Galileo?"

Shen just chuckled. This reminded him of how back in Paris, Thévenot, who prided himself on being a philosophe, took wicked pleasure, whenever the opportunity presented itself, in provoking Couplet.

There were other names Hyde thought Shen should be aware of if he was going to meet Boyle. They also were members of this Royal Society. There was an astronomer turned architect who was responsible for designing the dome that was presently being erected atop St. Paul's cathedral in London. Shen had caught sight of it before boarding his coach at the Oxford Arms. That was Christopher Wren and then there was Isaac Newton who had just published a treatise that was causing quite a stir. Hyde hadn't read it yet. His impression was that it was heavy going. He'd however been told on good authority that the book's purpose was to demonstrate that mathematics was the language best suited to precisely describing the phenomena of motion and gravity. These were rules, Newton had apparently set out to argue convincingly, that applied universally. To everything! From the motion of the earth around the sun to the way a ripe apple falls off a tree.

Shen took note.

Then Hyde, as though seeking to deliberately steer the conversation toward a more controversial topic, evoked the role of the Jesuits in China. The Bodleian Library had copies of Ricci's remarkable journal as edited by Trigault. Of course, it did. Hyde had also been shown the strikingly detailed maps of China produced by Martino Martini together with their accompanying descriptions. These maps had contributed to the increasing awareness of the importance of China in a world with expanding horizons. No doubt about it. Martini must have been brilliant, and Shen mentioned that he was the very man whose lecture at Louvain had so inspired Couplet and Ferdinand Verbiest, the astronomer extraordinaire who had Emperor Kangxi's ear back in the Forbidden City.

Portrait of Thomas Hyde holding Chinese inscribed scroll at the Bodleian Library

Yes, Hyde couldn't help being impressed by all that the Jesuits had achieved, and he was of course devoting as much time as he could to reading the Confucius Sinarum Philosophus that Shen had so kindly brought with him from Paris. He was grateful for that. He didn't by the way agree with everything that was said in the rather lengthy Preface. Well, Shen, responded, nor did he but then he was a mere aspiring scholar and in no position to challenge his superiors. Hyde didn't necessarily agree with such expressions of humility but that was a topic for another day.

What was frustrating Hyde and what he really wanted to get to, was to argue that it was high time that others, the Protestant English in particular, begin taking China seriously and do their own pioneering work. Hyde quite frankly resented the Jesuit stranglehold on the information coming out of China.

At this, Shen tactfully remarked that while he sympathized with Hyde's frustrations it didn't make sense to blame the Jesuits for having attempted what no one else had even thought of doing. It was a risky business. Look at how Schall had been mistreated and consider that the Jesuits were willing to devote their whole life to the task. They did so aware that they were unlikely to ever make the return voyage to Europe. And then it wasn't as if the Jesuits were having an easy time of it. On the one hand they were being blamed for paying too much attention to Chinese traditional rituals and on the other they were frustratingly aware their presence in China was dependent on their demonstrating that they were useful. Useful to the extent that they were keeping the Chinese informed regarding all this scientific progress Hyde was so enthused about.

So, it was Shen's turn to voice frustrations. Hyde had mentioned the mathematicians the Sun King had sent to Emperor Kangxi. Of course, Hyde was resentful. It's not as if the English and the French weren't intensely wary of each other. Shen had by now spent enough time in Europe to be aware of the intensity of their rivalry. Did Hyde realize that the latest news was that rather than having arrived in Beijing, the Sun King's mathematicians were stranded in Siam? How many mathematicians did Hyde know right here in Oxford who would be willing to put up with such dangers and hardships?

The fineness of Hyde's port-wine—it was Portuguese from Catholic Oporto—contributed significantly to restoring peace, good humor, and academic congeniality to the evening's discussion. By the end of it all the two men were discussing why it was that in the ancient and venerable game of Go, black plays first unless it waives that privilege in exchange for a few extra stones. Was that a fair exchange? It was a weighty matter that commanded their undivided attention well into the late night hours.

Arrangements had been made for Shen, on his return to London from Oxford, to visit the court painter whom James II had charged with executing his full-length portrait. That such a portrait should have been commissioned by the king was recognized as being the most unusual of honors. The painter whose name was Godfrey Kneller was German born but was by now well known to London society. He had been appointed to his present official post some eight years earlier by King Charles II. He had reputedly studied under Rembrandt and, not known for his modesty, made much of having perfected his art both in Venice and in Rome. He was still in his forties and his willingness to make a virtue out of producing large numbers of commissioned portraits had already made him a wealthy man. Shen was awed to learn that only a few years earlier, Kneller had journeyed to Paris for the specific purpose of painting none other than the Sun King.

Shen was instructed to visit the great man's studio. It was in a spacious house overlooking the piazza at Covent Garden. The piazza was a large open square to the west of which was an imposing recently built church resembling a Roman temple. Both church and square had been designed in the years following Charles II's restoration by a famed classical architect whose name, Shen was informed, was Inigo Jones. The square owed its Italianate name to the handsome style of the tall rows of commodious houses built to the north and south and whose upper floors were designed to allow for columned arcades open to the public. Covent Garden was an attractive and lively London neighborhood. It was distant enough from the medieval city to have survived the Great Fire. It had therefore become a regular gathering place for hawkers and merchants selling fruits, herbs, roots, and flowers. Mingling among the crowds were enterprising buskers and performers eager to earn a living by displaying their animated puppets. The daily walk toward and around the piazza afforded Shen much pleasure. There were spots along the way where he would make a point pausing to take it all in and do so by leaning unobtrusively against a shaded column.

It was Kneller's habit to delegate to the up-and-coming aspiring artists in his employ much of the time-consuming work required to portray his formally clad sitters in whatever elaborate setting and posture befitted their rank. He reserved to himself the final inspired details and naturally did his sitters the honor of personally committing their facial features to otherwise near completed canvases. So, as might be expected, his studio was a busy place. Cynics were wont to observe that wig wearing among his gentlemanly clientele had further minimized the need for Kneller's personal involvement. The wigs had become standardized accoutrement. So, what about Shen's portrait?

Well, for one, Shen was no wig-wearer and Kneller was not about to entrust to an underling the delicate task of painting the splendid gown embroidered by Candida Xu in Shanghai. The more so since the king had decreed that it was in that very gown that Shen was to be portrayed. Kneller was also taken by the young man's demeanor.

An English Summer

This was no ordinary commission. There were times when the great man took it upon himself to meet a particular challenge and execute a painting fully reflective of his genius. This was one of them. It was one thing to make money out of satisfying the needs of wealthy courtiers and quite another to foster his artistic reputation. So, come September, Shen was summoned to regularly make his way to Kneller's studio. Once there, he was invariably requested to sit in a comfortable chair set discretely away from the bustle and enjoined to wait patiently. With luck the great man would in time come sweeping by, brush in hand, gaze dramatically and intently at his sitter and go to work on the imposingly large canvas propped up on a nearby easel. The arrangement was such that it afforded Shen the even greater pleasure of observing the courtly flurry whipped up by the many gentlemen present together with the fetchingly dressed chattering ladies accompanying them.

Then there was the visit Shen was to pay to the famed Robert Boyle. By the time the invitation had come, it was already October. Boyle lived in a fine house along Pall Mall. The house belonged to his sister Katherine. She'd acquired it thanks to the family's considerable wealth. Pall Mall had become one of London's most prestigious neighborhoods. It was all due to the extensive rebuilding that had taken place following Charles II's restoration to the throne, and to the fact that it bordered St. James Park. Its name derived from pallamaglio, a popular ball and mallet game of Italian origin played in the nearby park. At Pall Mall's western end was the palace of St. James. A stroll across the park in a southerly direction led to Westminster Abbey and a walker turning more to the east would soon enough reach the majestic buildings that were readily recognizable as forming part of the palace of Whitehall many of which overlooked the Thames.

Boyle's sister Katherine was also intellectually inclined and had caused the house to be furnished with an elaborate laboratory designed by none other than her brother's old friend and fellow experimenter at Oxford, Robert Hooke. At the time of Shen's visit, Boyle was 60 and no longer in the best of health. He had become something of a recluse and was notably choosy about who he deigned to meet with. He wasn't one to suffer fools gladly.

Shen's nervousness was understandable. Beyond what Hyde had already told him in Oxford, he'd been warned that Boyle was known to be an insatiably curious polymath and relentless interrogator for whom no subject was beyond his ken. In fact, the young man was cordially welcomed by both Boyle and his sister. Yes, Boyle did ask Shen how many Chinese characters he'd mastered, and how many he hoped to know by the time he reached the age of wisdom and enlightened understanding. His sister also wanted to know to what degree characters in current use differed from those with which philosophers of antiquity such as Confucius, Mencius and Laozi had expressed themselves. Shen was only too happy to oblige, and he was relieved to note that since his time at Oxford in Hyde's company, his Latin was not only more fluent, but that he was also having less difficulty comprehending the strangeness of the way the English intoned it.

Would, Boyle asked Shen, like to ask him a question of his own? Yes, Shen would. He'd been told of how Boyle took pleasure in speculating that machines would in time be capable of flying through the air like birds and perhaps even ply the oceans without being at the mercy of winds and currents. So, when might such miracles come about? And then what message Boyle might like to have him carry back with him to China.

"Tell them," Boyle said with hardly repressed enthusiasm, "that it's just a matter of time. Those who experiment enough will get there and you can add that nothing good ever comes out of holding on to unproven theories."

That was the parting shot. Shen had indeed been told about how Boyle had set out to debunk Aristotelian dogma that held that all substances were composed of earth, water, fire, and air. Shen was no less aware of belonging to a culture that placed emphasis on the interplay of five forces, that also included those of earth, water, and fire. Those forces, while not used to explain the composition of substances, were nonetheless held to influence vital cycles such as those determining the courses of heavenly bodies, of human affairs and of living bodies.

Time perhaps to rethink concepts hallowed by the passage of time. Boyle's experimental approach had inclined him to the view that matter was in fact built up from combinations of rudimentary particles or corpuscles. Shen was reminded of his conversations with Thévenot in Paris and then with Hyde regarding the Yi Jing. Might it be possible to account for the complexity of nature by thinking of it in terms of an infinity of combinations that could be achieved by simply juxtaposing a negative and a positive… a yin and a yang… a black and a white counter in the game of Go? Shen was grateful to Thomas Hyde for having introduced him to Boyle and to his gifted sister.

Godfrey Kneller had done his magic. James II had approvingly reviewed his masterpiece and ordered an unassuming but handsomely robust frame befitting the sitter's uplifting spiritual gaze. The portrait was, at the king's suggestion, to be referred to as The Chinese Convert. It was ready to be transported to Windsor Castle where the king would direct the exact place at which it was to be hung.

Shen continued to correspond with Hyde. Insatiably curious, the great man kept peppering him with questions relating to Chinese weights as well as soliciting his insights into opening Go strategies. Shen was asked to attend London dinners and other social occasions deemed useful to promote awareness of the China missions. He did so dutifully and also answered questions posed by those curious enough to have begun reading the now more readily available copies of the Confucius Sinarum Philosophus. It was, however, time to move on. Should he and Spinola return to Paris or was it still Couplet's intention to join them in London so that all three might at long last board a ship bound for Lisbon? Even Spinola, cordial and congenial as ever, was growing visibly frustrated,

Then, just a few weeks before Christmas, the welcome news reached Shen and Spinola that Couplet had likewise accomplished that which he had set out to do. Confucius Sinarum Philosophus was being read among the Parisian intellectuals of the day and in fact beyond the borders of France reaching luminaries such as Gottfried Leibniz in faraway Leipsic. And, yes, the corrected galleys of Histoire d'une dame chrétienne de la Chine had been delivered to the printer. Couplet, following a brief return to his native Mechlin and a visit to his beloved Louvain, had secured a Channel crossing and arrived in London in time to celebrate Christmas.

By the end of March, the three men were ready to embark on the last stage of their European journey. There were frequent sailings linking the Port of London to Lisbon. Their frequency was attributable to a political and commercial alliance that went back to the 14th century. The English, as Shen knew from his Oxford sojourn, had taken a liking to port wine, and wool from the British Isles was popular with the Portuguese. Then there was money to be made at both ends. The English did so by trading in the goods flooding into Lisbon from Portugal's far-flung colonial enclaves, and most especially from Brazil. And then, not so long ago, James II's elder brother Charles II had married Catherine of Braganza. It was she who had famously helped the English East India Company establish itself in India by handing over Portuguese held Bombay as part of her dowry.

The three men were packed and ready to go.

Confucius says:

In the ceremonies of mourning, it is better that there be deep sorrow than in minute attention to observances.

Things that are past, it is needless to blame.

Analects III

If a man takes no thought about what is distant, he will find sorrow near at hand.

Analects XV

It is said in the Book of Poetry: What needs no display is virtue.

Doctrine of the Mean

IX
Lisbon
1688 to 1691

*T*he tall-masted ship Shen, Couplet and Spinola had boarded at the Billingsgate wharf just south of Thames Street and within sight of London Bridge, docked in Lisbon in April of 1688. It was then that Shen became aware of the reality that his journey had now taken him to a very different place.

Each of the three men faced a set of very different challenges.

Couplet had hoped to board a Portuguese carrack bound for Macao via Goa, but he was out of luck. The convoy making up that year's Carreira da India had already left Lisbon. He soon found out, however, that he faced a far more serious impediment to his return to China. He was notified by the Portuguese authorities administering the Padroado that an authorization for the following year's spring sailing, namely that of 1689, would not be forthcoming. What had gone amiss? Couplet knew that by subscribing to the oath of subjugation demanded of him by the Propaganda in Rome, he had taken on an enormous risk. He was now being made to pay an exorbitantly high price for having done something that in Rome was expected of him. To complicate matters even further his compatriot Charles de Noyelle, the Order's superior general who had encouraged him to publish Confucius Philosophus Sinarum under Louis XIV's patronages and then return to China via Lisbon, had died while he and Shen were still in Paris. Couplet was getting older, and he was aware of his increasing physical frailty. He was desperate to get back to China while still able to do so. China was his raison d'être. He felt trapped.

Shen faced no such problem. Before dying, Charles de Noyelle had made the necessary arrangements for him to be enrolled in Lisbon's Jesuit novitiate. It was a small step taken to placate the Portuguese. Sadly, it had done nothing to alleviate Couplet's predicament. Shen took up residence in the novitiate shortly after arriving in Lisbon. He was ready to join the class of novices that had been convened for the late summer.

Cotovia Novitiate in Lisbon: Late 17th century Portuguese engraving

The novitiate had been built some fifty years earlier and overlooked a large well planted olive grove set on a hill. The Lisboans had two names for this lovely hill. They referred to it as Monte

Olivete or Cotovia which is the Portuguese word for a lark. It offered pleasing distant views and yet was close enough to the city to be within sight of São Roque, Lisbon's Jesuit mother church. The novitiate was built in a Baroque architectural style with which Shen, having spent a year in Rome, was by now familiar. He knew full well that it was a Jesuit-inspired style and was designed to give an overall impression of classically restrained harmony and elegance to a large building.

Shen's challenges were of a very different nature to Couplet's. He'd now been absent from his native China for almost seven years and he, naturally enough, experienced moments of intense homesickness. Would he ever again walk the streets of Nanjing and be reunited with his family? Also, the excitement of the journey had given way to the sobering reality that he now faced a course of intensive study requiring him to achieve fluency in Portuguese—in addition that is to the working knowledge of Latin he had so painstakingly acquired over the years. He would also be living and studying under intentionally austere conditions in the close proximity of complete strangers. He'd already crossed into his thirties, seen more of the world than most of his fellow humans could expect to experience in a lifetime and his classmates would be young and brash. Not all would see in him one who having come from a distant land was to be welcomed and honored. Others, surely, would give in to the all-too-human tendency to bully and belittle those thought of as different. These were things he and Couplet talked over whenever they met and conversed in the novitiate's exiguous and spartanly furnished parlor. Shen increasingly looked forward to these occasions as an opportunity to speak in his native Chinese and relieve his deeply felt homesickness.

On arriving in Lisbon, Spinola announced that he had business in Rome, unexpectedly so it seemed, and that instead of waiting until the following spring for a passage to China, he'd be on his way to the Eternal City. Maybe that wasn't, after all, so surprising, Couplet had remarked to Shen. Spinola's zealous and ambitious nature had already come to his superiors' notice. Wasn't that why he'd been chosen, presumably by both de Noyelle and Père la Chaise, to attend the nuncio's episcopal ordination in London? Spinola was surely up to something.

In his distress, Couplet had found refuge within a Jesuit residence and being by nature an assiduous correspondent, took to letter writing. His letters were addressed mostly to those who in France, Germany and beyond had made a start of reading the Confucius Sinarum Philosophus and knowing him to be holed up in Lisbon had taken the opportunity to engage him in an extended academic discussion. Then there was his Histoire d'une dame chrétienne de la Chine, his eulogy dedicated to Candida Xu, that, to his great satisfaction, had been enthusiastically received and commented on not only in Paris but also in other capitals. He'd heard word from Madrid that plans were being made for a Spanish edition. Would he be willing to travel to Madrid? His superiors, knowing that nothing would give him more pleasure, had readily acceded to his wish.

The year went past quickly enough and by October of 1689 news came through that Pope Innocent XI had died. Shen was saddened. This was the pope whose feet he'd kissed and who had thanked him as well as Couplet for having had the courage and dedication to affront the many perils facing those bridging the great chasm separating China from the West.

Then, in the spring of 1690, the second year of Shen's residence in the Lisbon novitiate, further news came out of Rome. The new pope who'd adopted the name of Alexander VIII had taken a bold decision. He'd decreed that China should have two bishops—one in Beijing and the other in Nanjing. His intention was to broker a truce with the Portuguese by placing the new bishoprics nominally within Lisbon's jurisdiction. The move, inevitably, was seen by the Propaganda as a regrettable compromise weakening Rome's control over the China missions and prolonging the age-old Church-versus-state jurisdictional conflict that was at the root of much ecclesiastical intrigue. The priest in Nanjing in charge of administering the missions in southern China was a native of Fujian who although a Dominican—he'd been converted by Spanish friars based in Manila—was liked and well-regarded by the China Jesuits. He was now, as a consequence of Pope Alexander's decision, a bishop and would go down in history as the first Chinese to be so named. Given, however, that he had not only reached his 80th year but was also in poor health, it made sense for the pope to appoint a successor bishop.

Couplet at first thought it was a prank, a lighthearted spoof, but no, it wasn't. Spinola was the one named successor bishop of Nanjing…that's right…Spinola, who hadn't even taken his last and fourth vow as a Jesuit…who was only 35…only three years older than Shen…and irony of ironies, Nanjing was Shen's birthplace. Couplet was in a state of disbelief.

The news was real enough because before long Couplet heard from Spinola. Of course, Spinola was now in a position to help Couplet get back to China. Good news, indeed, but Couplet would have to wait. Spinola had embarked on a tour of Europe hoping to recruit a group of seasoned yet still physically vigorous Jesuits for the China missions. He needed Couplet. Spinola had never been to China and the little Chinese he knew he'd learned from Shen on the fly. Spinola wouldn't have assembled his recruits until the spring of 1692. That was two years from now and he wanted Couplet to be part of the voyage. Only Couplet could teach these men Chinese and prepare them for what lay ahead. How could Couplet refuse? Anyway, how else was he going to get back to China?

❖

By the early spring of 1691, Shen had spent almost three years in Cotovia. He was given his own piece of good news in that he was now deemed ready to take his first vows. He did so in the company of his classmates in the church of São Roque in the heart of Lisbon. It was reputedly one of the earliest Jesuit churches built anywhere. Couplet was present and it was the most moving of occasions. After the ceremony the two men lit a votive candle dedicated to Shen's ancestors and another in memory of Couplet's mother who had died too young for her to tell him of her love for him. To Shen the candles appeared as smoldering incense sticks set upon the altar in the great hall of his Nanjing home.

The other good news was that Shen would without further delay be boarding a carrack bound for Goa where, at one of the Order's most prestigious seminaries, he would for several years be receiving a thorough grounding in philosophy. Philosophy was, of course, a vitally important component of the rigorous and lengthy curriculum to which aspiring Jesuits were required to subject themselves. India's Malabar Coast would be the midpoint and obligatory stopover on his long journey back home.

That evening Couplet treated Shen to a glorious dish of flaked cod mingled with egg, chickpeas, onions, and olives. Lisboans had a name for it—Bacalhau à Brás. More tears were shed. It was an occasion that brought back memories of that evening five years earlier spent in a Roman tavern as guests of the now departed and much missed Charles de Noyelle.

There was something Couplet wanted to tell Shen, a parting and fatherly piece of advice.

"Michael, I want you to promise me something. The last time you and I gazed on your homeland was on that early misty December morning more than nine years ago when the Santo António sailed out of Macao. Not in my wildest dreams could I have imagined where this journey would take us. You realize, don't you, that you have lived more richly than any emperor? Well, yes, I'm glad you do. Allow me to go even further and suggest that even Confucius would have reason to envy you. Yours has been the most memorable of journeys. You agree? Good! So, here's what you are going to promise me. When you get back to China, tell your story. It's a story that needs to be told. You'll be the first among your countrymen to have such a story to tell. I'm proud of you beyond words."

There followed an emotional parting at the quayside of Lisbon's sheltered harbor at the mouth of the mighty Tagus River. Spring, as Couplet knew only too well, was the preferred departure time for the ships of the Carreira da India. The hope was that by leaving early in the season the ships would encounter favorable winds as they rounded the Cape of Good Hope. Each March and April, Lisbon and its port were at their busiest.

Couplet had every reason to hope this would be the last year of his exile so that, God willing, he and Shen would meet again in Goa. From Goa, Couplet, together with Spinola, would continue on to China and he would, naturally, do his utmost to visit Shen's family in Nanjing. He would bear the good tidings of the young man's remarkable journey and of his success in mastering the subtleties of Thomistic and Platonic philosophy in Goa's most prestigious seminary. It was the least Couplet could do. He would be Shen's long-hoped-for messenger.

Lisbon's harbor at the mouth of the Tagus: Late 16th century German-Dutch engraving

Shen's voyage began auspiciously enough. The winds were fair and there was every reason to hope that his ship would round the Cape of Good Hope by June, thereby reaching the midpoint of the East African coast not later than August. August was the best month at which to catch the southwesterly monsoon winds which mariners relied on for that last and crucial leg of the voyage that entailed sailing across the Indian Ocean toward Goa. There was tenseness to the rounding of the Cape that went beyond the skill and the luck required to steer a steady course. After three months at sea, food rations tended to turn rancid and the drinking water had a way of taking on a stale, almost sour, taste. Some of the men sickened. There was an anguishing unpredictability to the onset of the fevers. At first only a few members of the crew were stricken, but then the fever spread to some of the passengers huddled around the hammocks on the main deck and in time, even to a number of those fortunate enough to have cabins in the forecastle. The heat seemed to have intensified making the presence of rats, lice, and other bugs all the more irritating and ominous.

Shen knew that the fevers were most often preceded by chills, headaches, and aching muscles. It could, of course, be dysentery, in which case the ignominy was concentrated in a man's gut, but the fevers could also come accompanied by an irrepressible itching that was then followed by the appearance of a pestilent red rash. The rash had a way of spreading from a man's back to the rest of his aching body.

Shen wasn't sure at first but then he could no longer wish it away. It was the rash; intense and unforgiving. Some of the men had recovered and there was hope still since the ship was, at the most, ten days from Mozambique, but then his condition worsened. He was propped up in a bunk in the corner of an improvised sick bay on the main deck. He asked to be given the Eucharist one more time after which he received the last anointing. His mind remained disconcertingly alert and then, suddenly, the memories came flooding into his consciousness.

He was back in Nanjing beside his mother, he was a child holding on to his grandmother's skirts and there they were bowing before the Shen family ancestral tablets...the smell of incense...the red lanterns flickering in the darkness...then he was dipping his brush into an inkstone and now it was poised above a blank sheet...he was in a flat bottom boat gliding silently over the canals and misty lakes of his childhood...he was in the presence of Candida Xu in Shanghai...her long bejeweled hands were fitting the silken gown across his back...he was sitting at Dona Inês' dining room table watching her smile benignly and contentedly...he smelled the polished teakwood...now he could see the belltowers of Flanders...the rounded arches of the church in Montmartre...the hills of Rome...Queen Christina, motherly, and solicitous...Corelli's violin...books... books in great piles, on shelves in libraries, spread in disarray over the floor of the little room in the rue Vivienne...the Yi Jing...the rolling of dice...Daoist temples...Sieur Melchisédec, impish and ironic...Confucius imagined...benign and peripatetic...the rhythmic clatter of the press overlooking the rue Saint Jacques...Hyde inquisitive and donnish...cloistered quads and bells ringing out the hours...the portrait in the studio overlooking Covent Garden and the courtiers in their powdered wigs...the votive lights in São Roque and Father Philippe...Father Philippe who never gave up dreaming of China...caring, yet frail...the best of guides for without him none of this would have come about...yes, Father Philippe was right...it had been a journey like none other.

Michael Alphonsus, or rather 沈福宗 to his ancestors, had strength enough for one last radiant smile and then it was all over. He was home. The journey had ended. It would fall to others to tell of it.

Philippe Couplet: engraving at Mechelen Museum by unknown artist

X
Epilogue

Couplet, who was now in his 70th year, set out from Lisbon on the 25th of March 1692, the feast of the Annunciation. He did so together with Spinola and fourteen Jesuits newly recruited for the China missions. The omens were highly favorable. The men had been invited to join the ship that was taking the newly appointed Portuguese Viceroy of the Indies to his official residence in Goa. This kindly and pious man had even arranged for them to be presented to King Peter II and his consort Maria Sophia at a farewell audience held at the Ribeira Palace that overlooked the very Tagus River at which their ship was anchored.

There was no reason for the ships on that year's Carreira Da India to deviate from the time-honored itinerary which was to head south for the Cape of Good Hope and with good fortune round it with enough time left over to reach Mozambique well before August. Mozambique was a small island within sight of the African coast that had become an essential stopping off point. It had been part of the Arab dominated East African Swahili coast, but as far back as the early 16th century, the Portuguese had succeeded in settling it and fortifying it. It was a haven for the weather-beaten carracks that had negotiated the stormy and treacherous waters leading up to the Mozambique channel that separated Madagascar from the African continent. It was on the island of Mozambique that they hoped to dock, repair their broken timbers, and replenish their exhausted supplies. Only then could they undertake the last, but excruciatingly long, stage of the journey that would take them across the full length of the Arabian Sea to Goa.

It was after stopping off in the Canaries and heading south that things began to fall apart. Near the equator the ship unexpectedly ran into intense heat and becalmed waters. Sickness struck both crew and passengers so that by the time it had rounded the Cape and docked in Mozambique twenty-seven of those on board had died. Couplet was too sick to go ashore, and it was from those who came aboard to care for and comfort him that he learned that the one he referred to as his devoted son Michael had died on board ship almost exactly a year earlier.

The island of Mozambique and Fort São Sebastião: 1598 Flemish engraving

Epilogue

Couplet, devastated by the news, did eventually disembark but then suffered several strokes in quick succession. By the time he had recovered, the winds were adverse to the point that Spinola's party was stranded in Mozambique. Only the following April were they able to enter the Arabian Sea and set sail for Goa. In May 1693 and now within only 150 miles off the Malabar coast, the ship ran into a monster storm. Couplet was lying in his bunk. A piece of luggage tumbled off an overhead rack and as it fell bruised his head. Had he been young and healthy he might have survived, but he didn't.

❖

Of the original sixteen Jesuits that had departed Lisbon in March 1692 only four ultimately reached China. Two remained in Mozambique and one in Goa. The other nine sickened and died on the way including Spinola as his Macao-bound ship sailed up the Vietnamese coast into the Gulf of Tonkin. Spinola never reached China, let alone Nanjing, nor did he receive the sacramental anointing that would have made him a consecrated bishop.

Had Shen made it all the way back to his native Nanjing, he would no doubt have been warmly embraced by his proud and aging parents. Had he lived, he'd have had the opportunity to write his own account of the more than nine years that elapsed between his sailing out of Macao in December of 1681 and his departure from Lisbon in the Spring of 1691. He would have been the first from his homeland to write such a narrative, and what fascinating reading it might have been. But as so often happens in human affairs, it turned out otherwise. His short life was nonetheless one well-lived. Of course, it was!

He cannot have looked back on his journey as anything other than the most extraordinary of adventures. He was, in some ways, exceedingly fortunate. His journey had begun with a shipwreck, but thanks to his youth and enthusiasm he'd survived it, and it turned out to be the first of a series of chance events that would lead to his encountering not only the richness and beguiling complexity of cultures other than his own, but also to his being ushered into the presence of some of Europe's most influential monarchs and thinkers. He had chanced on a time in history that was, to paraphrase Charles Dickens, both the best and the worst.

It was the most exhilarating of times in the sense that the journey Shen found himself engaged in was designed to bring awareness of Confucian wisdom to a wider world. It was a world on the threshold of a momentous awakening that would expand the boundaries of what humans knew of the natural world far beyond that which had hitherto been imaginable. It would do so at an exponential rate and in time challenge to the core the worldviews inherited from the tradition-bound cultures of the past.

Three and a half centuries have gone by since Shen sailed out of Macao—a mere proverbial blink of the eye—and here we are confronting the awesomely challenging consequences of that accelerating evolutionary process.

It was by any measure an extraordinary journey. Louis XIV, reputedly Europe's most powerful monarch, had caught sight of Shen while he was being shown around the fabled Hall of Mirrors and honored the young man by summoning him into his presence and engaging him in conversation. In Rome, Shen had been fussed over by Queen Christina of Sweden, one of the leading intellects of her era. He'd also kissed the feet of Pope Innocent who had expressed compassionate concern for those who, like himself, put their lives at risk whenever they journeyed to or from China. In Paris, he had the immense satisfaction of watching as copies of the great Confucian Treatise he had so meaningfully contributed to came off the press. In London, he met and conversed with Robert Boyle, a founding member of the Royal Society, and in Oxford, while indulging his love of books in one of Europe's great libraries, he played chess with one of the era's leading oriental scholars. In

Epilogue

one last flourish, he was asked by none other than the English King to submit to having his portrait executed by one who had studied under Rembrandt and was regarded as the foremost portraitist of his time. There was indeed much to be proud of and the more so in light of the fact that we have every reason to believe that Shen was one of the very first intellectually alert scholars from China to engage meaningfully with European culture.

It might not have been the very worst of times, but there was more than enough discord afflicting Europe in the late 17th century for young impressionable Shen to come up against the disturbing shadow side of the human journey. There was the political absolutism that inspired the same Louis XIV who had welcomed him to Versailles, to so abusively crush religious dissent that he inflicted a deep and lasting wound on his great nation. There was the religious dogmatism that so clouded the good judgment of the same James II who had commissioned Shen's portrait that he suffered the loss of his crown. Then, and for good measure, there was the hubris of those in Rome who conceived of themselves as the sole guardians of ritual orthodoxy. To their lasting shame, they failed to discern the presence of the sacred within cultures which were just as venerable and arguably even more ancient than their own. Finally, there was the enduring delusion of self-sufficiency fostered by a succession of Chinese emperors who saw themselves as embodying an all-powerful and eternal mandate of heaven. It blinded them to the inevitability of having to come to terms with a wider world whose querulous barbarians could not indefinitely be kept at bay. Intolerance born of denial was thriving. We moderns know it for what it is—a hardy, noxious weed that continues to plague the human journey.

What to make, though, of the tragic dimension of Shen's and Philippe Couplet's lives? They were certainly not the only ones. Ricci died of exhaustion without so much as meeting the emperor he'd dreamt of conversing with in the very Chinese language he'd selflessly dedicated the best years of his life to mastering. Ricci never accomplished what he imagined to be his life's ultimate purpose: to sow within the fertile soil of Confucianism the seeds of the religion he'd been brought up to believe was destined to encompass the whole of struggling humanity. Then there was the life of the youthful last Ming Emperor who, rather than face the Manchu invaders, killed himself in the hills outside the Forbidden City. Nor can we forget the linguistically gifted Father Trigault, whose depressive tendencies were exacerbated by his obsessive pursuit of unattainable philosophically derived truths. What of the life of the promising young Manchu emperor whose cultural aversion to variolation caused him to die of smallpox? What of Michael Boym, the most observant of naturalists whose fate it was to be undone by chasing a delusional dream he'd been put up to by those desperate to hold on to a sliver of power in the face of the Manchu onslaught? There is Adam Schall, so absurdly persecuted by those who felt threatened by his intellectual brilliance. And perhaps most tragically of all, there were the Japanese martyrs who were helplessly entrapped by historical events far beyond their making.

Shen and Couplet were an odd couple, but they became virtually inseparable companions and cared greatly for each other. In the end, facing his grief for the son he had lost, Couplet was comforted by knowing the value of Shen's life was not diminished by its untimely end.

Though tragically cut short, Shen clearly lived an intensely eventful life. He did not travel alone nor in vain. His extraordinary journey invites us to relive what he experienced through our own eyes. The paths of those who have preceded us enrich our lives and allow us to perceive ourselves in their reflections.

Historical Notes
Chronology and Subsequent Events

In attempting to place 17th century events in context it helps to bear in mind that this was a preindustrial world with a global population estimated at some 600 million, roughly a quarter of which would have inhabited the Middle Kingdom—compared to 8 billion today of which 1.4 billion live in China. The northern regions of the globe were also suffering from an intensifying Little Ice Age that was restricting traditional food production and was responsible for a level of human hardship that needed to be addressed. This arguably contributed to socially transformative trends such as the acceleration of urbanization, the development of long-distance commerce, the colonization of distant lands in warmer climates, new approaches to food production, openness to new worldviews and to scientific and medical experimentation and innovation that would lead to the development of hitherto unimaginable technologies.

China's Early History

50000 BCE	Or earlier, appearance of modern humans in China's river valleys.
2952 BCE	According to Couplet's *Tabula chronologica Sinicae* published as an appendix to *Confucius Sinarum Philosophus*, the reign of Fuxi, the first of China's *Three Sovereigns and Five Emperors* began in 2952 BCE. According to most modern scholars, Fuxi is a purely mythical character and accounts predating the Zhou Dynasty are largely legendary.

China's Principal Dynasties

c.2000 BCE	**Xia**
1046-256 BCE	**Zhou**
221-206 BCE	**Qin**—known today for terracotta army commissioned by Emperor Shi Huangdi
206 BCE-220 CE	**Han**
618-907	**Tang**—An artistic Golden Age exalted in classical poetry
960-1279	**Song**
1271-1368	**Yuan (Mongol)**
	1264-1294: Emperor Kublai Khan's reign (during Marco Polo's travels)
1360-1644	**Ming** (traditional and wary of foreigners)
	1572-1620: Emperor Wanli's reign (during Ricci's Chinese sojourn)
	1644: Emperor Chongzhen suicide during encirclement of Beijing by Manchu-supported rebels
1644-1911	**Qing (Manchu)**
	1644-1661: Emperor Shunzhi's reign—Adam Schall his tutor, premature death from smallpox
	1661-1722: Emperor Kangxi's reign—Ferdinand Verbiest his advisor
	1735-1799: Emperor Qianlong's reign—Kangxi's grandson—dismissive of Macartney's embassy

Other Notable Dates

c.500 BCE	Lives of **Siddhartha Gautama** in India and **Laozi** in China founders of the Buddhist and Daoist traditions
551-479 BCE	Life of **Confucius**
100 BCE-100 CE	Early Indian Buddhist missionaries arrive in China via Silk Road
1271-95	**Marco Polo**'s travels

The Portuguese Century

1488	Rounding of Cape of Good Hope by Bartolomeu Dias
1492	Columbus' First Journey to Caribbean
1494	Treaty of Tordesillas between Portugal and Spain allocating—under Papal sanction—the lion's share of lands to the East to Portuguese exploration and conquest
1510	Portuguese colonization of Goa
1511	Portuguese conquest of Malacca
1514	Papal confirmation of the *Padroado* arrangement granting to the Portuguese Crown administrative authority over Church matters within the *Império Ultramar Português*
1543	Portuguese awareness of Japan
1557	Portuguese lease of Macao from Ming dynasty

Dutch and Other Challenges to Portuguese Dominance

1598-1663	Dutch-Portuguese War
1609-21	VOC takeover of Spice Islands, displacing the Portuguese and outmaneuvering the British East India Company causing it to turn to India

1619	Dutch settlement of Batavia
1622	Creation of office of the Propaganda Fide in Rome in attempt to assert measure of Papal control over missions including those administered by Portugal under the Padroado
1639	Banning of missionaries from Japan and martyrdom of Christians, culminating with the Tokugawa Shogunate's expulsion of Portuguese and all foreigners (Sakoku)—except for the Dutch on Dejima Island in Nagasaki Bay
1641	Dutch wrest Malacca from the Portuguese
1652	Settlement of Cape Colony by Dutch Boers (farmers)
1660	Capture of Ceylon by the Dutch
1661	Bombay ceded by Portugal to England—as Catherine of Braganza's dowry on marrying Charles II—thereby becoming one of the East India Company's early strategic Indian settlements

Timelines of Notable Personalities
(In Alphabetical Order)

Michael Boym (1612-1659)

1644	Arrival in Macao year of Manchu invasion of Beijing
1650	Ambassador of Ming court in exile hoping for papal and European support
1656	After challenging journey and facing European refusal to side with Ming against victorious Manchu Qing, attempted return to China
1656	Authoritative and magnificently illustrated *Flora Sinensis* published in Vienna
1659	On overland stage of journey from Goa to China death from exhaustion in Guangxi province
1667	Inclusion of his *Flora Sinensis* in Kircher's *China Illustrata*
1682	Publication in Frankfurt by a German physician of his *Specimen Medicinae Sinica*

Historical Notes

    1686   Publication in Nuremberg of his *Clavis medica ad Chinarum Doctrinam de pulsibus* as edited by Couplet

Philippe Couplet (b. 1623)—until departure from Macao with Michael Shen

    1640   Acceptance into Jesuit novitiate in native Mechlin (Spanish Netherlands)

    1648   Deemed, together with his classmate Verbiest, unfit by Spain as missionary for Mexico

    1654   Attended, together with Verbiest, Martino Martini's China lecture at Louvain

    1656   Departure for China in group led by Michael Boym

    1659   Arrival in China and immersive study of Confucian texts as one of *The Four Translators*

    1665   Following Adam Schall trial, confined for several years along with other missionaries in Canton—occasion of reunion of *The Four Translators*

post-1671   Assignment to missionary posts in different Chinese provinces, among them Shanghai home of Candida Xu

    1679   His naming as procurator

Próspero Intorcetta (1625-1696)

    1659   Arrival in China and immersive study of Confucian texts together with Francis Rougemont (1624-1676), Christian Herdtrich (1625-1684) and Couplet coming together as *The Four Translators*

    1662   Publication in China of bilingual Latin Chinese *Sapientia Sinica* inclusive of selected Confucian texts

    1665   Following Adam Schall trial, confined with other missionaries in Canton—occasion of reunion of *The Four Translators*

              Publication in Canton (1667) and in Goa (in 1669 on his way to Rome) of *Scientia politico moralis* which includes Confucius' *Doctrine of the Mean*

    1674   Procurator in Rome reporting on events—back in Hangzhou

    1676   And onward, promotions to increasingly senior positions within the China missions

Matteo Ricci (1552-1610)

1582	Arrival in Macao and study of Chinese and Confucian texts
1582	Through 1601, 19-year northward progression thru Chinese coastal provinces
1595	Residence in Nanjing
1601	Reaches Forbidden City
1603	Publishes in Chinese, *True Meaning of the Lord of Heaven*
1610	Death and burial in Beijing

Michele Ruggieri (1543-1607)

1583	Arrival in China (1579) and works with Ricci
1583	Through 1588, publication of Chinese catechism and creation with Ricci of Portuguese Chinese dictionary
1588	Departure for Rome with Ricci-translated Confucian text and charged with arranging Vatican mission to Beijing
1592	Following lack of success in Rome, retirement in Campania writing Chinese poems

Adam Schall (1591-1666)

1630	Beijing assignment in recognition of mathematical and astronomical skills
1644	Remains in Beijing following fall of Ming dynasty to invading Manchu
post-1644	Manchu recognition of his ballistic design capabilities, appointment as head of Beijing Board of Astronomy and in time counselor to youthful Manchu Emperor Shunzhi (b. 1638)
1665	Accusation of astronomical malfeasance by regents following emperor Shunzhi's premature death due to smallpox.Imprisonment, death sentence, subsequent pardon but exile of all Jesuits including *Four Translators* to Canton
1666	Fatal stroke after release from prison

Shen Fuzong (b.1657)

Shen Fuzong baptized in his native Nanjing as Michael Alphonsus

Historical Notes

Nicolas Trigault (1577-1628)

- 1611 Arrival in Nanjing
- 1614 Mission to Rome (as procurator) with manuscript of Ricci's journal
- 1615 Publication of *De Christiana Expeditione apud Sinas* in Augsburg
- 1617 Portrayal by Peter Paul Rubens
- 1619 Return to China—In Macao during Nanjing Incident (outlawing of missions)
- 1626 Composition of groundbreaking Romanized Chinese dictionary
- 1628 Fatal depression due to Name-of-God controversy

Ferdinand Verbiest (1623-1688)

- 1658 Arrival in China
- 1660 Summoned to Beijing to assist Adam Schall at Board of Astronomy
- 1664 Imprisonment—together with Schall—death sentence and subsequent pardon
- 1670 Friend and tutor of youthful Emperor Kangxi following dismissal of his autocratic regent—rehabilitated and appointed head of Board of Astronomy
- 1673 Rebuilding of Beijing observatory and design of scientific contraptions at Emperor Kangxi's behest
- 1680 Endorsement of Couplet as procurator
- 1688 Death in Beijing just before arrival of the *Mathématiciens du Roi* requested by Kangxi

Francis Xavier (1506-1552)

- 1525 Through 1530, student in Paris and meeting with Ignatius of Loyola
- 1542 Arrival in Goa
- 1549 Through 1551, in Japan
- 1552 Death off-shore Guangzhou (China)

Timeline of Shen's and Couplet's journey

- 1681   December 4, departure from Macao
- 1682   Late January 1682 to February 1683, shipwreck off Banten and year in Batavia
- 1683   October 8, arrival in Enkhuizen (Dutch Republic)
- 1684   Winter, homecoming at Mechlin
- 1684   Summer to early fall, arrival in Paris, meetings with Père la Chaise, Melchisédec Thévenot and the future *Mathématiciens du Roi,* presentation to Louis XIV at Versailles

  September, departure for Rome and arrival before Christmas
- 1685   Year in Rome, encounter with Queen Christina and audience with Pope Innocent XI (June)

  October, revocation of the Edict of Nantes by Louis XIV
- 1686   Spring, departure for Paris from Rome

  Spring 1686 to spring 1687, working year in Paris with Thévenot and other scholars—linguistic advice, translation, cataloging
- 1687   March, Shen's departure from Paris for London with Spinola as guide

  April, Shen's attendance at St. James' palace of episcopal consecration of Papal nuncio and reception by James II at Whitehall

  May, Couplet still in Paris—printing by Horthemels and publication of *Confucius Sinarum Philosophus*

  Summer, Shen at Oxford with Thomas Hyde; Publication in London of Isaac Newton's *Principia Mathematica:*

  Likely in fall, Shen's meeting with Robert Boyle and sittings for portrait by Godfrey Kneller in London

  Likely late summer, Couplet still in Paris—printing and publication of life of Candida Xu

  Late fall, Couplet's departure from Paris—reunion with Shen and Spinola in London before onward journey to Lisbon

1688	April, Shen, Couplet and Spinola depart London with ship arriving in Lisbon
	Likely in fall, Shen's enrolment in Lisbon Jesuit novitiate
1689	Spring, Couplet having incurred displeasure of Portuguese for subscribing an oath of subjugation to the Propaganda denied permission to sail to China
1691	Spring, Shen's first vows and departure from Lisbon for Goa
1692	March 25, Couplet, as member of group led by Spinola, departs for China from Lisbon in his 70th year

Personalities Shen Met on His Journey

James II fled to France a few days before Christmas **1688**. The following January, the English parliament not only named William of Orange and Mary to succeed James, but it also adopted a *Bill of Rights*. Its purpose was to permanently bar Catholics from the throne and transform parliament into a legislative and representative body whose laws could no longer be overridden by royal authority. An *Act of Settlement* adopted in 1701 further restricted access to the throne by Catholics and eventually led to the Hanoverians replacing the Stuarts. James died in exile in Saint-Germain-en-Laye that same year. His grandson 'Bonnie Prince Charlie' led the unsuccessful Jacobite Rising of 1745.

Queen Christina of Sweden died in Rome in **1689**, age 62 of complications related to diabetes. She had continued to advocate for the rights of Jews and wrote Innocent XI an indignant letter deploring the shortsightedness of Louis XIV's revocation of the Edict of Nantes.

Innocent XI, the pope whose feet Shen had kissed, died in **1689** without having addressed the issue of the Chinese Rites that so vexed the Jesuits.

Robert Boyle, whose health was already deteriorating at the time of Shen's visit died on the last day of **1691** just one week following that of his scientifically gifted sister Katherine who owned the house in Pall Mall.

Melchisédec Thévenot died in **1692**, the same year as Couplet but peacefully in a Paris suburb. He was 72. The philosopher Gottfried Leibniz reputedly said of him that he was one of the most inquisitive men he had ever met.

Historical Notes

Thomas Hyde, a few years following Shen's visit, was named professor of Arabic at Oxford. He kept his position as librarian until **1701** when he retired. His portrait can be found hung in an ill-lit, narrow corridor deep inside the Bodleian library. He's wearing a pitch-black clerical cassock. Only his benign oval-shaped face, a white double-banded collar tab and a wound-up scroll inscribed with two Chinese characters held in his right-hand, peer out of the gloom. One character is probably 古 voiced as *gu* denoting things of great antiquity. The other 甲 or *jia* likely refers to the tortoise shells on which some three-and-a-half-thousand-years ago, the Chinese experimented with writing. It's a fair bet that it was Shen who told him about the tortoises and that he took note.

Père la Chaise, or rather François de la Chaise remained Louis XIV's confessor till the bitter end. He died in **1709** at the venerable age of 84. He owes his exceptional name recognition to a chance event. Napoleon in 1804 decreed the transformation into a cemetery of a tract of land on a hill in Ménilmontant. It happened to have been adjacent to the house in which Père la Chaise had lived and to which I imagined him welcoming Couplet and Shen. Thus did the Cimetière du Père-Lachaise come about. As a result, he has a metro station named after him which is more than can be said for the king he served so unreservedly.

Louis XIV died in **1715**. His reign of seventy-two years was among the longest of any sovereign. He'd ascended the throne as a four-year-old and was succeeded by a five-year-old great grandson also named Louis. The pious Madame de Maintenon who was three years his senior outlived him by yet a few more years.

Godfrey Kneller was knighted in 1715 by George I, the first Hanoverian king. He died in London in **1723** wealthy and famous. He was 77. The first paragraph of his Wikipedia entry mentions The Chinese Convert as one of his greatest artistic achievements. Also mentioned is his portrait of Isaac Newton.

Publications and Events of Related Historical Significance

Following its publication in **1687**, *Confucius Philosophus Sinarum* was widely and positively commented on by Europe's learned journals that were at about this time emerging as significant disseminators of scientific developments. While it was by all accounts successful in stimulating genuine and widespread interest in Chinese culture among the culturally curious, its readership was nonetheless limited to philosophically inclined thinkers—Gottfried Leibniz among them—so that it was neither reprinted nor translated into the principal European languages that were beginning to supplant Latin. According to a small but vocal coterie of anti-Jesuit detractors who opposed any form of accommodation with Chinese rites, it erroneously, self-servingly, and dangerously characterized ancient Chinese beliefs and moral principles as reflective of those enshrined in the biblical tradition. Also, Couplet in compiling the elaborate historical appendix—Tabula chronologica Sinicae—had relied on Chinese sources indicating that Emperor Fuxi's reign stretched back to a time that, according to the Vulgate version of the Bible, predated the biblical flood. Given that most 17th century Europeans uncritically and literally believed that the flood had wiped out all humans save Noah and his brood this added fuel to the fire of a developing controversy.

The **1687** publication of **Candida Xu**'s biography, *Histoire d'une dame chrétienne de la Chine*, appears to have commanded a wide readership since a Spanish translation appeared in Madrid in 1691. There followed Flemish and Italian editions and versions adapted to Chinese readers appeared during the course of the 19th and 20th centuries.

In the aftermath of Louis XIV's **revocation of the Edict of Nantes** and in the years during which Shen was in Lisbon (**1688-1691**), several hundred thousand professionals and industrious craftsmen left France choosing permanent exile rather than forced conversion. Some historians have suggested that it not only led to France's economic impoverishment but also sowed seeds of resentment and distrust toward the absolutism that came to characterize the Ancien Régime. It was a resentment that arguably contributed a century later to Europe's first radical social revolutionary bloodbath and to a lasting wariness among many French people toward anything suggestive of clerical influence over the body politic.

The six **Mathématiciens du Roi** whom Shen and Couplet had met on first arriving in Paris in 1684 had been instructed to begin their China-bound journey by joining an impressive embassy dispatched by Louis XIV to the king of Siam. The expedition sailed from Brest in March 1685 and while it reached the Siamese capital with little difficulty, the onward journey to Beijing was marked by a series of delays and frustrating setbacks. When five out of the six finally reached Beijing in February of **1688**—one had remained in Thailand—and were welcomed by Emperor Kangxi, almost three years had gone by since their departure from France. It was a difficult beginning to an initiative that would allow a small group of Europeans who happened to be Jesuits to retain a foothold in China and, despite the daunting challenges involved, act as a fulcrum for a two-way exchange of scientific information. Shen and Couplet thanks to their fortuitously timed journey, thereby contributed in no small measure to establishing a lasting presence in China that would play a leading role in fostering East-West cross-cultural awareness throughout the 18th century.

Clement XI was elected pope in 1701 and in **1704** decided to deal head on with the Rites issue by condemning the mere suggestion that it might be acceptable for Chinese converts to ritually honor their ancestors. For good measure he outlawed any further discussion on the topic. He also formally forbade referring to God as either by the single Chinese character Tian or by the doublet Shang-di. He obviously hadn't taken kindly to the thoughts expressed in the preface of *Confucius Sinarum Philosophus*. Clement was the third pope to have succeeded Innocent XI.

Emperor Kangxi, who managed to outlive all those popes, was so exasperated by the whole business that in **1721**, the year before his death aged 69, he issued his own stern decree in which he famously said of Pope Clement's declaration that he'd never seen a document containing such nonsense. Despite a **1724** imperial ban expelling all foreign missionaries from China, an exception was made for those residing in Beijing who were members of the French scientific mission. Kangxi's eventual successor and grandson the famed and long-reigning Emperor Qianlong, was only too happy to benefit from the mathematicians' technical expertise and artistic talents and from that of the Jesuits who followed in their footsteps. These dedicated and highly gifted men continued to impress. Measured in such terms their mission would, in the fullness of time, be thought of as having been spectacularly successful. The missionary ban remained in effect until the mid-19th century when it was relaxed in the aftermath of the Opium Wars. The fact that many of the Christian communities founded by the Jesuits outside Beijing remained active was largely due to the existence of lay groups and associations of the type promoted by influential women such as Candida Xu.

Beginning in 1759 and culminating in **1773**, popes succumbing to the political storm raised up by Europe's Enlightenment thinkers and most particularly by the reform-minded Marquis of Pombal, Portugal's chief minister, took steps to suppress the **Jesuit Order**. The China Jesuits, including those who had stepped in the shoes of Louis XIV's mathematicians, held on to the hard-won positions they had staked out for as long as they could. It was a losing battle. it is difficult to imagine a more self-destructive act. The Order was restored in the early 19th century.

Historical Notes

In **1792**, Emperor Qianlong, in his dismissive response to an impressively large delegation sponsored by George III—the Macartney embassy—the purpose of which was to open China to British traders, famously declared that his Celestial Empire "… possesses all things in abundance and has no need to import the manufactures of barbarians" and effectively ended **western trade with China**. Europeans, alas for Qianlong's successors, were not so easily put off. They returned a half-century later, infamously led by the British with gunboats, imposing on the Chinese an unequal exchange of Indian-grown opium for chests of the tea they had grown addicted to. Matteo Ricci's dream of gaining access to the Forbidden City through study and reverencing Confucius was permanently put on hold.

Today, no Chinese child graduates from elementary school without having learned the Romanized alphabet. Not because there is any thought of replacing characters with an alphabetic writing system but because **Pinyin**, a sound transcription system adopted in the 1950s, relies on Romanization and is used to teach throughout China the standardized version of spoken Chinese most often referred to in the West as Mandarin and achieve near universal literacy. Its distant ancestor is the Ricci-Trigault method that was the first to rely on the Latin alphabet to represent Chinese syllabic sounds and match them to written characters. I have used the Pinyin transcription consistently, hence spellings such as Beijing, Nanjing (Nanking), Qing (Ching) dynasty, Daoism (Taoism), and the Yi Jing. I have made an exception for Tai Chi which in Pinyin is Taiji.

Ricci's tombstone inscribed in both Chinese characters and Latin can be seen in the backyard of a Communist Party school in Central Beijing. At the height of the Cultural Revolution, it was about to be hacked to smithereens by Red Guards but, thanks to the intervention of a reverential caretaker, was granted a last-minute reprieve.

Nicolas Trigault, while in Antwerp promoting Ricci's journal following its publication in 1615, came across the already famous Dutch painter **Peter Paul Rubens**. Rubens sketched him wearing a cylindrical hat broader at the top than at the base just like the one worn by Ricci on the title page of the book. Trigault stands erect and solemn, enfolded within a generously proportioned scholarly gown with hands tucked inside its wide sleeves. Rubens used pen and ink and thanks to pastel-colored chalks infused a sense of dreaminess and lightness into his artistic creation. Fate would have it that it ended up in the care of the Metropolitan Museum in New York City—perhaps as ironic as having Shen's portrait hang in Windsor Castle and then in Abu Dhabi.

Places Shen Visited

The **palaces, libraries and churches** Shen visited in Europe have for the most part survived into the modern era with a few exceptions:

A few years after Cardinal Mazarin's death in 1661, his protégé Jean-Baptiste Colbert took steps to accommodate the **Bibliothèque du Roi** in a townhouse he had acquired in the rue Vivienne and had remodeled by none other than Louis le Vau, the designer of Versailles' Hall of Mirrors. This was the Colbert who not only became the Sun King's chief minister but who also founded both the Académie des Sciences and the Compagnie française des Indes. It was there that Thévenot, Couplet and Shen put the final touches to the Confucius Sinarum Philosophus. It was not until 1721 that the entire royal collection was moved across the street to the far larger and now vacant Palais Mazarin. Sadly, Colbert's townhouse was torn down in the 1820s to make way for the Galerie Colbert that now houses the Institut National de l'Histoire de l'Art. A visitor can nonetheless take pleasure in admiring the impressive dome of the Galerie Colbert, snacking at the brasserie Le Grand Colbert and then crossing to the opposite side of the rue Vivienne where it is possible to sit quietly for a while within the awe-inspiring magnificence of the 19th century Salle Ovale of the Bibliothèque nationale in what was once the Palais Mazarin.

The **Cotovia novitiate and the Ribeira Palace** were reduced to rubble by Lisbon's 1755 earthquake.

The **Palace of Whitehall** in the decade following Shen's visit was ravaged by the spread of a fire caused by a servant's ill-advised attempt to dry linen by hanging it too close to burning coals. So thorough was the devastation that the only building to have survived to this day is Inigo Jones' famed banqueting house. Fortunately, Shen's portrait was at Windsor.

The **Palazzo Riario** where Queen Christina resided during the year Shen spent in Rome was several decades later expanded beyond recognition and renamed the Palazzo Corsini. It is today a fine arts museum. Had she not brought to Rome the manuscripts amassed by her father King Gustavus Adolphus as booty during the Thirty Years War, they would have perished in the fire that in 1697 destroyed Stockholm's royal palace. They are now part of the Vatican's famed collection of rare books.

Author's Notes
and Sources

In my telling of Shen's journey, I have given due regard to the principal events, chronology and underlying facts characterizing each of its stages as reflected in published academic sources. I cite below and gratefully acknowledge my debt to these sources since without them the writing of this historically based novel would not have been possible. I also set out to situate the journey within its broader historical context. That said, I have freely fictionalized the particulars of the human interactions narrated, the dialogues underlying them, the contexts within which they occurred, and the details of the journey as well as those reflective of late 17th century everyday life. I have also exercised judgment in coping with conflicts among the sources cited. All the characters mentioned by name have a historical basis with the notable exception of Dom João and Dona Inês. Since there was scant evidence on how the year in the Dutch East Indies following the shipwreck was actually spent, I chose to rely on my imagination and on my past experience of living in Southeast Asia. I also used that year as an opportunity to narrate the historical background I deemed relevant to gaining a fuller appreciation of the significance of Shen's and Couplet's journey. The details of the voyage on the Dutch ship that follow that episode and even its name are likewise imagined.

Beyond Ricci—*www.ricci.bc.edu*: A website dedicated to rare books from the Jesuitica Collection at Boston College which includes a wealth of notes relating to many of the historical figures mentioned including Ferdinand Verbiest, Adam Schall, Nicolas Trigault, Xu Guangxi (Candida Xu's grandfather) and, of course, Matteo Ricci and Couplet.

Dijkstra, Trude: *Confucius in Dutch-Made Learned Journals—in Printing and Publishing Chinese Religion and Philosophy in the Dutch Republic, 1595-1700*. Chapter 4, Brill, Leiden, 2021

Gallagher, Louis J.: *China in the sixteenth century: The journals of Matteo Ricci: 1583-1610*. Random House, New York, 1953.

Heyndrickx, Jerome: Editor of *Philippe Couplet S.J. (1623-1693), The man who brought China to Europe*, Steyler Verlag, Nettetal, 1990. This book is a collection of authoritative academic papers connected with a conference organized in 1986 by the Ferdinand Verbiest Foundation at the University of Leuven. I relied in particular on the papers authored by Peter Gordts (*Philippe Couplet of Mechlin, a Jesuit in Belgium*), Theodore N. Foss (*The European Sojourn of Philippe Couplet and Michael Shen Fuzong 1683-1692*), Edward J. Malatesta S.J. (*The Last Voyage of Philippe Couplet*) and Claudia von Collani (*Philippe Couplet's Missionary attitude toward the Chinese*).

King, Gail: *A Model for All Christian Women: Candida Xu, A Chinese Christian Woman of the Seventeenth Century*. Collectanea Serica, New Series 2, Routledge, New York, 2021.

Meynard, Thierry: *Confucius Sinarum philosophus (1687) : the first translation of the Confucian classics*. Institutum historicum Societatis Iesu, Rome 2011.

Morin, Benoît: *Les mathématiciens du Roi, première mission scientifique et de connaissance de la Chine*, published in 2016 on the website *france-chine-international.fr*.

Mungello, David E.: *Curious Land: Jesuit accommodation and the origins of Sinology.* University of Hawaii Press, Honolulu, 1989.

Murta Pina, Isabel: *Shen Fuzong (Michael Alphonsus),* a paper published in Luisa M. Paternicó, *The Generation of Giants 2,* Centro Studi Martino Martini, Trent, 2015.

Poole, William: *The Meeting of Shen Fuzong and Thomas Hyde in 1687.* A lecture at the Oxford Bibliographical Society, 2010.

Spence, Jonathan D: *The Memory Palace of Matteo Ricci,* Viking Penguin, New York, 1984.

Spence, Jonathan D: *When Minds Met: China and the West in the Seventeenth Century.* Text of the 2010 Jefferson Lecture in the Humanities, Washington, DC.

17TH CENTURY PUBLICATIONS

Thanks to the high-resolution scanning of a wealth of rare books and their being made freely available on a number of public interest websites, it is possible to view, read and appreciate the high-quality typesetting and illustrations of many 17th century publications. Cited below are six of the books specifically referred to in my recounting of Shen's journey.

First and foremost is the masterpiece around which the journey revolves and which I initially refer to as the *Confucian Treatise*. It is, of course, more accurately described by its Latin title as *Confucius sinarum philosophus, sive, Scientia sinensis latine exposita* and was printed in Paris by Daniel Horthemels and published in 1687. It is accessible on the *archive.org* website. I was given permission to consult and photograph the splendid copy held at Yale University's Beinecke Rare Book and Manuscript Library. It is an in-quarto volume measuring approximately 8 ½" x 13 ¼" and bound in a plain vellum-covered rigid binding. Its large format brings out the clarity and elegance of the typesetting. Nolin's copper engraving of Confucius facing page 117 is particularly pleasing.

Also available on *archive.org* is Nicolas Trigault's remarkable transcription into Latin of Matteo Ricci's diary which he published in Augsburg in 1615 under the title *De christiana expeditione apud Sinas suscepta ab Societate Jesu. Ex P. Matthaei Ricii eiusdem Societatis Commentariis.*

The other book of interest on *archive.org* is the 1696 two-volume reedition of Melchisédec Thévenot's monumental *Relations de divers voyages curieux : qui n'ont point esté publiées, et qu'on a traduit ou tiré des originaux.* Thévenot published his collected documents in a series beginning in 1663. The inclusion of greatest relevance to our story is the Latin translation of Confucius' *Doctrine of the Mean* which did not appear until 1672. This is the text titled *Sinarum Scientia Politico Moralis* Thévenot had lifted from the version published by Próspero Intorcetta in two parts: first in Canton (1667) and then in Goa (1669). It can be found in the second volume of this 1696 reedition of Thévenot's *Relations* and begins on page 446.

Reference is made to Alexandre de Rhodes' autobiography published in Paris in 1653 in which he recounts his hair-raising experiences in Batavia. It is titled *Divers voyages et missions du père Alexandre de Rhodes de la Compagnie de Jésus en la Chine et autres royaumes de l'Orient, avec son retour en Europe par la Perse et l'Arménie* and is available on *gallica.bnf.fr*.

Philippe Couplet's biography of his Shanghainese patron Candida Xu which he published in Paris in 1688 and titled *Histoire d'une dame chrétienne de la Chine, ou par occasion les usages de ces peuples, l'établissement de la religion, les manières des missionnaires, & les exercices de piété des nouveaux Chrétiens sont expliquez* is available on *books.google.com*.

Michael Boym's *Flora sinensis*, which he dedicated to Leopold of Hungary, and published in Vienna in 1656, includes delightful

Author's Notes

illustrations. It is available on the Smithsonian's *biodiversitylibrary.org* website.

The Confucian quotes used throughout are from the three of the *Four Books* attributed to Confucius that were included in the *Confucius Sinarum Philosophus*, namely: *The Great Learning*, *The Doctrine of the Mean*, and *The Analects*. They are taken from James Legge's monumental *The Chinese Classics* published in 1861. Legge was a Protestant missionary who in later life was named to Oxford's newly instituted chair of Chinese Language and Literature. He was passionately opposed to Britain's opium policy and his advocacy of higher education for women contributed to the foundation of Oxford's Somerville College.

Illustrations

*U*nless otherwise stated, the illustrations are of two-dimensional period prints, engravings, paintings, or coins and are therefore in the public domain. In cases where the images were not downloaded from a Wikimedia Commons digital file, the webpage hosting the file is indicated.

List of Illustrations by Page Number

p.4-5   Carte Universelle du Monde by Pierre Du Val (1619-1683), geographer to Louis XIV, published posthumously in 1684—Wikimedia Commons sourced from Barry Lawrence Ruderman raremaps.com

p.12   Age of Sail Portuguese carrack: 1897 print—Line drawing from Joaquim de Mello's *Marinha histórica do século* XV e XVI

p.14   The straits of Sunda and of Malacca: 1683 French map—From Alain Manesson Malet's (1630-1706) volume II of *Description de l'univers* published in Paris—www.archive.org

p.19   Plan of Batavia showing Dutch Kasteel and docks: 1681 Dutch engraving—National Archive, The Hague—www.nationaalarchief.nl

p.22   Southeast Asia depicting range of VOC's activities: late 17th century Dutch map —Attributed to Nicolaes Visscher II (1649-1702) and included in *Atlas van Dirk van der Hagen*, a five-volume collection of maps and prints assumed to have been compiled around 1690—Koninklijke Bibliotheek, The Hague

p.27   Spice Islands East of the Straits of Sunda: 1683 French map—From Alain Manesson Malet's (1630-1706) volume II of *Description de l'univers* published in Paris—www.archive.org

p.38   Mechlin cathedral: 18th century English print—Thomas Rowlandson (1757-1827)—Boston Public Library collection—www.picryl.com

p.43   Port of Macao: 18th century French drawing—Gaspard Duché de Vancy (1756-1788)—www.gallica.bnf.fr

p.45   Calligraphic rendering of Shen's family and personal names—Author PHGCOM licensed under Creative Commons

p.48   Nanjing's porcelain pagoda: 1664 Dutch engraving—Johan Nieuhof (1618-1672) in *Het gezantschap der Nederlandse Oost-Indische compagnie*, an account of the VOC's 1665 embassy to Beijing

p.49   View of outskirts of Nanjing: 1683 French engraving—From Alain Manneson Malet's (1630-1706) volume II of *Description de l'univers* published in Paris—www.archive.org

p.50   Inner court of the Forbidden City: 1664 Dutch engraving—Johan Nieuhof (1618-1672) in *Het gezantschap der Nederlandse Oost-Indische compagnie*, an account of the VOC's 1665 embassy to Beijing

p.53   The Three Vinegar Tasters—16th century painting attributed to Kano school—Tokyo National Museum

p.73   Manchu archer on horseback: 18th century painting—Giuseppe Castiglione (1688-1766), Jesuit painter resident at imperial court—National Palace, Taipei—www.gwongzaukungfu.com

p.78   Squirrel chasing a green haired turtle from Michael Boym's *Flora Sinensis* (1656)—Bibliothèque universitaire Moretus Plantin, Namur, Belgium

Illustrations

p.78 Mango from *Flora Sinensis* (1656)—Bibliothèque universitaire Moretus Plantin, Namur, Belgium

p.89 Matteo Ricci, Adam Schall and Ferdinand Verbiest: early 18th century French engraving—Plate from volume 3 of *Description de la Chine* by Jean-Baptiste du Halde (1674-1743) published in The Hague (1736)

p.90 Emperor Kangxi—Anonymous Qing dynasty painter—Palace Museum, Taipei

p.97 Michael Boym's *Clavis Medica ad Chinam doctrinam de pulsibus* as edited by Couplet: title page—Published 1686—www.archive.org

p.98 Michael Boym's *Clavis Medica:* illustrative plate—Published 1686—www.archive.org

p.100 Tiger's Canal (Tijgersgracht) in Batavia: late 17th century Dutch engraving—Johan Nieuhof (1618-1672) included in the *Atlas van Dirk van der Hagen,* a five-volume collection of maps and prints assumed to have been compiled around 1690—Koninklijke Bibliotheek, The Hague

p.104 Ricci's *De Christiana expeditione apud Sinas* (Augsburg 1615), edited by Nicolas Trigault: title page— www.archive.org

p.108 Nicolas Trigault by Peter-Paul Rubens likely sketched in Antwerp in 1617—On paper with chalk and pastel—New York Metropolitan Museum of Art

p.114 Latin and Chinese bi-lingual edition of Confucian-inspired *Sapientia Sinica*: 1662 printed in Jiangxi with woodblocks on double leaves and published at Próspero Intorcetta's initiative—New York Public Library—www.digitalcollections.nypl.org

p.134 Charles de Noyelle: 17th century Flemish print—Arnold van Westerhout (1651-1725)—Biblioteca Nacional de España

p.143 François de la Chaise: 17th century French engraving—Anonymous from *Iconography of two-hundred portraits acquired in France*, a collection of period engravings published in 1840

p.155 Jesuit house on hill overlooking Ménilmontant: 17th century French engraving—Anonymous—www.leftinparis.org

p.161   Palace of Versailles: 1682 French—Engraving by Israel Silvestre (1621-1691)—New York Metropolitan Museum of Art—www.metmuseum.org

p.172   Church of the Gesù in Rome with (to the right) the Casa Professa: 17th century Italian engraving—Giovanni Battista Falda (1643-1678)—www.info.roma.it

p.175   Queen Christina of Sweden: 18th century French engraving—Pierre-Alexandre Tardieu (1756-1844) after portrait by Sébastien Bourdon (1616-1671)—National Gallery of Art, Washington DC—www.nga.gov

p.176   Palazzo Riario nella Longara, Queen Christina's residence in Rome from 1659 to 1689: 18th century Italian engraving—Anonymous—Rodolfo Lanciani collection of the Biblioteca Nazionale di Archeologia e Storia dell'Arte, Rome—www.searchworks.stanford.edu/view/cd950fp4361

p.181   Pope Innocent XI: memorial coin—Attributed to a member of the celebrated Hamerani family of engravers—Photographer: cgb

p.185   Belvedere courtyard linking the Vatican palace (left) to the Villa Belvedere (right) with the Sistine library (center, dark and narrow) named after Pope Sixtus V (1521-1590): 1618 Italian etching—From a set of plates by various artists depicting Roman gardens published by Greuter & Scaichi in 1623—www.britishmuseum.org

p.187   Sistine Hall (Salone Sistino) of Vatican Library—Detail of October 2008 photograph by Michal Osmenda available under Creative Commons attribution

p.198   *Bibliothèque du Roi* in the rue Vivienne: detail (medallion 2nd from the right) from *The Glory of the Might of Arms*—See next illustration—www.gallica.bnf.fr/blog/29082019/colbert-et-la-bibliothèque

p.200   *The Glory of the Might of Arms, Science, and the Arts under the auspicious reign of Louis the Great*: 1676 French engraved almanac—Henri Noblin—www.gallica.bnf.fr

p.212   Chronology of Chinese Monarchs: title page to Couplet's treatise—Photo by author

p.216	Siamese delegation received by Louis XIV at Versailles' Hall of Mirrors in 1686: 1687 French engraving—Almanac by unknown artist
p.223	Confucius: engraving by Jean Baptiste Nolin (1657-1708) facing *Life of Confucius*—Photo by author
p.233	The sixty-four hexagrams underlying the philosophy of the Yi Jing included in the preface to *Confucius Sinarum Philosophus* (1687)—www.gallica.bnf.fr
p.234	*Confucius Sinarum Philosophus* (1687): title page—Photo by author
p.237	Couplet's *Histoire d'une dame chrétienne de la Chine* (1688) depicting Candida Xu: engraved frontispiece—www.books.google.com
p.253	King James II: detail of 1686 portrait by Nicolas de Larguillière (1656-1746)—National Maritime Museum, Greenwich, England
p.255	Palace of Whitehall: 1696 Anglo-Dutch engraving—Leonard Knijff (1650-1722) from Volume VII of *Survey of London*
p.263	Bodleian with Duke Humfrey's Library above the Divinity School (left facing) and the Schools Quadrangle (right): 1675 English engraving—David Loggan (1634-1692) from *Oxonia Illustrata*—www.images.collections.yale.edu
p.266	Breakfast, lunch, dinner, drink and a snack (dim sum) in Shen's handwriting while at Oxford—Photograph by Theresa Thomson (October 15, 2018) taken at time of a special exhibition memorializing Shen's visit held at St. Hugh's College, Oxford that included documents from the Bodleian Library—www.timeless-travels.co.uk
p.277	Thomas Hyde's portrait at the Bodleian Library with him holding Chinese inscribed scroll—Unknown artist on the occasion of his retirement in 1701—Photo by author
p.288	Cotovia Novitiate in Lisbon: late 17th century Portuguese engraving—www.lisboadeantigamente.blogspot.com

p.293   Lisbon's harbor at mouth of Tagus: late 16th century German-Dutch engraving—Detail from print included in Georg Braun (1541-1622) and Frans Hogenberg's (1535-1590) *Civitates orbis terrarum* (1572)

p.296   Philippe Couplet: medallion-shaped engraving—unknown artist—website of the Koninklijke Kring voor oudheidkunde, Letteren en kunst van Mechelen (Royal Society for archeology, literature and arts of Mechlin)—www.oudheidkundigekring.be/mechelen/node/460

p.298   The Island of Mozambique and Fort São Sebastião: 1598 Flemish engraving—Pieter van den Keere (1571-1646)

Acknowledgements

I'm grateful to those who encouraged me to venture beyond the dryness of the historical record and try my hand at bringing out the human dimension of a story that, as one friend put it, deserved to be rescued from the drawer into which aspiring storytellers all too often consign their dispiritingly feeble early attempts. A big thank you to my wife Lisette who was my indefatigable reader and to Caren Polner who went far beyond contributing her consummate skills as a professional graphic designer and took on the role of inspired editor, thereby challenging me to seek out that elusive mean—Confucian?—at which imagination and rigorous historical research happily intersect.

About the Author

Robert Henrey has, since retirement from an international financial consulting career based in New York City, pursued through writing, and lecturing his lifelong scholarly interest in history and linguistics. He has traveled extensively throughout Europe, Latin America, and the Middle East, and gained a heightened awareness of Far Eastern cultures while living in Singapore in the 1970s.

In *Shanghai 1980* he recounts his experience of China as it emerged from the trauma of the Cultural Revolution, and in his previously published *Bloodshot Mountain* he analyses the profound social and economic impact on early colonial Latin America of the discovery in the remote Andes of the world's richest silver mine. In *Through Grown-Up Eyes*, he reflects on his varied life experience and how fate landed him, an unsuspecting eight-year-old, in the starring role of the 1948 British film classic *The Fallen Idol.*

Robert and his wife Lisette met at Oxford as undergraduates and have for the longest time lived in Connecticut.

Printed in Great Britain
by Amazon